Progress in

EXPERIMENTAL PERSONALITY RESEARCH

VOLUME 12

PSYCHOPATHOLOGY

CONTRIBUTORS TO THIS VOLUME

LOUIS J. COZOLINO

PHILIP D. HARVEY

BRENDAN A. MAHER

THEO C. MANSCHRECK

JOHN M. NEALE

WILLIAM M. WAID

PROGRESS IN
Experimental
Personality Research

Edited by
Brendan A. Maher and Winifred B. Maher

DEPARTMENT OF PSYCHOLOGY
AND SOCIAL RELATIONS
HARVARD UNIVERSITY
CAMBRIDGE, MASSACHUSETTS

VOLUME 12

PSYCHOPATHOLOGY

1983

ACADEMIC PRESS

A Subsidiary of Harcourt Brace Jovanovich, Publishers

New York   London

Paris   San Diego   San Francisco   São Paulo   Sydney   Tokyo   Toronto

ACADEMIC PRESS, INC.
111 Fifth Avenue, New York, New York 10003

United Kingdom Edition published by
ACADEMIC PRESS, INC. (LONDON) LTD.
24/28 Oval Road, London NW1 7DX

LIBRARY OF CONGRESS CATALOG CARD NUMBER: 64–8034

ISBN 0–12–541412–9

PRINTED IN THE UNITED STATES OF AMERICA

83 84 85 86   9 8 7 6 5 4 3 2 1

CONTENTS

A Tentative Theory of Schizophrenic Utterance

BRENDAN A. MAHER

Psychopathology of Motor Behavior in Schizophrenia

THEO C. MANSCHRECK

The Oral and Written Productions
of Schizophrenic Patients

LOUIS J. COZOLINO

The Specificity of Thought Disorder to Schizophrenia:
Research Methods in Their Historical Perspective

PHILIP D. HARVEY AND JOHN M. NEALE

Psychophysiological Processes
in Delinquency-Prone Young Adults

WILLIAM M. WAID

CONTRIBUTORS

Numbers in parentheses indicate the pages on which the authors' contributions begin.

LOUIS J. COZOLINO, *Department of Psychology, University of California, Los Angeles, Los Angeles, California 90024* (101)

PHILIP D. HARVEY, *Department of Psychology, State University of New York at Stony Brook, Stony Brook, New York 11794* (153)

BRENDAN A. MAHER, *Department of Psychology and Social Relations, Harvard University, Cambridge, Massachusetts 02138* (1)

THEO C. MANSCHRECK, *Department of Psychiatry, Massachusetts General Hospital, Harvard Medical School, Boston, Massachusetts 02114* (53)

JOHN M. NEALE, *Department of Psychology, State University of New York at Stony Brook, Stony Brook, New York 11794* (153)

WILLIAM M. WAID*, *Institute of Pennsylvania Hospital and Department of Psychiatry, University of Pennsylvania, Philadelphia, Pennsylvania 19104* (181)

*Present address: New Jersey Psychological Institute, 93 West Main Street, Freehold, New Jersey 07728.

PREFACE

In this the twelfth volume and the twentieth year of this series, we continue our policy of publishing volumes on topics in psychopathology alternating with volumes on normal personality processes. The present work is mainly concerned with the area of experimentally based research on the disorders of schizophrenia. Chapters deal with theory and findings from the study of language utterances, from motor behavior and its anomalies, and thought disorder. One paper examines the concept of delinquency proneness.

Research strategies that are currently being applied to the study of schizophrenia have emphasized the possible central role played by cognitive processes in the production of manifest clinical anomalies. This constitutes a departure from the earlier predominance of concern with motivational and affective aspects of the patients' behavior. In this respect it may be seen as a natural consequence of both the major improvements in methodology associated with cognitive psychology, and a reaction to the disappointment that has been experienced from the results of purely dynamic conceptions of the research problems of schizophrenia.

While this appears as a newer development against the background of work of two or three decades ago, it is essentially a return to a formulation of the task of experimental work in schizophrenia that dates back to the beginnings of such efforts in the late nineteenth century. The problem has not changed, but the techniques available to tackle it have developed significantly. It seems reasonably clear that this trend is likely to be with us for a long time to come.

Of particular interest in this volume is the exploration of the possible links between language anomalies and motor symptoms in schizophrenia. These have typically been treated theoretically as separate but parallel aspects of the schizophrenic picture, but until recently little has been done to examine the extent to which both might be reflections of a more unitary pathological process, perhaps related to the role of efficient deployment of attention in any serial output of behavior. Although the work reported here is only a beginning, the possibilities appear to be encouraging of further effort.

Delinquency, the subject of the final chapter of this volume, has long posed a problem that is to be found in all areas of psychopathology, namely the relative importance of biological factors in creating vulnerability to the behavior versus the role of social learning influences in shaping and maintaining antisocial behavior in persons of essentially normal biological endowment. The present contribution presents the evidence for a biopsychological position. In a later volume we expect to publish explanations of this behavior that argue for a more environmental and "normal" view of this behavior.

At the close of this Preface we would like to remind readers of this volume that although many papers that have appeared in this series have been a result of invitations addressed to individual research investigators, we do consider for publication any relevant paper from any source and invite potential contributors to address papers to us directly for editorial reflection.

BRENDAN A. MAHER
WINIFRED B. MAHER

CONTENTS OF PREVIOUS VOLUMES

Progress in

EXPERIMENTAL PERSONALITY RESEARCH

VOLUME 12

PSYCHOPATHOLOGY

PROGRESS IN EXPERIMENTAL PERSONALITY RESEARCH, VOLUME 12

A TENTATIVE THEORY
OF SCHIZOPHRENIC UTTERANCE

Brendan A. Maher

DEPARTMENT OF PSYCHOLOGY AND SOCIAL RELATIONS
HARVARD UNIVERISTY
CAMBRIDGE, MASSACHUSETTS

I. Diagnosis, Definition, and Clinical Characteristics

It is scarcely necessary to emphasize the complexity of the problems presented by schizophrenic behavior. No other topic within psychopathology has received so much attention from theorists or so much effort from empirical research investigators. Sheer volume has made mastery of the scientific literature dealing with schizophrenia almost impossible. With this in mind, we develop any theoretical formulation of any area of schizophrenic pathology with an acute sense of the temerity required for such an enterprise and an awareness of the pitfalls that have plagued previous attempts of this kind. We approach, therefore, with considerable trepidation, the task of developing a theoretical formulation of schizophrenic utterance, knowing that it will be limited in scope and likely to be lacking in data on some crucial points. Nonetheless, the accumulation of information from a wide range of sources, relevant to the problem of schizophrenic utterance, seems to warrant the task of generating at least a tentative theory at this time. In this chapter, the writer makes such an attempt, an extension and elaboration of a more schematic outline presented in previous papers (Maher, 1968, 1972).

Before proceeding to the main burden of the chapter, we must consider some preliminary matters. They are, in order (*a*) the problem of the reliability and validity of schizophrenia—or the schizophrenias—as a diagnostic entity, (*b*) the definition of *utterance* that is to be used, (*c*) the anomalies to be explained, and (*d*) the specifications appropriate to a theory of schizophrenic utterance.

A. SCHIZOPHRENIA AS A DIAGNOSTIC ENTITY

In recent years there has been an increasingly vigorous attack upon the validity of psychopathological diagnostic entities in general and upon that of schizophrenia in particular. Although the reader is undoubtedly familiar with the main thrust of the criticisms that have been made, it may be helpful to review them briefly here. The prime criticism is that interjudge agreements about diagnoses of schizophrenia are too low to warrant serious acceptance of the validity of the entities that these diagnoses are intended to identify. Space limitations preclude a review of the many studies that have been reported, but it will be useful to note that interjudge agreements on schizophrenia have been recorded as 78–90% (Schmidt & Fonda, 1956) for the gross diagnosis and 51% when less experienced clinicians are making the judgment. Beck (1962) reported 53% agreement between experienced psychiatrists; Sandifer, Pettus, and Quade (1964) found 74% agreement.

Discussing these figures, Ullman and Krasner (1975) comment, quite properly, that it is difficult to set a standard of agreement that is acceptable without regard to the uses to which these diagnoses will be put. They do, however, comment that "the chance of significant and useful research results when there is a 40 percent error of classification is probably slight."

Much the same sentiment, advanced from an explicitly ideological base, is to be found in the work of such writers as the sociologist Scheff (1975). Researchers who employ the term *schizophrenia,* Scheff claims, may be "unknowingly aligning themselves with the status quo; for example, by accepting the unexamined diagnosis of schizophrenia, they may be inadvertently providing the legitimacy of science to what is basically a social value judgment [p. 11]." This assertion of Scheff's is based upon his earlier conclusion that "because of the all but overwhelming uncertainties and ambiguities inherent in the definition, 'schizophrenia' is an appellation, or 'label.'" Schizophrenia, then, according to Scheff, does not exist in the way emphysema exists, but is a fiction designed to suppress people who break society's rules.

The use of "low" diagnostic reliabilities as a basis for rejecting entity concepts in psychopathology arises from a rather simple-minded assumption—namely, that the critic knows a priori what percentage of interjudge agreement should be found when there *is* a disease entity underlying the external signs and symptoms. Thus, the Ullman and Krasner conclusion that 40% error in diagnostic agreement of schizophrenia is too large to warrant further research into the entity is purely arbitrary, being an assertion unaccompanied by any empirical evidence that established entities invariably produce interjudge agreements with lower error margins. What must be emphasized here is that there is as yet no laboratory test for schizophrenia—nor can there be until research has followed the usual historical progression from diagnosis by external symptoms, to a formulation of the primary pathology and the ultimate development of laboratory tests directed at the pathological process itself. A proper basis for judging the meaning of interjudge agreements in diagnosis is through comparison with interjudge agreements (with and without laboratory test) for known disease entities.

Fortunately, we have examples of such agreements in a paper by Falek and Moser (1975). Their figures are instructive. A scrutiny of eight studies reveals, for example, that agreement between physicians about the diagnosis of angina reaches only 45% and that interjudge agreement about the presence of pathology on the electrocardiogram ranges from a high value of 79% to a low of 30%. They conclude that "diagnostic concurrence for many physical disorders is oftentimes as inaccurate as that observed in studies of schizophrenia [p. 64]." In fact, in some of the studies they cite, the diagnosis of physical disorder emerges as less reliable than that of schizophrenia. Clearly, we need not take too seriously the recommendation that 40% error of classification renders a proposed disease entity too dubious to warrant research.

Unreliability of diagnosis in any disease is a matter for concern. An appropriate response to the problem is effort directed at improving and refining the diagnosis, and this is a current focus of much effort by psychopathologists. Thus, Schneider's (1959) concept of first-rank symptoms and the work of the International Pilot Study of Schizophrenia (World Health Organization, 1973), of Carpenter, Strauss, and Bartko (1974), and of Feighner, Robins, Cruze, Woodruff, Winokur, and Munoz (1972) provide examples of work aimed at improving the definition and reliability of the diagnostic categories of schizophrenia.

It is important to note that, even where a well-established pathology is involved, completely reliable diagnosis without a laboratory test is unlikely. Some at least of the symptoms may arise from other causes. We know that some schizophrenic-like phenomena are to be found in cases of organic, toxic, and drug-induced psychoses; that some delusions are based not upon disordered perceptions but upon adaptation to actual threat and the like. Nonetheless, we may conclude that current diagnostic reliabilities *do* warrant research into and theorizing about schizophrenia. Improvement is obviously necessary, and concerted efforts are under way to bring that about. We may, however, turn to our examination of the problems of schizophrenic utterance at this point without undue concern that we may be pursuing the chimera.

B. SCHIZOPHRENIC UTTERANCE DEFINED

By *utterance* we shall mean the production of language, spoken or written, whether spontaneous or in response to questions or other task instructions. Our analysis will focus upon the linguistic aspects of utterance, such as word order, word meaning, and sentence structure. Secondary aspects of utterance, such as pause patterns, handwriting, and the like, will be touched upon in a limited way only.

Utterances of schizophrenic patients have been typically regarded as pathological on the basis of two quite different sets of attributes. The first of these is the credibility of the content. Thus, a schizophrenic patient who states *My brain has turned to molten lead* is exhibiting delusional beliefs while employing language that is entirely adequate. The sentence structure and semantic meaning of the utterance are quite clear. Subject, verb, and object are properly placed; the adjective is appropriate to the noun, and so forth. We regard the statement as evidence of pathology because the content is incredible, not because it is linguistically deficient. A model for the understanding of delusions has been presented by the present writer elsewhere (Maher, 1974; Maher & Ross, 1983). It will not be considered here.

A second set of attributes arises from linguistic anomalies in the patient's utterances. That is to say that we recognize that there is something amiss with the utterance regardless of any judgment about the validity of its content. For example, such sentences as *Right now, I'm thinking of Pike's Peak for a rehaul of the Korean thing* [Chaika, 1974] or *Thanks everlasting and Merry New Year to the Mentholatum Company for my nose, for my nose, for my nose, for my nose, for my nose, for my nose* [Maher, 1968], are regarded as anomalous not because we doubt that the first speaker is thinking about Pike's Peak or that the second is grateful for the treatment of his nose. They are anomalous because they deviate from normal rules of utterance. Our theory will be concerned with this kind of deviation.

C. THE ANOMALIES OF SCHIZOPHRENIC UTTERANCE

At this point we can turn to a description of the major anomalies that have been found in the utterance of schizophrenic patients. No catalog can be exhaustive, and we provide only a description of the major categories. These will form the basis of the theoretical explanation that will follow.

1. Repetition of Linguistic Units

A frequent observation is that the utterances of schizophrenic patients tend to include many repetitions. These repetitions may be of complete phrases, words, or syllables; they may be immediate or separated by other segments of an utterance. Examples come from many sources. The first of those that follow has already been cited in part in a previous paragraph.

1.   *I am of I-Building in the State Hospital. With my nostrils clogged and Winter here, I chanced to be reading the magazine that Mentholatum advertised from. Kindly send it to me at the hospital. Send it to me, Joseph Nemo,[1] in care of Joseph Nemo and me who answers by the name of Joseph Nemo and will care for it myself. Thanks everlasting and Merry New Year to Mentholatum Company for my nose, for my nose, for my nose, for my nose, for my nose* [Maher, 1968, p. 30].

Here we can see the repetition of the writer's name, *Joseph Nemo* and the phrase *for my nose,* and the repetition of *care,* with a slightly different connotation on the two occasions.

---

[1] The real name has been changed in this excerpt and in any other similar quotations in this chapter.

2.   *I hope to be home soon, very soon. I fancy chocolate eclairs, chocolate
     eclairs donuts. I want some donuts, I do want some golden syrup, a tin of
     golden syrup or treacle, jam* [Critchley, 1964, p. 361].

Here repetitions of one- and two-word phrases are clear. The same kind of
process can be seen in the responses of a patient to vocabulary items presented to him:

3.   **Cruel**—*to try to believe what you really are. It's cruel sometimes to be
     kind.*
     Near—*to cure kindness you've got to be keen on kindness. Sometimes it's
     cruel.*
     Shrivel—*you shrivel up if you don't believe in what you say.*
     Chivalry—*it's sometimes more cruel to act age instead of beauty* [Raven,
     1958, p. 224].

In this sequence of utterances, we can see the frequent reappearance of *cruel*
as an intrusion and the repetition of *kind*—originally appearing as an association to cruel, perhaps.

4.   *The subterfuge and the mistaken planned substitutions for that demanded
     American action can produce nothing but the general results of negative
     contention and the impractical results careless application, the natural
     results of of misplacements, of mistaken purpose and unrighteous position,
     the impractical serviceabilities of unnecessary contradictions* [Maher, 1968,
     p. 30].

In this passage the repetition is at the level of syllables as well as words.
Thus, *mistaken, results,* and *impractical* appear twice, while *mis* also appears in *misplacements, -ion* appears in substitu*tion*s, ac*tion*, conten*tion*,
applica*tion*, posi*tion*, contradic*tion*s; *sub* in *sub*terfuge, *sub*stitutions, etc.

5.   A German language sample reads:

     *Das ist vom Kaiserhaus, sie haben es von den Voreltern, von der Urwelt,
     Frankfurt-am-Main, das sind die Franken, Frankfurter Wurstchen,
     Frankenthal, Frankenstein* [Mittenecker, 1951, p. 366].

Quantitative measures of repetition (or *perseveration*) of syllables have been
reported by Mittenecker (1951, 1953) with samples of German language and
by a variety of investigators in English using the type–token ratio. This
latter measure consists of the ratio of the number of different words used
in a passage to the total number of words in the passage. The more frequent
the repetitions, the fewer different words per passage of a given length.

Because whole words are counted, and not syllables, the measure is somewhat cruder than Mittenecker's technique. A detailed summary of work with this technique is to be found elsewhere in this volume (Cozolino, Chapter 3).

Nevertheless, both measures generally indicate more repetitions in the language of schizophrenic patients than in the language of normal controls. An additional, important report was made by Mittenecker to the effect that repetition is higher in the normal language of schizothymic individuals, suggesting that the processes that give rise to repetitions are operating prior to any overt clinical manifestation of schizophrenia.

2. Associative Intrusions

A second, common observation about schizophrenic utterances is that they often contain associative intrusions. Some of the examples given above illustrate this. Thus in example 3, we find the intrusion of *kind* as an association to *cruel,* the association enduring into the response to *near* to the extent of dominating the response and making it irrelevant to the question. These associative intrusions may be in the form of simple association chains, or they may occur as spasmodic intrusions in later parts of the utterance.

Examples of associative intrusions follow:

6.   *My mother's name was Bill . . . and coo?* [Chaika, 1974].

7.   *I like coffee, cream, cows, Elizabeth Taylor* [Maher, McKean, & Mc-Laughlin, 1966].

8.   Bleuler's patient, when listing the members of her family included, *Father, son . . . and Holy Ghost* [Bleuler, 1950].

9.   Arieti (1967) quotes the example of a patient who would recite a morning prayer as follows:

   Sweetness angel, gentle, mild, mellow, gladness, glory, grandeur, splendor, bubbling, babbling, gurgling, handy, candy, dandy, honor, honey, sugar, frosting, guide, guiding, enormous, pure, magnificent, enchanged, blooming plumes [p. 280].

10.   Examples of associational intrusions at segments of an utterance would include:

   Here a man has lost his staff, his right arm is locked behind his back without a leg to stand upon. Is that right, there should be a nurse or other staff to see to his rights. Why not consider the rights of all of the people who make up this country of ours. What is their wish for their future, their family, their community, our nation.

In the rather complex example 10, we see the appearance of association to opposites (*arm–leg*), and double-entendre associations to *staff* (as a supportive pole and as a ward employee) and *right* in three meanings of location (*right* arm), of propriety (is that *right*), and in the legal sense (to see to his *rights,* the *rights* of all people).

The demonstration of associative intrusions of this kind is inevitably a matter of inference. There is no definitive way in which we can be sure that *arm* and *leg* appeared in the previous paragraph by associational processes: It simply seems more likely that this was the case than that the entire sentence was intended and completed as a meaningful utterance.

Before proceeding further, we should note that one set of characteristics of schizophrenic utterance may overlap with another. If a patient utters a sentence containing a clang association, it will appear both as an example of repetition of syllables and as the intrusion of an association.

3. Punning

The appearance of intruding associations into an utterance may occur when a word has been employed that is susceptible to more than one valid meaning. When this happens it creates the general impression of a pun, or play on words. In a letter sent to the writer, addressed originally to the complaint department of a large store in a midwestern city, the following passage occurs. It was written by a schizophrenic patient.

11. *To Wise and Company,*

If you think that you are being wise to send me a bill for money I have already paid I am in nowise going to do so unless I get the whys and wherefores from you to me. But where fours have been then fives will be and other numbers and calculations and accounts to your no-account no-bill, noble, nothing.

12. PHYSICIAN: *That's a cigarette you're smoking.*

PATIENT: *It's a holy one . . . it goes in one hole and out the other and that makes it holy* [Chaika, 1974, p. 268].

We have already seen an example of the same kind of process in example 10 above, with the multiple use of the word *right*. In both cases, the appearance of associations to the second meaning of the critical word leads the patient off into a digression from the apparent intent of the original utterance. Thus, the patient in example 10 begins to talk about a man's right arm and wanders off into a discussion of civil rights. In example 11, the writer is continually diverted by double meanings. *Whys and wherefores* brings up *where fours,* which in turn brings up *fives, numbers, calculations,* and so forth. One is tempted to speculate that *no-account, no-bill,* and *noble* are chained together because of the meaning of the word *count* as a title of nobility.

Systematic quantitative investigation of the vulnerability of schizophrenic patients to double-meaning words has been reported by Chapman and his colleagues (Chapman, Chapman, & Miller, 1964). Their findings indicate that intrusions are more likely to occur when the intruding meaning of the double-meaning word is of more common usage than the intended meaning. In a test developed by Chapman for this investigation, the patient is asked to select the correct meaning of a sentence containing a double-meaning word, where the rest of the sentence provides a context that makes clear which meaning is intended. Thus, in the test sentence *The farmer wanted a new pen for his cattle,* the subject is given the choice of an explanation such as *The farmer wanted a new writing implement, The farmer wanted a new enclosure,* or, irrelevantly, *The farmer wanted a new overcoat.* If the word *pen* is most commonly used to mean *writing implement,* the schizophrenic patient is likely to opt for this meaning even though the context words, *farmer* and *cattle,* indicate that the meaning *enclosure* is intended. The process of intrusion is less likely to occur if the context calls for the most common meaning—thus, the sentence *The writer wanted a new pen and paper* would not lead to misinterpretations of the meaning of *pen.* It is interesting in this connection to note the observation of Arieti (1967, p. 280) of a patient who, when shown a pen and asked to name it, said, "A prison," presumably because of the meaning *penitentiary* as *pen.*

4. Object Chaining

Schizophrenic patients sometimes utter sentences in which the position of the object (but not the subject or verb) is occupied by several nouns or noun phrases often lexically appropriate and not necessarily in the form of obvious associations. The following are from the writer's files.

13. *I have no way of knowing how much difference of opinion different editors, politicians, historians, sexologists, astrologers, or theologians might have to say about this very unusual, very controversial letter.*

14. *I have put out some beautiful things, the bust of Lincoln, the bust of Washington, the Thinker, strawberry teapot and sugar bowl, some ashtrays.*

Several of the examples cited already for other purposes also include instances of this multiple-object sequence. Thus, examples 1, 2, 4, 6, 7, 8, and 10 all contain some object chaining in their structure. Maher *et al.* (1966) have reported the results of empirical studies of utterances consistent with the hypothesis that object chaining is significantly related to the diagnostic judgment that an utterance is schizophrenically disordered.

5. Word Schemes

Any observer of schizophrenic utterance will have noticed occasional examples of written language productions in which the patient appears to be using such components as letters, numbers, syllables, or sounds to generate a complex pattern or scheme. The following example will illustrate such a case:

15.   *My name is Aaron, first and last Jewish high priest . . . I believe in*
      Abraham, father of the Hebrew race . . . an acid is a chemical compound
      which contains hydrogen and which dissolves metals. The adrenal gland
      produces cortisone and adrenaline. The Aegean sea connects Asia with
      Europe, the Hebrews with the Greeks. Africa is the land of the dark peo-
      ples. Agriculture is the art and science of raising vegetable crops in order
      that people may eat. From the books of Moses to the five religions of
      Aaron, God is very interesting. In this day of the airplane religions need
      to unite. Jewish, Catholic, Protestant glorify man; Moslem, Hindu,
      Buddhist glorify animal . . . . Alcohol is formed by fermentation and is a
      powerful stimulant and antiseptic. America is a place for God to wear a
      New Jersey. The anatomy of God has miles of smiles to go with years of
      tears . . . . The apostles are the twelve disciples of Jesus. the Lord. Aqua
      means water from which fish, symbol of Christ, came. Arabia is a desert
      from which Islam came [Document received by the writer, cited in
      McKean, 1963, p. 1].

As the emphasis (added by the present writer) suggests, the patient appears to have been working his way, more or less systematically, through the alphabet with two letter combinations each beginning with *A*. Thus *Aaron, Abraham, acid, adrenal . . . Arabia,* follow in approximate sequence. The utterance is also marked by certain content themes, mainly the desire to unify certain religions. We have no way to know whether the alphabetical sequence that we see in this instance was the result of a controlled conscious plan of utterance in which the religious theme intrudes or in which the double A beginning the patient's own name provokes an associational process based upon letter sequences, with occasional digressions into religion together with some clang associations (*miles of smiles and years of tears*) and one punning association (*a place for God to wear a New Jersey*). At a later part of this chapter, the writer will argue that word and numbers schemes of this kind represent a compound of a basic pathology of utterance combined with an interpretive process of the kind found in delusions.

II. Specifications for a Theory of Schizophrenic Utterance

Ultimately, a theory is judged by the data that are obtained when it is tested. The judgment is made in comparison with whatever other theories are available, defective theories falling not from their own weakness but because of the presence of a better alternative. Theoretical formulations of schizophrenic utterance are not yet, however, in a state where telling comparisons can be made; hence, we approach the questions of the specifications for a theory of schizophrenic utterance by laying out some a priori criteria rather than by pointing to an existing theory that must be bettered.

A. PARSIMONY

Parsimony requires that theories about pathological processes invoke the fewest possible factors to account for the widest range of symptoms. This is the appropriate operating criterion until such time as this minimum number of components fails to account for as wide a range of facts as may be explained by a less parsimonious theory. In practice this means that a theory of schizophrenic utterance should begin with the assumption that the pathological processes already seen to operate in a wide range of nonlanguage symptoms (such as perception, motivation, and learning) are also at work in producing the language anomalies and should not abandon this assumption until the data compel a more complex set of assumptions.

B. SPECIFICITY

Specificity of prediction is a second important criterion. Theories that can only "postdict" the phenomena are, in principle, untestable. Thus, an adequate theory must specify the conditions under which linguistic anomalies will occur, where in an utterance or passage they are likely to occur, what semantic or syntactical features they are likely to possess, and what nonlanguage symptoms are likely to accompany them. To take a case in point, an adequate theory must explain why we much more often get object chaining than subject or verb chaining, or why punning intrusions generally consist of the strong meaning disrupting the weak meaning of a word rather than vice versa.

Precision of prediction also requires an adequately detailed and *positive* description of what will happen. If we predict that a schizophrenic, asked to discuss a parent, will speak "gibberish" or "nonsense," we have provided merely a negative description by noting that whatever is said will *not be* "sense." We have failed to be precise because an almost infinite set of word patterns could be uttered by the patient and still be consistent with the prediction. On the other hand, if we specify that under conditions likely to elicit schizophrenic utterance we will find object chaining with associational characteristics, only a small class of utterances could confirm the prediction but a very large range would falsify it. Our earlier example 6, *My mother's name was Bill . . . and coo,* is equally consistent with the prediction that the patient will talk "nonsense" and with the prediction that there will be associational object chaining. The second prediction is much more easily falsified than the first, and hence the theory that gives rise to it is more testable, more precise, and thus preferable.

Explanations of pathological behavior that focus upon the reaction of other people to such behavior run the risk of weakening prediction by confusing effects and causes. We might, for example, note that the behavior of a drunken person is embarrassing and annoying to others present. From this we might prematurely conclude that, as drunken behavior has this effect, it is reasonable to suppose that the slurred speech and stumbling gait of the intoxicated individual are best understood as due to a failure to be sensitive to the reactions of others and/or a motive to cause them distress. No doubt these explanations might have some merit in individual cases, but we would be wise to seek first for explanations in the pharmacology of alcohol and its effects upon neuromuscular coordination. By the same token, we should hesitate to assume that the fact that schizophrenic utterance often causes listeners to be confused means that the utterances take the specific form that they do *because* they succeed in confusing listeners. No doubt disordered behavior is sometimes maintained by the consequences that it creates: It is rash to assume that this is always the case.

C. TEMPORAL FLUCTUATIONS

Third, a theory of pathology must deal with the fact that many symptoms fluctuate over time and that patterns of symptoms may change even though the underlying pathology does not. Huntington's disease, for example, shows a clear family history and systematic deterioration of motor and intellectual deterioration, but four different subtypes can be identified, each with different symptom patterns. In the same family, different individuals may have different subtypes, and the same patient may, over a period of time, display a change in subtype. Applied to schizophrenia, this consideration makes it likely that not all patients with a diagnosis of schizophrenia will exhibit schizophrenic utterance on demand or that the particular anomalies exhibited on one occasion will always be the same as those revealed on another.

D. PROPOSITIONS FOR A THEORY OF SCHIZOPHRENIA

Certain reasonable propositions can be advanced as a result of schizophrenia research. They have guided the formulation of the theory repeated in this chapter. Full discussion of all of them is beyond its scope, and so they will be presented here in summary fashion. However, the analysis of evidence relevant to the attentional deficit hypothesis and language anomalies, summarized in item 5 below, will form a substantive part of this chapter.

1. Schizophrenia has a substantial genetic etiology.

2. The genetic component is most plausibly regarded as a diathesis or vulnerability such that the manifestations of clinical schizophrenia are precipitated and exacerbated by stress. Stress may include threat, rejection, fatigue, physical illness, loss of employment, and many other such psychological and situational factors.

3. This diathesis is quantitively variable from one affected person to another so that in some cases only severe stress will suffice to produce clinical schizophrenia while in others minor stresses will do so.

4. As a corollary to the preceding observation, we should expect that extreme vulnerability will mean that a constant and continuing schizophrenic syndrome is likely to arise early in life as minor stresses tend inevitably to be of frequent and repeated occurrence. Per contra, identifiable major stress, rapid onset, later average age of onset, brief duration, and low recidivism are most likely to be found when vulnerability is low, as such stresses are rarer in occurrence and less likely to occur repeatedly to the same individual.

5. While the biological mechanisms that mediate the response to stress are perhaps the most primary in the causal chain, one early link in this chain entails disruption in the efficient and rapid adaptation of attentional focusing to the demands of the external environment. We shall propose here that the same disruption impairs the ordered selection and editing of internally stored stimuli required for communication and other patterned forms of response.

6. A distinction can be drawn between basic pathological processes and those anomalies of behavior that arise as a secondary consequence of them. These latter will vary considerably as a function of the individual characteristics of the patient, such as intelligence, education, prior experience, and current social milieu. Secondary consequences may develop in reciprocal steps, affecting the patient's own behavior and that of others, especially the patient's immediate family. Thus, a patient with difficulty in language utterance may begin to avoid situations that call for communication. Where

this cannot be done, the patient's verbal behavior will elicit anomalous communication patterns in those trying to converse with the patient, and this in turn will exacerbate the disruptions of the patient's communications.

III. Attentional Deficit

A. SCHIZOPHRENIA AND THE ATTENTIONAL DEFICIT HYPOTHESIS

In one form or another, it has long been hypothesized that a part of the primary pathology of schizophrenia consists in a deficit of attentional deployment. The observations upon which these hypotheses have been based acquired an experimental form in the early work of Kraepelin's associate, Reis, and later in the work of Hoch. As early as 1904, Hoch suggested that the clang associations seen in patients were due to an attentional disorder and that this could explain a diverse range of other anomalies (Hoch, 1904; Maher & Maher, 1979). Early clinical observations along the same general line had been offered by Kraepelin and by Bleuler. Bleuler, for example, commented: "The selectivity which attention exercises over normal sensory impressions may be reduced to zero so that almost everything that meets the senses is registered [Bleuler, 1950, p. 68]."

This theme has appeared in various forms through the succeeding decades. David Shakow proposed that the attentional difficulties of schizophrenic patients were reflected in their inability to hold a preparatory mental set in reaction-time tasks. His early formulation of this problem was reported in Huston, Shakow, and Riggs (1937) and was extended over many papers in subsequent years (e.g., Shakow, 1962, 1963, 1971). Chapman and Chapman (1973) were to criticize the mental set model, mainly on the grounds of its vagueness. It does, however, occupy an important position in the history of the development of experimental psychopathology.

In their review of the literature on attention and schizophrenia to that date, Lang and Buss (1965) concluded that "schizophrenics have difficulty in focusing on relevant stimuli and excluding irrelevant stimuli, in maintaining a set over time, in shifting a set when it is necessary and in pacing themselves. . . . These difficulties are pervasive, occurring over a wide range of perceptual, motor and cognitive tasks [p. 97]."

Difficulties in attentional focusing, deduced from the nature of the tasks upon which schizophrenic patients perform with most evident deficit, were also reported by the patients themselves. In a series of innovative studies, McGhie and his colleagues (Lawson, McGhie, & Chapman, 1964; McGhie & Chapman, 1961; McGhie, Chapman, & Lawson, 1965a, 1965b) obtained first hand accounts of the experience of schizophrenia. Examples of their reports include the following:

> *I can't concentrate. It's diversion of attention that troubles me—the sounds are coming through to me but I feel my mind cannot cope with everything. It's difficult to concentrate on any one sound—it's like trying two or three different things at one time.*

> *It's as if I'm too wide awake—very, very alert. I can't relax at all. Everything seems to go through me. I just can't shut things out.*

> *Everything seems to grip my attention although I am not particularly interested in anything. I'm speaking to you just now but I can hear noises going on next door and in the corridor. I find it difficult to shut these out and it makes it more difficult for me to concentrate on what I am saying to you. Often the silliest things going on seem to interest me. That's not even true; they won't interest me but I find myself attending to them and wasting a lot of time this way* [McGhie & Chapman, 1961, cited in McGhie, 1970].

The difficulty in screening out external stimuli was paralleled for some patients by a difficulty in screening internal irrelevancies out of consciousness. Thus:

> *My thoughts get all jumbled up. I start thinking or talking about something but I never get there. Instead I wander off in the wrong direction and get caught up with all sorts of different things that may be connected with the things that I want to say but in a way that I can't explain. People listening to me get more lost than I do* [McGhie & Chapman, 1961, p. 108].

> *Half the time I am talking about one thing and thinking about half a dozen other things at the same time. It must look queer to people when I laugh about something that has got nothing to do with what I am talking about, but they don't know what's going on inside and how much of it is running around in my head. You see I might be talking about something quite serious to you and other things come into my head at the same time that are funny and this makes me laugh. If I could only concentrate on the one thing at the one time I wouldn't look half so silly* [McGhie & Chapman, 1961, pp. 109–110].

Many similar reports have come from other investigators (e.g., Freedman, 1974) and reflect phenomena summarized by Shakow (1962) in this way:

> It is as if, in the scanning process which takes place before the response to a stimulus is made, the schizophrenic is unable to select out the material relevant for optimal response. He apparently cannot free himself from the irrelevant among the numerous possibilities for choice. In other words, that function which is of equal importance as

a response *to* stimuli, namely the protection *against* the response to stimuli, is abey-
ant. . . .
   . . . irrelevant associations to which the normal is also subject but to a much lesser
degree would appear to arise from three sources: chance distractors from the environment; irrelevancies from the stimulus situation; and irrelevancies from past experience—the mere presence of these irrelevant factors—seem to lead the schizophrenic to
give them focal rather than ground significance, signal rather than noise import [pp.
2-3].

It is important to note here that the notion that an individual "selects" a
response to make does not necessarily imply a *conscious* process of selection. There is little or no reason to believe that, when utterances are formed
in ordinary speech, they represent the end point of a process of conscious
examination of various alternative words and phrases—although this may
well occur under some circumstances, as when the speaker is seeking to
make a very specific impression on the listener and is monitoring the listener's progress from point to point in this regard. In the production of
written language, of course, considerable degrees of conscious editing may
be involved both at the point of the actual writing and from one draft to
another.

A thorough review of the data supporting the usefulness of the attentional deficit hypothesis is beyond the scope of this chapter. We may simply
point out that a wide range of experimental findings, clinical observation,
and patients' first hand accounts suggest strongly that the condition of the
schizophrenic patient is marked by serious problems in excluding from consciousness irrelevant stimulus material from both the external environment
and from inner stored associations. Later in this chapter, we shall refer to
possible loci of the defect responsible for this condition. However, we must
first consider the processes by which the identification of relevancy and
irrelevancy appears to be conducted in normal circumstances.

B. Adaptive Aspects of Attention

Selective attention is commonly assumed to operate through the mechanism of a filter (Broadbent, 1958) that serves to screen irrelevant stimuli,
preventing them from entering the information-processing sequence that
would normally terminate in recognition and identification in consciousness. Cognitive psychologists have offered several models of the process of
filtration and access, varying in terms of the proposed locus of the filter,
the completeness of suppression of irrelevant input, and the fate of this
input (e.g., Broadbent, 1958; Moray, 1959; Treisman, 1960). Whatever the
mechanics of the selection process, we suggest that effective responses to
environmental stimuli involve a balance between two opposing alternative
filter settings. One setting is maximally open and hence facilitates the de-

tection and identification of novel or changing stimuli in the environment. The other, a narrow setting, is insensitive to stimuli other than those immediately relevant to the current motive state of the individual. At times psychopathologists have been impressed by the apparent inability of schizophrenic patients to exclude irrelevant stimuli (i.e., by their distractibility). At other times investigators have emphasized the apparent tendency of patients to perseverate in attending to a limited portion of the stimulus field, seemingly unaware of changes elsewhere in the environment. We propose that neither of these two settings, wide or narrow, is a fixed characteristic of schizophrenic attention, but that it is the rapidity and adequacy of the adjustment of the filter setting to the changing task demands of a situation that is deficient.

An organism acting in a complex environment is faced with conflicting sets of demands upon attention. One set of demands arises from the necessity to be alert to any new stimulus entering the immediate environment, for such stimuli may pose a threat to life or an opportunity for eating, reproduction, or other activities favoring survival. No organism could ignore dangerous predators or edible prey and still survive. But, by the same token, any new stimulus must be examined and identified if an adaptive response is to be forthcoming. Examination and identification take time and require the momentary suppression of attention to other stimuli in the environment. This takes place at some risk to the organism, for this suppression of attention may entail failure to notice a predator approaching from another direction. The longer the identification process takes, the greater the danger to the organism. Rapid identification requires that the observer make maximum use of any *redundancies* in the features of the stimulus that are to be identified. Features are redundant to the extent that they correlate with other features. Once we have ascertained that the car parked by the highway carries a flashing blue light on the roof, the further observation that the word *Police* is painted on the door is redundant. Any stimulus characteristic may be said to be completely redundant if observation of it adds nothing to our knowledge of the identity of the stimulus concerned, beyond what has already been found out.

When the information value of the features of a single stimulus may be ordered in terms of the amount of information each conveys, it is most effective to scan them in that order, the aim being to reduce uncertainty by the largest possible amount at each successive point in the sequence. When the uncertainty remaining at any point falls below some significant value, there may be more to be gained by widening attention to scan the environment broadly before returning to the next feature of the original stimulus. Thus, a ground gunner noting a distant plane in time of war may scan for a feature that has a high correlation with its status as friendly or hostile.

If 90% of all airplanes with twin fuselages in the combat zone are friendly, scanning for this feature first may be effective in indicating a high enough probability that it is friendly to permit the gunner to scan the horizon for other possible intruders before returning to examine the features that will determine whether it is one of the 10% of such planes that are hostile.

The use of redundancies to permit the optimum deployment of attention, from narrow to wide, requires instant adaptation to redundancies. In a complex and rapidly changing environment, no time must be wasted in examining stimulus characteristics that are highly correlated with those already scanned for; in a primitive natural habitat, such time wasting could be fatal. On the other hand, there is danger for the organism if it abandons the narrow scan of a single stimulus in favor of a wide scan of the environment before the harmlessness (or indigestibility) of the single stimulus has been established at a safe level of probability.

Certain activities may require focusing of attention in a narrow range for extended periods of time. Eating and sexual activity are possible examples of these. Under these circumstances the survival of the organism may depend not upon effective attentional adaptations but upon conducting the activity in secure and private settings in which the risk of external threat is minimal and the need for attentional flexibility thereby diminished. It is tempting to speculate that the customary standards of privacy and modesty that generally surround these activities are reflections of the primitive vulnerability of the participants rather than of purely moral codes of conduct.

Whatever the evolutionary origin of patterns of attentional deployment may be, it is clear that disruption of them must bring much behavioral disorganization in train and that this will be likely evidenced in, among other areas, the use of stimulus redundancies to optimize responses.

In any given situation, the variable of redundancy interacts with the current costs and benefits of various responses: These, of course, reflect the nature of current motive states. Under some extreme conditions, prisoners in concentration camps risked death to steal food, indicating that the cost of definitely failing to find food at that point was functionally greater than the cost of risking execution. We know from the early classic studies of Atkinson and McClelland (1948) that hungry subjects judge an ambiguous stimulus to be food related on the basis of less information about the stimulus than do nonhungry subjects. Many examples of shooting from the hip on the basis of inadequate stimulus identification come to mind. It is sufficient here to reiterate that the degree of redundancy that leads to identification and termination of scrutiny will vary with the motive state of the observer.

The main point of this discussion is to suggest that there is an intimate and inverse relation between the redundancy of a stimulus and the demand that it will place upon attention. Such relations have been pointed out, for example, for motor movement (e.g., Fitts, 1954; Posner & Keele, 1969; Salmoni, Sullivan, & Starkes, 1976) and for animal behavior as well as for other response systems. Among the many approaches that may be made to the investigation of attentional processes in schizophrenia is one that emphasizes the failure of attentional focusing to respond to stimulus redundancy. Such failure may consist of slowness in terminating observation of a given stimulus when maximum redundancy has been established—with accompanying failure to respond to new, low-redundancy stimuli in the environment. It may consist of failure to continue scrutiny of a low-redundancy stimulus to the point that an identification can be established. The first is the clinical phenomenon of *perseveration* and the second that of *distractibility*.

It is our intention here to apply this rather general model of attention redundancy dissociation to the analysis of the phenomena of schizophrenic utterance to see how broad a range of findings might be consistent with it.

IV. Language, Redundancy, and Attention

A. REDUNDANCY

In our discussion we employ the term *redundancy* as it is used in the context of information theory. Any event, signal, stimulus, or other change in the environment may be empirically correlated with one or more following events. Sounds of a siren are highly likely to be followed by the appearance of an emergency vehicle; thunder is often followed by lightning and by rain; the sound of a car in the driveway by a knock on the door and so forth. To the extent that any event A is likely to be followed by another event B, the occurrence of B is redundant; that is, it is predictable. The redundancy of B may be quantified, being directly related to the empirical frequency with which B actually follows A. If B always follows A, it is completely redundant; if B follows A on 90% of occasions, it is more redundant than another event, C, which follows A on only 40% of occasions.

Redundancy of this kind is of significance in the study of language. Hearing the beginning of a sentence: *I pledge allegiance to the flag of the United* _____, the missing final words could readily be predicted. They are thus redundant. Given the sentence *I will now put on my hat and* _____, there is a reasonable probability that the terminal word will be *coat* or at least some article of clothing. A listener could make such a prediction with some probability of being correct. On the other hand, given a sentence beginning

I will now _____, it would be very difficult to predict the missing words and thus the word *put* is not redundant.

Redundancy in this sense must be sharply distinguished from the literary meaning of the term—namely, the duplication of meaning in an utterance. If a speaker were to say *I will now put on my hat and hat,* the second *hat* would be completely redundant in the literary sense, but, being quite uncommon and unpredictable in ordinary speech, would be of low redundancy in the information theory sense.

B. SERIAL ORDER

For reasons that appear intuitively plausible, the redundancy of a word in a sentence is likely to increase as a function of the position that it occupies in the serial order of the sentence. Thus, the reader who successfully predicts the missing word in the sentence given in the preceding section might find it very difficult to predict correctly the second word in a sentence given only that the first words are *I will*_____. Data bearing on this issue were presented over 20 years ago by Aborn, Rubenstein, and Sterling (1959). They studied the predictability of words as a function of serial order in sentences of 6-, 11-, and 25-word lengths. Unfortunately, they did not control for sentence structure, combining simple and compound sentences in the same data analysis. Nonetheless, their data are pertinent to the present discussion. In 6-word sentences—those least likely to be compound—they found that the predictability of nouns (the largest class of words) increased steadily from the initial position to the final position. They comment on their overall results: ". . . predictability increases with sentence length regardless of sentence position. This is in accord with the observation of information theorists that constraint increases with the increase in context [pp. 177–178].'' Predictability in this study turned out to be a complex matter. The probability that a word could be correctly predicted increased if it occupied a position late in the sentence, but this effect was reduced if the word in question was from a class with many possible members. Nouns, for example, formed the largest single class of words. Hence, the prediction of exactly which noun is going to occur in a sentence is made difficult by the very large number of alternatives from which a choice is to be made.

These investigators noted that, in general, the maximum effect upon predictability was achieved when the prediction was made within a context of between 5 and 10 words. Longer contexts did not improve predictability. Similar data were reported by MacGinitie (1961). He also commented that contexts of more than 5 words had little better effect than 5-word segments in improving predictability. However, he noted that long-range effects might occur where the words to be predicted are taken from a continuous passage.

Under these circumstances the predictability gained by increasing exposure to a context may be cumulative such that sequential exposure of a reader to segments of the passage makes it possible to predict with increasing accuracy even when the immediate context is fewer than 5 words. MacGinitie cites the related finding of Carroll, Carton, and Wilds (1959) showing that the predictive advantage of 5-word contexts was significantly better when the segments came from a sequenced paragraph than when the same segments were rearranged in random order. MacGinitie points out, further, that if groups of contiguous words are removed from text their predictability is irretrievably reduced: "In reading . . . although understanding may often be gained without seeing every word clearly, if a *group* of words is missed, the loss is generally irretrievable from context [p. 128]."

Much the same effect has been found where the unit of study is the single letter in the context of printed English. Thus, Burton and Licklider (1955) reported that there was increasing predictability of single printed letters with increasing length of contexts up to a maximum of 32-letter sequences. Longer contexts provided no improvement in predictability. Aborn *et al.* (1959) concluded that their maximum context of predictability of 5–10 words corresponds reasonably to a context of 23–45 letters, with a mean very close to the 32 letters cited by Burton and Licklider.

We might summarize these findings as follows: In sequential passages of language, each successive unit is increasingly redundant (i.e., predictable) for sequences of up to either 32 letters or approximately 5–10 words. This general function is subject to modifications. Other factors being equal, a word drawn from a large word class (such as a noun) is less predictable in the same sequential position than a word drawn from a small word class (such as a function word—article, preposition, etc.). If the passage from which the words are to be predicted is long and drawn from a continuous systematic source, there is a cumulative gradual increase in predictability. High-frequency words are more redundant than low-frequency words in the same context.

C. Order of Approximation

In the studies cited in the preceding discussion, the contexts were normal printed English sentences. These sentences are constrained by the rules governing the formation of English sentences. The rules are instrumental in generating the redundancies that operate to improve predictability. Thus, we know that, in an adequate sentence, an article such as *the* is highly likely to be followed by a noun. The words that provide the context of predictability do not do so by sheer virtue of their total number, but because they are organized according to grammatical rules. Miller and Selfridge (1950) developed a technique for varying the degree to which any given string of words approximates the rules of normal sentence structure. At one extreme, that of zero-order approximation, five words are selected randomly from a dictionary and put together to form a string. Strings of similar length are constructed such that any two words in sequence have actually occurred together in a real sentence, any three words, and so forth on up to a complete sentence. Subjects heard these word sequences read aloud and then were required to repeat them. Percentage accuracy of recall increased with the order of approximation for any given length of word sequence up to a maximum of fifth-order levels. Increasing the order of approximation beyond five—including long sequences of complete sentences—did not increase recall efficiency further.

Increasing the order of approximation is clearly increasing the redundancy of words in the sequence. In the zero-order condition, no word could be predicted from the previous word, because the transitional probabilities between each word and the next were purely random. When the fifth-order condition was present, any series of five words in a sequence would possess the redundancy gradients of a simple sentence, and, as in the case of the work of Aborn et al. (1959) already cited, this seems to have been the ceiling value of redundancy that a sequence could attain. The work of Miller and Selfridge demonstrated that order of approximation—and hence redundancy—affected the recall of heard word sequences. Inferior recall may, of course, arise from variables at many points in the input–output chain. Initial processing of the words throughout the input chain, retrieval of the words once processed, and transmission of the retrieved words to the motor responses involved in communicating the recall are some of the obvious elements in which impairment might arise. Whatever the locus of impairment, it is clear that redundancy affects it. As we shall see shortly, the beneficial effects of redundancy on recall are not found in some kinds of schizophrenic patient.

D. REDUNDANCY AND LISTENING

A good many years ago the Danish psychologist Rubin suggested that systems of various kinds evolve redundancies in their operation as a form of safety margin serving to ensure against the effects of failures of part of the system. Examples that he gave (Maher, 1973; Nielsen, 1956) included the labeling of poisonous medicines as such, locking them up in a special cabinet, and the provision of training in their use to the personnel who will have reason to administer them. Bridge builders, airplane designers, and others set load working capacities that are well above the maximum loads likely to be applied. This safety margin, Rubin suggested, could be discerned in the development of language. In order to ensure that such factors as ambient noise, listener fatigue, and poor speaker articulation did not corrupt the intelligibility of a communication, redundancy evolved to provide the necessary margin of safety. Where these factors are likely to be present to an unusual degree, as in combat radio communications, additional redundancy is added to crucial messages through the use of phonetic voice codes of the "A-Alpha, B-Bravo" variety, thereby making it possible for the listener to hear only a part of a transmission—"Alph . . ." or ". . . ravo"—without losing comprehension. Rubin commented on these factors as follows:

> Where conditions make comprehension difficult it can be achieved by straining to pay close attention. This happens, for example, when one is listening to a lecture in a foreign language—as long as one makes an effort one can understand what is being said—but if one tires or relaxes the whole thing, more or less, goes over one's head.
>
> We have no precise description of how these efforts are made and we know nothing of their psychophysiological mechanisms. For our purposes here it is sufficient to state that we know that comprehension can be obtained by exertion where it would otherwise fail. However, we should note that attention often adapts itself to the demands of a situation. Involuntarily, we concentrate more where comprehension is difficult than where it is not. This concentration is not a general arousal of attention but is focused and directed at understanding the speaker and excluding disturbing factors [cited in Maher, 1973, pp. 80–81].

Rubin notes here that attentional focusing is achieved at some cost of "exertion," "straining," or "effort," and that, presumably, this kind of effort is harder to make when the listener is already fatigued. He went on to observe that the speaker also adapts the rate, volume, articulation, and word choice of utterance to compensate for the presence of difficult listening conditions. Neither the attentional adaptation of the listener nor the utterance patterns of the speaker were assumed to be voluntary, although they might be in particular cases. Rubin conducted some studies of redundancy using a crude device that periodically interrupted a microphone–loudspeaker circuit so that only portions of the transmitted utterance were heard. Interruptions were at rates between 20 and 50 per second, eliminating up to half of the total transmission. He reported that listeners did not lose comprehension, even at the maximum loss ratios, when the utterance was in the listener's native Danish. The tolerable loss ratio dropped substantially when the utterance was in a foreign language, even though the languages used were known to the listeners and comprehensible to them when transmitted without interruption.

These findings, rather loosely documented in Rubin's work, have been amplified and extended with considerable sophistication in later years. Denes and Pinson (1963) summarize a large body of research that has established the survival of intelligibility of heard speech even when large frequency ranges are filtered out, when waveforms are distorted, when partial units of utterance are eliminated, and so forth. It is also clear that this survival of intelligibility depends in the main upon the listener's use of transitional probabilities that apply to the text being transmitted.

From all of the foregoing, we may suggest that adequate listening is achieved by a pattern of attention employing segment sampling of the source of a message, the sampling being repeated most rapidly at those points in which the utterance is least redundant and vice versa. Here again, adequate listening will require an effective and instant adaptation of the pattern to the varying redundancy characteristics of the message.

E. SYNTAX MARKERS, ATTENTION, AND LISTENING

We have already seen that language utterances tend to exhibit a gradual rise in redundancy from the beginning of a unit (such as a clause or a simple sentence) to the end. In a passage this indicates that redundancy just before a comma or period is most likely to be high but drops rapidly immediately following such a mark. From this we would deduce that attentional focusing by a listener should be maximal at the beginning of a clause but become minimal at the end of a clause. This statement is one that should apply *ceteribus paribus*—that is, if other variables affecting redundancy, such as word frequency, are uniform in value across the clause and if the use of language does not depart from typical transitional probabilities.

Two sets of data support this inference. Fodor and Bever (1965) presented audible clicks to subjects listening attentively to an oral message. They subjectively located (i.e., "heard") clicks as occurring closer to a neighboring syntax marker than they were. Thus, a click located actually in the middle of a clause "moved" toward a nearby comma or period. Intrusion of the click into the conscious awareness of the listener seems to have been governed by the syntax utterance, a syntax break being at a point at which the consciousness of the listener was most vulnerable to intrusion. Somewhat earlier, Ladefoged and Broadbent (1960) had showed that such errors of location of clicks are larger when intruded into sentences than when placed in a series of spoken randomly ordered digits. This, of course, suggests that in the latter case, where the transitional probabilities are constant throughout the sequences, no one point is more vulnerable than another.

The auditory click technique is very much akin to that of dichotic listening, the click constituting a secondary channel of input for a listener who is attending to the primary channel. Maher and Berman (in press) applied the dichotic listening procedure to groups of normal subjects. They were required to shadow (repeat) a message transmitted orally on the main channel of a two-channel recorder. These messages consisted of compound sentences, with the comma dividing clauses being located after either the sixth or seventh word in the sequence. Thus in some cases the sixth word, being at the end of a clause, should be highly redundant, while the seventh would have low redundancy; in others the seventh would be highly redundant, with the eighth being of low redundancy. On the second channel of the recorder were uttered random unrelated words so placed as to occur on either side of the comma in the primary channel. At the end of the transmissions, subjects were asked to recall any word that they had heard from the secondary channel. Words placed just before a syntax marker in the primary channel were recalled significantly more often than those placed immediately after such a marker. These data support the conclusion that high-redundancy points in an utterance are vulnerable to a decline in attentional focusing and, hence, permit an intrusion into consciousness of other stimuli present in the environment at that moment.

F. SYNTAX AND SPEECH PAUSES

Ordinary speech does not, of course, include explicit utterance of syntax markers. The effects reported above are most likely conveyed through the relationship between the syntax of an utterance and the pattern of pauses that accompanies this. Goldman-Eisler (1958), for example, has shown that hesitation pauses in speech occur in anticipation of sudden increases in the information or uncertainty in the message being transmitted. She wrote:

> The close relation found to exist between pauses and information on the one hand and fluency of speech and redundancy on the other, seems to indicate that the interpolation of hesitation pauses in speech is a necessary condition for such an increase. . . . Fluent speech was shown to consist of habitual combinations of words such as were shared by the language community and as such had become more or less automatic. Where a sequence ceased to be a matter of common conditioning or learning, where a speaker's choice was highly individual and unexpected, on the other hand, speech was hesitant [p. 67].

More recent work by Goldman-Eisler (1972) indicates that the sentence is a unit that is relatively invulnerable to disruptions, the breaks between sentences that are marked by period points being, however, positions particularly prone to pauses and disruptions. Work by Beattie and Butterworth (1979) strongly indicates that in natural speech (recorded from spontaneous dyadic discussions) words of either low redundancy or of low frequency are preceded more often by pauses than is the case for words of high redundancy or high frequency. As low-frequency words also tend to be of low contextual probability (low redundancy), it was necessary to separate these factors statistically. This indicated that both redundancy and word frequency exercised independent effects in generating pauses.

The significance of a pause in speech is open to several interpretations. One of these is that the pause serves to alert the listener that a low-redundancy element is about to be uttered and thus creates attentional focus in the listener. From this perspective it may act like the sudden cessation of ticking in a clock, in that the listener now attends to it. Such pause patterns need not be voluntary on the part of the speaker but may develop in the course of early language acquisition and, in this sense, be quite unconscious. A second possibility is that the pauses reflect a search process going on whereby the speaker needs more time to find the right word when he or she has no immediately prior set of transitional probabilities to delimit the search. These two possibilities need not be mutually exclusive. Beattie and Butterworth have emphasized the lexical search as a main source of pause production, whereas Rubin had pointed out the role of pauses, together with volume and pitch, in attracting the listener's attention.

G. REDUNDANCY AND INTRUSIONS

We may summarize what has been said so far by noting that language utterances follow sequences from low to high redundancy. These shifts in redundancy are accompanied by corresponding changes in attention to the utterance by both listener and speaker. Correspondence between low redundancy and focused attention is high at the beginning of an utterance unit, such as a clause, with a gradient of change toward high redundancy and diminished attention toward the end of the unit. The sequence recycles when a syntax marker, such as a comma or period, is reached. Those points at which diminished attentional focusing is operating are the points at which irrelevant stimuli, such as clicks and other channels of speech, are noticed.

To apply these observations to the problem of schizophrenic utterance, two further assumptions are necessary:

1. The patterns of attentional deployment operating in the listener are also operating in the speaker—that is, the speaker's attention is most focused upon the low-redundancy elements of his or her utterances and least upon the high-redundancy elements, with a concomitant vulnerability to the intrusion of irrelevant stimuli into consciousness during the utterance of these latter elements.

2. Intrusions into consciousness, in either listener or speaker, may arise from internal preoccupations or fantasies and, most importantly, from activated associations to prior units of the utterance. It is to these latter that we shall now turn.

V. Associational Processes in Utterance

Seeing, hearing, or speaking a word, or other linguistic unit, activates associations that have been acquired to that word. These associations do not ordinarily enter consciousness. Were they to do so, the conduct of normal speech would be extremely difficult. It will be a part of the thesis of this chapter that they do enter into the utterances of a speaker under certain circumstances. One such set of circumstances may be found in the speech of normal persons; another is to be found in the utterances of some schizophrenic patients. Let us first consider the evidence that might justify the assumption that associations are activated in the manner described.

A. LEXICAL DECISION

Meyer and Schvaneveldt (1971) demonstrated that when subjects have recognized a word that has been presented visually they can more easily recognize newly presented words that are related to the one presented initially. The first word is said to *prime* the recognition of others that have a relationship to it. These relationships are mainly of an associational nature. To explain this effect, a model has been postulated whereby it is assumed that access to a lexical item (a word) occurs only when the item has been activated to a level that has risen above some critical threshold. Activation is triggered by any prior cognitive process that is related to the item. We might regard this process of threshold crossing as somewhat analogous to what happens to the threshold for the recognition of external stimuli under conditions of high motivation.

The technique employed to study lexical access is one in which the priming word is presented first and the thresholds of recognition for other words, related and nonrelated, are compared. There is no suggestion that the activation of related words has entered consciousness, but only that it has reached a level that facilitates recognition. This technique has been referred to as the *lexical decision* technique and is of immediate significance for our present discussion.

B. LEXICAL ACCESS AND AMBIGUOUS WORDS

In our previous discussion of the work of Chapman *et al.* (1964), we have noted the importance of ambiguity of word meaning in the genesis of schizophrenic utterance. Patients were likely to give the most common meaning of an ambiguous word whether the context called for it or not. Ambiguous words present a question of particular importance to our discussion—namely, whether all sets of meaning and associations are activated when such a word occurs, or only those appropriate to the context in which the word appears. Thus, we may ask, when the sentence *He sold his stock because his broker advised him to do so* is uttered, do only those associations to *stock* that are context relevant become activated—such as *bonds, dividend, Wall Street,*—or do all associations to other meanings of *stock* also become activated. In this latter case, associations to livestock, stock theater, inventory, riding, etc. would be activated, even though they are not relevant to the context of the sentence. The first alternative—context-relevant associations only—has been termed the Direct Access model; the second model—activation of all associations regardless of context—has been termed the Complete Access model. A review of this distinction may be found in Swinney (1979).

Data obtained by Swinney (1979) and Swinney, Onifer, Prather, and Hirshkowitz (1979) indicate that both context-relevant and context-irrelevant meanings are activated when anbiguous words occur, but, most importantly, the context-irrelevant meanings decay quite rapidly, whereas the relevant ones last longer. This process of decay is inferred by the fact that the priming effect terminates sooner for irrelevant meanings than for relevant ones. However, the decay may perhaps also be seen as arising from the active suppression of irrelevant associations rather than as a passive fading away. For individuals with impaired efficiency of suppression, we might expect these irrelevant associations to remain active for longer periods of time, thereby prolonging the probability that they may intrude into an utterance.

C. ASSOCIATIONS IN EVERYDAY SPEECH

An additional line of information comes from the observation of associational processes in everyday speech. At an extremely simple level, let us consider the utterance of a sentence of the elementary subject–verb–object form, such as the statement *Bees make honey.* We will take this as the core meaning, or *utterance plan,* that the speaker intends to communicate. Acceptable transformations are such that the essential, or deep structural, meaning may be adequately conveyed by any one of several other actual sentences. Thus, *Honey is made by bees* and *It is by bees that honey is made* would be acceptable versions of the intended utterance. By "acceptable" is here meant that the speaker uttering either of these two forms would regard him- or herself as having said what was intended: There would be no discrepancy between the intent or plan of the utterance and the actual content of what was uttered.

A second form of transformation involves the use of synonyms. There are few synonyms for *bee* or *honey,* but there are some for *make.* Thus, the utterance *Bees manufacture honey* would be an acceptable version of the intended utterance. In a sentence of this kind, it would be difficult for an activated association to be employed in the utterance without distorting it in relation to the intended form of the utterance. Associations to *bee* might include *sting, wasp,* or *hive,* and to *honey* might include *sweet* and *comb.* None of these are synonyms for a unit of the intended utterance and could not therefore appear in the utterance without changing the intent to a critical degree. Were such an association to intrude into the spoken utterance, such as in the form *Bees make sweet,* the sentence would strike the ear of the listener as odd and would appear to the speaker as uncomfortably discrepant with the kind of message that he or she was trying to convey. To the listener the thought processes of the speaker might appear vague and tangential. To the speaker the discrepancy might demand some explanation, perhaps in terms of thought control by others.

The fact that associations do not intrude into normal speech, by definition, tells us something about the processes that may be necessary to achieve clear utterance. From the results of the classic technique of word association testing, we know that, to the instruction "Say the first word that comes into your head" upon hearing a stimulus word, subjects generally respond quite rapidly with a word, some words being much more common than others. Classifications of these responses have been established using such groupings as opposites (*black–white*), categories (*knife–eating utensil*), synonyms (*dress–gown*), empirical contiguities (*sea–boat*), and rhyming or clang associations (*boat–float*).

Associations come easily and rapidly when elicited in this way. They appear to be readily provoked, and this should give us reason to reflect upon the difficulties that should arise in uttering an ordinary sentence. Given the strong associative relationship between, let us say, *black* and *white,* it seems reasonable to assume that the utterance of the word *black* activates to some degree the potential of uttering *white.* The successful utterance of a sentence such as *The black sheep was eating the grass* depends therefore upon the failure of associations to be activated sufficiently to intrude into the overt utterance. If this were not the case, and all activated associations were to intrude, then the sentence might well be disorganized by the appearance of the word *white* and perhaps *goats* as an association to *sheep, drink* as an association to *eat,* and so forth. Thus, we might conceive of the utterance of a complete and organized sentence as a feat achieved by the effective exclusion of the associations that lie like a web of distractions around each element in the sentence. Among the associations activated by any element is the element itself. Thus, uttering the word *black* not only activates such associated words as *white* but also activates the word *black* itself.

Putting the matter more simply, the utterance of any word increases the probability that any other word associated with it, including the initial word itself, will be activated and have the potential for entering consciousness within some limited period of time thereafter. That they do not do so in normal speech may be ascribed to the operation of effective inhibitory processes brought into play by the plan of the utterance that the speaker intends. Hence, there is, normally, no consciousness of the activated associations and no conscious inhibition of them. We recognize their activation only under the special circumstances provided by the lexical decision task: We recognize the role of the inhibition of associations only by its evident failure in some kinds of pathology of utterance.

However, even in normal speech, there exists the possibility for the activated association to be incorporated into language when it happens to carry the meaning that the speaker intends. This is possible whenever an activated association is also a synonym for a later component of the sentence. We might schematize the process as shown in Figure 1. Several examples of this kind of associational activation are provided by B. F. Skinner in his *Notebooks* (Epstein, 1980). He writes:

> From a review of a TV program:
> "Lamp at Midnight," to put it plainly, had a touch of greatness, catching a moment of irreconcilable conflict in Catholic Church history with a burning eloquence worthy of the vast and timeless issues at stake.
> Apparently this appearance of *burning. . . at stake* was quite unconscious. (If not it is a rather macabre bit of humor) [p. 78].

And later,

> J. K. Galbraith in Ambassador's Journal: "a dog once bit me on the leg adjacent to the left testicle. . . . " Two sentences later: "They are old friends but I listened with all proper patience to the State Department view of their crotchets." Is the *crotch* of *crotchets* thematically determined by *leg adjacent to testicle*? [p. 79].

Yet another example comes from the work of David Joravsky, *The Lysenko Affair* (1970). Referring to stock-breeding policies that followed from the Lysenko influence, the author writes of the insistence of Stalin that science serve practical interests: "If any one wondered how broadly Stalin and his lieutenants conceived service of production, the answer was given by Iakovlov, then Party chief of agriculture. A favorite young stockbreeder, telling how he had transported bull sperm 8 kilometers to inseminate 800 cows, caused Iakovlev to ejaculate: 'Now, that's real science' [p. 98]." We can speculate fairly plausibly that the word *ejaculate* appeared (in preference to *exclaim, proclaim, cry*) because of the influence of the prior reference to insemination.

It is important to note that in all the examples so far we are limited to plausible post hoc identification of associational links. The links are not

A. Plan of utterance:[1]

A career in art has problems.

Possible Connections:

	Associations		Synonyms
	Career	Art	Problems
	Work	Painting	Difficulties
	Employment	Sculpture	Disadvantages
	Job	Gallery	Hardships
	etc.	Artists	Obstacles
		Draw	*Draw*backs
		Engrave	Pitfalls

Actual utterance:

*A career in art has **drawbacks.***

B. Plan of utterance:[1]

*This book, written by a man awaiting execution
in Sing Sing prison, is quite amazing.*

Possible connections:

Book	Man	Execution	Prison	Amazing
Volume	Person	Gallows	Pen	Astonishing
Author	Woman	*Electrocution*	Jail	Stimulating
Library	Human	Hanging	Cell	*Electrifying*
Binding	Male	Death	Convict	Surprising

Actual utterance:

*This book, written by a man awaiting execution
in Sing Sing prison, is quite **electrifying.***

C. Plan of utterance:[2]

China is a giant looking cautiously at the world.

Possible connections:

China	Giant	Looking
Orient	Ogre	Watching
Emperor	Large	Gazing
Peking	Jack	Peering
Plate	Beanstalk	*Peeking*

Actual utterance:

*China: A giant **peeking** cautiously at the world.*

[1] Examples noted by the writer through personal observation.
[2] Cited by Skinner, B. G. In R. Epstein (1980, p. 291).

FIG. 1. A model of the associational influence process on word choice in normal utterance.

made explicit in the body of the utterance itself and, we propose, are not present in consciousness to the speaker or writer. Because of the obvious dangers of reliance upon a criterion of post hoc plausibility, so long a fatal flaw in the methods of psychodynamic interpretation of fantasy and other expressive productions, it is necessary to base the claim to plausibility upon *obvious* associations. Recourse to presumed idiosyncratic associational links in individual cases is a treacherous strategy to employ as it quite quickly becomes nonfalsifiable.

D. REPETITION AS ASSOCIATION

In the preceding discussion, we have been concerned with the incorporation of associations into normal speech when this is possible because of their character as synonyms. We should note, however, that any word spoken (or heard) may be incorporated into later utterance in the form of repetition, where such repetition does not violate the intended meaning of the utterance. Thus, a sequence such as *I love to sail. Let's go to the boat show and see if they have anything on sale* provides a repetition at the phonetic level, whereas such passages as *A stable economy requires continual reinvestment in industrial plant. Tax reductions given now are a case of locking the stable door after the horse has gone* provide examples of repetition with two meanings of an ambiguous word. Perhaps most persons who have been taught the elements of acceptable writing style learn to avoid repetition where this is possible without distorting the intended meaning of their utterances. To do this may require conscious editing, either at the point at which a sentence is being formulated or in the process of turning a preliminary draft into a final version. Mittenecker (1951) has pointed to a mechanism of associational repetition at the level of the syllable, using the hypothesis of subliminal activation to account for it. We should expect, then, that while there are inhibitions against the too frequent repetition of the same word in a passage of utterances (except for function words, prepositions, articles, and others that have few available synonyms), the process of associational activation will increase the probability of repetition. In patients who present other signs of language anomaly, such as disruptive associational intrusions and the like, we should expect a higher than usual rate of word repetition in their utterance sequences. The phenomenon of word repetition in the utterances of schizophrenic patients has long been noted in the clinical literature and forms the empirical justification for the original use of the Type–Token Ratio as an investigatory tool in this field. (See, for example, Chapter 3 in this volume.)

E. Associational Activation as Efficient

An admittedly post hoc case might be argued that associational activation serves a purpose in the behavioral economy of the individual. Associations are generally formed by experienced repeated contiguities. The fact that the word *white* is a common associate of the word *black* may reflect, not the operation of some mechanism whereby opposites are automatically associated, but the fact that in common language usage the two words may tend to appear in contiguity. Thus, *Here it is in black and white, You can't convince me that black is white, A black and white television set, Black and white photography,* and other such routine phrases provide a high probability that one word will be found in the same context as the other. The same principle would apply to other associates. By activating the associations to a heard word, the recognition of these associates is improved (as we have seen in the case of the lexical decision paradigm). By activating these associations, the task of the speaker is also facilitated through the improved and speedier availability of associated words, some of which the speaker is likely to need in the course of turning the utterance plan into an actual utterance. From this point of view, the phenomenon of associational activation is not a simple by-product of neurolinguistic activity, offering a potential hazard to clear expression and hence requiring control and inhibition by the operation of meaning and syntax rules. Rather it is a process that serves to improve the ease of word recognition in the listener and word finding in the speaker, readily channeled and constrained by the plan of the utterance.

F. Activation and Motivation

We have already noted that states of motivation operate to reduce the threshold for the recognition of relevant stimuli. It is perhaps prima facie plausible to suppose that motive states also affect the threshold of activation of associations that are relevant to the motive. The relationship between increased intensity of motive state and the pattern of associative response made to motive-relevant stimuli is very complex. Early work on this has been reviewed by Laffal (1965), leading him to conclude that, while there is substantial evidence that needs influence verbal behavior, "the process is not always the simple one of increasing the need-related responses, and that alterations of the conditions of the association task may change the whole hierarchical structure, placing otherwise weak responses in a dominant position and ordinarily dominant responses in a weak position [p. 62]."

Lexical decision paradigms and the other data that we have considered so far suggest that it is not necessary for subjects to be in any unusual state of motive arousal for associational activation to occur. Motive states may well operate selectively upon subsets of associates to render them more "active" than other subsets—either by adding an increment of activation to need-relevant associates or by suppressing need-irrelevant associates. Whatever the mechanism involved, it seems clear that, while motive states may affect *which* associates enter into language utterance, the entry of some associates is probable whenever the meaning characteristics of an utterance permit it.

It is important here to note that the formulation being offered differs in some respects from that developed some years ago by Laffal (1965). The main difference may be exemplified by considering an illustration of a slip of the tongue, used by Laffal to demonstrate the effect of motive states upon associational components of an utterance. From the work of Simonini (1956), Laffal cites the example of a radio–television fluff. The speaker remarked, describing the Battle of the Bulge in World War II: *His battalion was swallowed in the Bulgium belch.* Laffal concludes that the speaker was influenced by two sets, one of which was to describe a military event, and the other was the speaker's own alimentary needs. This latter, Laffal suggests, may have both influenced the choice of the word *swallow* to mean destroyed and, via associational links, the connection of *bulge* and *belch* produce the combination of words at the end.

> These examples of interferences in normal speech provide a link with language distortions in schizophrenia. However, to understand language distortions in schizophrenia, it is not enough to recognize that conflicting needs may disrupt the conscious intention, produce faults, and make unusual responses momentarily dominant, one must also take into account the surprising ways in which the conflicting needs may influence verbal forms while remaining hidden both to the patient and the observer [p. 83].

Later, he adds: "The associative chain has little regard for what we know as logic and proceeds on the basis of the most improbable relationships. One important effect of this process is that the relation of the response to the needs and conflicts of the patient is well hidden [p. 83]."

The present formulation differs from the foregoing in that it does not assume that schizophrenia is a condition induced by psychological conflict, and hence it eschews the notion that there need be any relation between associations of patients and such conflicts. Rather, we assume that the breakdown responsible for anomalous intrusions of associations into utterance is essentially neuropsychological and represents a failure of those mechanisms that ordinarily limit the entry of associations to those that are meaning congruent. We do not assume that activated associations proceed on any basis other than as a reflection of a general property of the underlying neural processes or that they proceed in ways designed to keep hidden from the speaker the nature of his or her own conflicts. On the contrary, it is assumed that activated associations remain below the threshold of consciousness because entry into consciousness would be disruptive of connected utterances and, hence, nonfunctional. The possible function of associational activation is to facilitate listening and uttering, and this does not require entry into consciousness.

VI. A Tentative Theory of Schizophrenic Utterance

A. CENTRAL PROPOSITIONS

The main thesis of our tentative theory of schizophrenic utterance is that the pathology of schizophrenia involves an inability to exclude from intrusion into consciousness material from either external stimulation or internally stored associations, that would normally be excluded on the basis of its irrelevance to the task situation in which the patient is performing. This process of exclusion normally depends upon (a) the control of the deployment of attention by redundancies in input, and (b) the inhibition of associated elements from entry into the plan or protocol upon which patterns of motor behavior—and in this case, specifically speech—are organized for execution.

In the case of language utterance, the two defective processes may interact, such that the speech of the patient may reflect not only the intrusion of internal associations but also the intrusion of external, irrelevant stimuli that may be co-occurrent with the act of utterance. By the same token, the patient's own utterance also operates as a potentially distracting form of sensory input, so that, under some circumstances, what was an associational intrusion into an early component of a passage of utterances becomes a stimulus upon which a later component is developed.

While individual states of motivation may affect the nature of the associations that intrude, the vulnerability to intrusion is hypothesized to be due to a neural defect. The etiology of this vulnerability is not presumed to reside in pathogenic conflicts of motive.

Associational bonds or networks in schizophrenic patients do not differ in their manner of development or their content from those of nonpatients. Thus, the problem is not one of bizarre associations, but of the intrusion of "normal" associations into utterance at inappropriate points. The inability to exclude intrusions may vary in severity from levels that seriously disrupt the intelligibility of utterances, to minor levels represented only by a higher than usual frequency of normal incorporations of associations into language. Variations in severity may be found in the same patient over time, corresponding to variations in the severity of other aspects of the symptoms of schizophrenia. We should also expect that disturbances in language should be associated with disturbances in the performance of sensory tasks that require optimal attentional deployments, and with motor performance of a coordinated or skilled kind.

One important modification should be noted, however. Extended experience of disturbed sensory input and disturbed associational utterance should, in due course, provide a core of anomalous associations: We should predict this on the principle that associational networks are formed by repeated experiences and will be reshaped should the character of experiences undergo significant changes. In chronic patients, then, we may be less surprised to find autistic or idiosyncratic associations than in patients whose schizophrenia is of recent onset.

In this theory we assume that normal utterances correspond to a pre-verbal plan or protocol, as illustrated in Figure 1. As the plan is transformed into specific components of utterance, words, phrases, etc., networks of associations are activated to them. It is proposed that this activation may occur simultaneously with the utterance of the relevant stimulus element, but an activated association will not appear as an uttered element unless it is congruent with the plan. All associated elements will be activated that have more than minimum strength in the individual's network. This strength will be a function of previous past experiences and may be increased by intense motivational states.

As an utterance proceeds, the rise of newly activated associations to succeeding elements will be paralleled by a decline in the level of activation of already activated associations. Any activated association will have a finite life such that its influence upon later parts of the utterance will diminish with increasing distance from the onset of activation. If the plan of utterance is very brief, activation of any associations will be impossible to detect, as there will be insufficient length of utterance for later portions to be affected by earlier ones. In brief, associational effects require a minimum length of utterance to be able to affect the content of an utterance.

It is also proposed that the components of an utterance require attentional deployments on the part of the speaker that correspond to those required in the listener. Focused attention is necessary to initiate the low-redundancy initial components of a syntactical unit, such as a clause, but is less necessary to carry out the utterance of the rest of the unit once it is in progress. Speaking, no less than listening, it is suggested, requires a constant shifting from broad to narrow focus of attention as the speaker moves from the completion of one unit to the initiation of another. Associations that are activated will intrude into consciousness on the same basis that external stimuli intrude—that is, when attention is not narrowly focused upon some limited segment of the environment. These conditions occur at the end of syntax units for the listener and, it is proposed, for the speaker also. However, this intrusion will enter disruptively into the utterance only when the capacity for normal recruitment of the focusing of attention upon the utterance of the next component is seriously impaired. This, it is suggested, is the case in schizophrenia.

We assume that the activation of associations has a functional value in normal language, in that (a) it increases the availability of elements likely to be used in an utterance for the brief ensuing period in which there is some probability that they may be appropriate, and (b) it improves the recognition of associated elements of an utterance by preparing the listener for their occurrence for the brief period in which there is a probability that they will occur. The termination of activation is assumed to be an active process of suppression akin to the process whereby irrelevant external input is damped or suppressed during attentional concentration upon a narrow range of the environment. The prolongation of activation beyond the brief period in which activated associations might be useful would lead, instead, to cumulative confusion, as there would be lowered thresholds for the production and detection of components unlikely to be a part of the later segments of the utterance. Suppression of activation is assumed to rest upon an appropriate neural mechanism, and in schizophrenia this mechanism is assumed to be defective to a greater or lesser degree.

B. Some Deductions

From the foregoing propositions, certain deductions may be derived.

1. Intrusions into utterance are most likely to occur at those points at which a rapid change of attentional focus is required. In both language utterance and language listening, these will include, especially, the point at which one clause or sentence ends and the next unit begins (i.e., at the location of a syntax marker, such as a comma or period). In English-speaking patients, these are likely to appear as associations to object-nouns, given the frequent use of the subject–verb–object sequence in sentence construction. In other languages, where the order subject–object–verb is permissible and common, associative chaining to the word before the syntax marker may include verb-associates, etc.

2. Intrusions into utterances at these points of vulnerability may consist of either intrusions of already activated associations, much like the normal incorporations already discussed (but differing from them in that the intended meaning of the sentence is disrupted), or short-term associative

chaining to the last word of a syntax unit, as described in the preceding paragraph.

3. A plausible, but not inevitable, deduction from the concept of vulnerability is that the pattern of pauses and hesitations usually found at clause boundaries in normal speech will be deviant in patients because the events occurring at clause boundaries (i.e., the intrusion of associations) differ from the processes occurring in normal speakers.

4. In connected discourse, the effect of associational disruptions will tend to be sequential. That is to say, succeeding sentences are likely to reflect associational carry-over from previous ones, thereby rendering the comprehension of the thread of discourse very difficult for the listener. Deviations from expected transition probabilities both within sentences and within passages will be reflected by poor ability of normal listeners to predict the actual sequence of utterance.

5. The phenomenology of the experience of disrupted utterance will be disturbing to the patient and will demand explanation. Essentially, the patient will experience hearing his or her own voice speaking an utterance that is discrepant with what was intended. Experiences of this kind may be explained in terms of "somebody is controlling my thoughts," "somebody is speaking through my mouth," and so forth. Such preliminary delusional processes may later be elaborated into beliefs that this control is being achieved by the use of radio waves, telepathy, or other invisible media.

C. SOME LIMITATIONS

While the diagnosis of schizophrenia is significantly affected by anomalies in the patient's utterances, many patients receive the diagnosis without the presence of florid language disturbance. The heterogeneity of the classification of schizophrenia means, inevitably, that any theory of schizophrenic utterance is a theory about a subset of patients. The presence of these anomalies in all patients bearing a diagnosis of schizophrenia is *not* predicted by this theory. What is predicted is that, where anomalies of utterance are found in schizophrenic patients—as distinct, say, from aphasic patients—they will have the characteristics described by the theory.

There is no basis in the theory for any strong prediction about the semantic content of specific associations that may intrude. A careful review by Schwartz (1978) of the content of associations uttered by schizophrenic patients leads him to conclude that there are no adequate grounds for believing that uncommon or deviant associations are characteristic of the schizophrenic. Indeed, the position of Chapman and Chapman (1973) would suggest that schizophrenic patients may tend to be biased toward the most common associations to verbal stimuli. However, we should note that the commonness of a word association response is an actuarial concept. For that proportion of normal subjects who give an uncommon association as their first response to a stimulus word, the uncommon association is their strongest association. This reflects, presumably, individual differences in the language experiences that accumulate to form associative bonds between verbal elements.

It is not necessary that an intrusion into utterance always strike the listener as strange. Our earlier discussion of normal intrusions illustrates the possibility that a meaningful utterance may contain associational elements and yet fit the speaker's plan of utterance. We may go one step further and recognize the possibility that associations may intrude into an utterance in a manner that creates a discrepancy between the plan of the utterance and its actual content (thereby creating some discomfort on the part of the speaker) but yet not be noticed by a listener.

D. Some Evidence

We may now turn to examine some of the evidence that is pertinent to the theory. Our examination will be confined to those studies that deal with language, its utterance and its comprehension, the very large body of information dealing with attentional dysfunction in nonlanguage areas having been mentioned already and being beyond the scope of this chapter.

1. Redundancy

a. *Contextual Constraint* The technique of Miller and Selfridge (1950) has been employed in several studies of information processing in schizophrenia. Lewinsohn and Elwood (1961), Lawson *et al.* (1964), and Gerver (1967) have reported that schizophrenic patients fail to gain from the increasing degree of contextual constraint provided in the Miller–Selfridge passages. However, the findings of these studies present complications, including failures to match for prior vocabulary competence and the presence of the deficit mainly in chronic—rather than acute—schizophrenic patients. The present writer and his colleagues (Maher, Manschreck, & Rucklos, 1980) have conducted an investigation on the ability of schizophrenic patients to profit from the increasing redundancy associated with increased contextual constraint in the Miller–Selfridge series, dividing schizophrenic patients into those who exhibited formal thought disorder (TD) and those without this clinical feature (NTD). Very significant impairment was found in the TD patients, but no significant differences between NTD, nonschizophrenic psychiatric patients, and normal controls. Differences between NTD and TD patients in simple immediate recall efficiency were controlled by equating performance in the zero-order condition. Thought disorder in this study was defined as a rating of 3 or higher on at least one of the four categories of thought disorder on the Schedule for Affective Disorders and Schizophrenia (SADS) (Spitzer & Endicott, 1977). These categories include incoherence, loosening of associations (or derailment), illogical thinking, and poverty of the content of speech. Differences between the mean performance of TD and NTD patients reached significance levels of $p < .005$ on each of the two measures employed in the study.

b. Predictability The predictability of the utterances of schizophrenic speakers has been studied at several different levels. One approach, mainly using the Cloze procedure (Taylor, 1953), records the predictability of words used by patients in sequential passages by asking normal readers to guess words eliminated from transcripts of these passages. Another approach (Rutter, 1979) requires normal readers to reconstruct the order in which a sequence of sentences was uttered; yet a third emphasizes the detection of connectors between one sentence and another in such passages (Rochester & Martin, 1979). We shall not describe these studies in any detail, as they are reviewed extensively elsewhere in the present volume (Cozolino, Chapter 3). However, it is useful here to note that impaired predictability at various levels is more typically found in TD schizophrenic patients than in those not exhibiting thought disorder.

c. Pause Length Earlier in this chapter we examined the relationship between pause lengths in spoken utterance and various aspects of the utterance itself, such as word frequency and redundancy. Maher, Manschreck, and Molino (1983) have examined the speech pause patterns of TD and NTD schizophrenic patients with reference to these two variables. The general tenor of the results of this investigation is that TD schizophrenic patients show a loss of the normal pattern of relationship between redundancy of their utterance and pause length, but they do not show any substantial loss of the normal relationship between pause length and word frequency. Schizophrenic patients not suffering from thought disorder displayed the normal pattern of relationships for both redundancy and word frequency. Rochester, Thurston, and Rupp (1977) examined patterns of pauses between clauses and within clause utterances in TD, NTD, and normal speakers. They concluded that the formulation presented by this writer (Maher, 1972) accounts nicely for their hesitation data.

We may summarize the findings from these three classes of investigation—contextual constraint, Cloze analysis, and pause length—as indicating a detectable impairment on the part of TD schizophrenic patients in the use of redundancies in either listening to or uttering sequences of language. This failure is not, of itself, compelling evidence of a failure in an attentional process. However, given the role of redundancy in influencing patterns of attentional deployment, the deficit in redundancy utilization is consistent with the general model of attentional deficiency.

2. Intrusion Points

The tendency of associational intrusions to occur at the boundaries of syntax units, such as clauses and sentences, has been shown largely by the earlier work of the present writer and his students (Maher, McKean, & McLaughlin, 1966). Examining written material from a wide range of psychotic patients across the country, we reported the presence of object chaining (and not subject chaining) to be a significant discriminator between TD and NTD patients. A replication of this analysis in a second sample achieved significance at a somewhat higher level than the original sample, thereby confirming and extending the finding. A detailed analysis of the distribution of subject–object ratios in these documents indicated that in all cases where the ratio of objects to subjects exceeded 3 the patients were independently judged to be thought disordered by the attending clinician; in cases where the ratio was between 2.00 and 2.99, five out of a total of six cases were judged to be thought disordered. Ratios of 1.99 and below were not discriminating. A retrieval of those texts that contained high subject–object ratios revealed that the effect was largely due to associative chaining at the end of the clause boundary. Examples of these are given earlier in this chapter (e.g., in Section I, C, examples 5, 7, and 8).

Negative evidence appears to come from a paper by Rochester, Harris, and Seeman (1973), who examined the propensity of schizophrenic patients and normal controls to misplace auditory clicks to a nearby syntax boundary when such clicks are presented dichotically in the middle of a clause. We might expect that patients whose attention is not controlled by the low redundancy typical of the middle of clauses should more accurately identify such clicks and reveal less shifting to the boundary of the clause. Unfortunately, although the investigators did examine the TD and NTD subgroups in their schizophrenic patients, they employed the Bannister and Fransella (1966) measure of thought disorder based upon the Repertory Grid Test. This test has been found to be lacking in any significant validity (Hill, 1976), and there is no basis for concluding that any of the patients of Rochester et al. were thought disordered. If this were the case, the similarity of performance between schizophrenic and normal subjects in this investigation is not surprising and would be in line with the rest of the literature pointing to the central importance of the thought-disorder factor in discriminating those patients in whom the problems of redundancy and associational intrusion are present.

3. Lexical Decision

An earlier discussion of the findings of the lexical decision task indicated that associations to words are activated in normal subjects even though they do not enter consciousness. The persistence of associational activation, in the presence of inappropriate context, was hypothesized to occur in schizophrenic patients, being a basis upon which associational intrusion might occur. Onifer (1980) has reported the results of a lexical decision study of schizophrenic patients, nonschizophrenic patients, and normal controls. He reported that schizophrenic patients demonstrated the predicted continuation of context-inappropriate meanings of ambiguous words, an effect not found with the other groups. However, the continuation was most reliably found when the inappropriate meaning was the primary, or most common, meaning of the ambiguous word. Incidentally, as the demonstration of the continuance of associational activation depends upon faster reactions by the subject (relative to his or her own base rate), it is difficult to explain the findings for schizophrenics as another instance of some undefined general deficit. Onifer concludes with the observation that an earlier formulation by the present writer—namely, that the utterance of normal, coherent speech may be seen as the result of the successful and instantaneous inhibition of associations to elements in the utterances, any failure of this inhibition leaving open the possibility of intrusion—is clearly congruent with his own findings.

4. High-Risk Children

An associational intrusion model does not lead to any necessary predictions about the premorbid state of cognitive processes in the future patient. Nonetheless, it naturally gains additional credence from any evidence that some mild version of associational intrusions may be found in populations known to be at risk for later schizophrenia. Two studies are of interest here. Oltmanns, Weintraub, Stone, and Neale (1978) studied the performance of children of schizophrenic patients, children of depressed patients, and children of normal parents on an object-sorting task. Children were required to compose groups of pictures of objects drawn from an array of 42 cards, on the basis that the selected cards were "alike in some way." The basis of the grouping was then elicited by questioning. Responses were categorized in several ways. Of importance to this discussion was the category of "complex response." This category was based upon realistic appraisal of attributes of the items and their relationships, but no single attribute or relationship defined the group. The authors cite as an example one child who grouped an apple, a pumpkin, a pie, and a candle, saying *You can make an apple pie and a pumpkin pie, and the pies need heat to cook. The candle burns and gives heat* [p. 241]. This kind of grouping seems to reflect a controlled associational process: It occurred significantly more often in the responses of the children of schizophrenics than in the responses of the other groups.

Oltmanns *et al.* conclude that their findings in respect to the complex response are consistent with an earlier finding, reported by Mednick and Schulsinger (1968), to the effect that children at risk for schizophrenia gave significantly more associative chains to stimulus words in a task that called for lists of direct associations to the same word. Adding the fact that drug-free adult schizophrenics also give more complex responses than normal controls do in the object-sorting task (Daut & Chapman, 1974), the general thrust of these studies is to suggest that associational intrusion into cognitive processes is an early feature of premorbid schizophrenia and occupies, presumably, a rather central place in the basic pattern of psychopathology that comprises the disposition to later schizophrenia.

5. Editing Deficit

Cohen and his associates (e.g., Cohen, Nachmani, & Rosenberg, 1974; Lisman & Cohen, 1972; Rosenberg & Cohen, 1966) have studied the production of communicative acts in schizophrenic patients with the aid of a model dealing with situations in which the speaker is required to describe an object in terms such that a listener could pick it out on the basis of the description. This model proposes a two-stage sequence. Given an object to describe, the speaker samples from his or her repertoire of descriptive terms associated with the "referent" object. These are then "edited" before utterance to eliminate those that are likely to be equally associated with some other "nonreferent" object. Ordinarily, we must assume, a speaker has no difficulty in simply naming the object concerned. Thus, *Pass me the butter* requires no more than that the speaker and listener share a common definition of *butter*. However, where several only slightly dissimilar objects are present, it may be necessary to add more descriptive terms. Thus, *Pass me the aluminum saucepan* is required when there are several possible saucepans present. Objects with very high degrees of similarity may require very specific qualifications in their description if they are to be correctly identified.

In the Cohen *et al.* (1974) sudy, schizophrenic and normal controls were asked to describe a specific color, from arrays of two or four disks varying in color and in the degree of similarity of color between items within the array. A panel of listeners was required to identify the selected color on the basis of the speaker's description. Patients performed as well as normal when the degree of disk similarity was low and discrimination thus easy. When the discrimination was difficult, the accuracy of the schizophrenics' descriptions dropped (as measured by the inability of the listener panel to identify the intended disk), reaction time increased, and utterances became longer. The patients were all classified as acutely schizophrenic, exhibiting thought disorder, and nonparanoid. Examples of disturbed schizophrenic responses included: *Green. Hold on, the other is too! In the garden such a green is unlikely. Too synthetic! The other is more gardenreal* [given as a single word], *piecemeal, oatmeal green, greenreal, filmreal, greenreal* [p. 11].

Response lengths were longer for normal subjects in the difficult discrimination task, although coherent and shorter than those of the schizophrenic patients. Thus, in an easy discrimination, between a purple-blue and a red disk, both normal and schizophrenic subjects gave one- or two-word answers. With the most difficult discriminations, the mean length of the schizophrenic response increases to 30 words (two-disk array) and 45 words (four-disk array). The respective values for normal response lengths were 18 and 33.

As the preceding example illustrates, initial elements in long schizophrenic responses were of a common character and related to the referent color, the later elements seeming to form chains of association to previous elements. Cohen *et al.* have interpreted their results to mean that the chaining arises from the difficulty of the task, this difficulty residing in the necessity to edit out common associations to the referent—as these are not sufficiently discriminating—and to select uncommon but more discriminating terms. This, they suggest, is typical of schizophrenic utterance under other difficult circumstances. "Whenever a schizophrenic samples a response he perceives to be ineffective or threatening in his everyday transaction, he is unable to edit it out and, as a consequence, manifests the same kinds of language disturbance observed in the present study [p. 12]."

Other interpretations of the data are feasible. Difficulty of the task produced longer responses in normals. This suggests that task difficulty and normative response length are inevitably confounded in this situation: They could only be unconfounded by requiring that subjects give a standard response length regardless of task difficulty—a condition that would be hard to meet without extreme artificiality in the responses to easy items. However, as it is, we do not know whether chaining arose because of the editing demands of the task or because the task had involved the patients in making prolonged utterances. Any prolonged utterance—however simple the task that produced it—carries with it an accumulating probability of associational interference.

In any event, the examples given by Cohen *et al.* point once again to the role of associational chaining in the utterances of schizophrenic patients with thought disorder and are, in this respect, in accord with the theory described in this chapter.

6. Language Disturbance and Motor Behavior

In the preliminary discussion of the criteria for a parsimonious theory of schizophrenic pathologies, it was suggested that an advantage accrues to explanations that permit the linking together of defects in response systems that are topographically separate but are served by a common system in which the pathology is hypothesized to reside. In a series of studies, the present writer with Manschreck and colleagues have examined the relationship between language features and motor features of schizophrenic patients (Manschreck, Maher, & Ader, 1981; Manschreck, Maher, Rucklos, Vereen, & Ader, 1981). The central findings of this series of studies are that, whether measured clinically or in the laboratory, the presence of motor symptoms is reliably associated with the presence of language and thought disorder. Not all measures were significantly related, and some other components of the syndrome were not correlated with either language or motor pathology, suggesting that something more specific than a general deficit is involved in mediating these relationships.

Studies from the experimental psychology of motor skill performance have long implicated attentional processes as of crucial importance to the timing and execution of motor sequences (e.g., Nickerson, 1980; Posner, 1980; Rosenbaum & Patashnik, 1980). While this does not warrant an unqualified conclusion that the correlations obtained between language and motor impairment in schizophrenia are due to a more basic defect in attentional efficiency, they are compatible with that possibility and may be seen as adding a slight increment of credibility to the attentional deficit theory of language disturbance.

E. Counter Theories

Alternative theories of language production in schizophrenia have appeared in the literature for many decades. Some of these have been presented in ways that do not provide a basis for empirical test and cannot therefore be evaluated in any direct comparison with the theory developed in this chapter. For the sake of exposition, we may look at the general strategy of explanation that particular theorists have adopted and attempt to compare them with the present theory in those terms.

1. Reinforcement of Noncommunication

One class of explanations turns to the effect that language anomalies have upon the listener and concludes that the production of this effect is responsible for the rise and maintenance of the anomalies themselves. Examples of this are to be seen in the work of Ferreira (1960). He suggests that the developing schizophrenic attempts to construct a new and personal language that will both defy understanding by others and yet permit the expression of feeling. In this respect his view is similar to that of Laffal (1965), already discussed, in that it assumes the possibility of a translation from the overt content of the schizophrenic's utterances to a "real" and coherent plan of utterance that the patient keeps hidden by linguistic disguise.

There is little doubt that the language utterances of schizophrenic patients can confuse the listener, as is indeed the case with the language of aphasic patients, acutely intoxicated patients, and others. By the same token, there is no doubt but that the observation of a grand mal seizure may be disturbing to the spectator, but the observer reaction does not compel us by any acceptable logic to conclude that this is what motivated the behavior. To establish that this is the case, we would need systematic studies in which observer reaction was manipulated to ascertain the effect of it upon the patient's language. No studies of this kind have been provided as evidence for the relevant theories.

At the clinical level, the prediction that language will be confusing to the listener is one that can be confirmed by an infinite number of word sequences and is, therefore, nonfalsifiable.

The "translation" of anomalous language into its supposed "real" meaning requires that we establish a consistent system of translation (rather than a new system made up ad hoc for each case) and some method, independent of the translation itself, for determining the validity of the new meaning thus revealed. Laffal's method of the analysis of contextual associates seems to meet the criterion of consistency of translation, but so far there has been no accompanying method for determining the validity of the translations that it makes.

2. Forrest and Poesis

David Forrest (1965, 1976) has suggested that the mechanisms underlying schizophrenic utterance resemble those seen in poetry. That is to say that the attributes of meter, word sound, rhyming, and other aesthetic qualities serve a purpose for the patient by conveying a significance to his or her statements that would be lacking in more prosaic forms of utterance. Here again, there is no doubt that some poets have employed associational techniques to heighten the poetic effect of their work: Dylan Thomas comes to mind as a source of examples of this approach. Against this view, however, must be set the very large number of rather drab, uninspired word strings, broken sentences, and so forth, coupled with the often evident distress of the patient at the quality of his or her own utterances. To accept the explanation that Forrest offers, we need explicit criteria for the judgment that an utterance is poetic and some method of assessing the manner in which these utterances convey more significance to the patient than normal utterances do. In brief, the hypothesis needs operational definitions and accompanying empirical tests if we are to accept it.

Before leaving this question we should, however, note one possibility that overlaps with the model proposed by Forrest. Earlier in this chapter, we commented upon the problem presented to patients by the fact that their own actual utterances do not correspond to their plans. To this extent, the language that patients hear themselves utter may be seen as likely to contain clues as to its own origin (i.e., the identity and purposes of whatever or whoever is responsible for the distorted utterances). Delusional explanations of the thought-control kind are understandable reactions to the recognition that the words coming from one's mouth are not what one intended—and are presumably the result of somebody else's influence. In the search for clues as to the origin of this situation, patients may turn to the utterances themselves for internal evidence, in the form of anagrams, palindromes, or anything else that might be informative. In this respect, patients may treat their own language as an alien object, the sound and form of which may be significant beyond the semantic content.

F. Relevance to Family Theories of Etiology

Some theories specify a proposed etiology for language disorder in schizophrenia that emphasizes communication incompetence but does not provide a fine-grain basis for predicting what types of language anomaly will occur and where they will occur. Most family-genesis theories are of this order (e.g., Bateson, Jackson, Haley, & Weakland, 1956; Lidz, 1973) in that they do not permit concrete prediction of the patterns of anomaly that should be found. The present theory is largely orthogonal to such approaches, as we do not attempt to define the first link in the etiological chain, beyond noting the role of genetic dispositions and assuming that a neural anomaly underlies the language anomalies. To the extent that language anomalies covary with other nonlanguage impairment in schizophrenia—such as the motor impairments noted already—the notion that the basic pathology was formed in the sphere of communication is so much the less convincing. It has not seemed particularly plausible to the present writer and his colleagues. The data relevant to biological factors in attention summarized by Matthysse (1977) seem to be more in accord with the findings reported here and to lend no encouragement to a search for genesis of the pathology purely at the level of interpersonal communication.

G. Some Conclusions

In this chapter the writer has presented a set of propositions relating language disturbance in schizophrenia to attentional dysfunction in that disorder. The propositions form a tentative theory about the pathology that underlies the language features of some schizophrenic patients. It does not specify a primary etiology of the disorder, although a neurological deficit is suggested as a reasonable candidate for this. Some suggestive evidence is reported, consistent with the theory and drawn from a range of methods and patient samples. Many deductions from the theory have yet to be tested, and such tests will, no doubt, suggest modifications in the theory.

Acknowledgments

My particular gratitude is expressed to my wife, friend, and colleague, Winifred Barbara Maher, for her many valuable suggestions and criticism at all stages of this work. I would also like to acknowledge the benefit that has accrued from discussions and collaboration with Theo Manschreck, William Milberg, Sherry Rochester, and Derek Rutter, and from the contributions of my former and present students William Berman, David Briggs, Louis Cozolino, Toni Hoover, Raymond Levy, Kathryn McKean, and Michael Molino.

References

Aborn, M., Rubinstein, H., & Sterling, T. D. Sources of contextual constraint upon words in sentences. *Journal of Experimental Psychology,* 1959, **57** 171–180.

Arieti, S. *The intrapsychic self.* New York: Basic Books, 1967.

Atkinson, J. W., & McClelland, D. C. The projective expression of needs: II. The effect of different intensities of hunger drive on thematic apperception. *Journal of Experimental Psychology,* 1948, **38**, 643–658.

Bannister, D., & Fransella, F. A grid test of schizophrenic thought disorder. *British Journal of Social and Clinical Psychology,* 1966, **5**, 95–102.

Bateson, G., Jackson, D. D., Haley, J., & Weakland, J. Toward a theory of schizophrenia. *Behavioral Science,* 1956, **1**, 254–264.

Beattie, G. W., & Butterworth, B. L. Contextual probability and word frequency as determinants of pauses and errors in spontaneous speech. *Language and Speech,* 1979, **22**, 201–211.

Beck, A. T. The reliability of psychiatric diagnosis: A critique of systematic studies. *American Journal of Psychiatry,* 1962, **119**, 210–216.

Bleuler, E. *Dementia praecox or the group of schizophrenias.* New York: International Universities Press, 1950.

Broadbent, D. *Perception and communication.* Oxford: Pergamon, 1958.

Burton, N. G., & Licklider, J. C. R. Long-range constraints in the statistical structure of printed English. *American Journal of Psychology,* 1955, **68**, 650–653.

Carpenter, W. T., Jr., Strauss, J. S., & Bartko, J. J. Use of signs and symptoms for the identification of schizophrenic patients: A report of the International Pilot Study of Schizophrenia. *Schizophrenia Bulletin,* 1974, **11**, 37–49.

Carroll, J. B., Carton, A. S. & Wilds, C. P. *An investigation of "Cloze" items in the measurement of achievement in foreign languages.* Cambridge, Mass.: Harvard University Graduate School of Education, 1959.

Chaika, E. A linguist looks at "schizophrenic" language. *Brain and Language,* 1974, **1**, 113–118.

Chapman, L. J., & Chapman, J. P. *Disordered thought in schizophrenia.* Englewood Cliffs, N.J.: Prentice-Hall, 1973.

Chapman, L. J., Chapman, J. P., & Miller, G. A. A theory of verbal behavior in schizophrenia. In B. Maher (Ed.), *Progress in experimental personality research* (Vol. 1). New York: Academic Press, 1964.

Cohen, B. D., Nachmani, G., & Rosenberg, S. Referent communication disturbances in schizophrenia. *Journal of Abnormal Psychology,* 1974, **83,** 1–13.

Critchley, M. The neurology of psychotic speech. *British Journal of Psychiatry,* 1964, **110,** 353–364.

Daut, R. L., & Chapman, L. J. Object-sorting and the heterogeneity of schizophrenia. *Journal of Abnormal Psychology,* 1974, **83,** 581–584.

Denes, P. B., & Pinson, E. N. *The speech chain.* Murray Hill: Bell Telephone Laboratories, 1963.

Epstein, R. (Ed.) *Notebooks: B. F. Skinner.* Englewood Cliffs, N.J.: Prentice-Hall, 1980.

Falek, A., & Moser, H. M. Classification in schizophrenia. *Archives of General Psychiatry,* 1975, **32,** 59–67.

Feighner, J. P., Robins, E., Cruze, S. B., Woodruff, R. A., Jr., Winokur, G. & Munoz, R. Diagnostic criteria for use in psychiatric research. *Archives of General Psychiatry,* 1972, **26,** 57–63.

Ferreira, A. J. The semantics and the context of the schizophrenic's language. *Archives of General Psychiatry,* 1960, **3,** 128–138.

Fitts, P. M. The information capacity of the human motor system in controlling the amplitude of movement. *Journal of Experimental Psychology,* 1954, **47,** 381–391.

Fodor, J. A., & Bever, T. G. The psychological reality of linguistic segments. *Journal of Verbal Learning and Verbal Behavior,* 1965, **4,** 414–420.

Forrest, D. V. Poesis and the language of schizophrenia. *Psychiatry,* 1965, **28,** 1–18.

Forrest, D. V. Nonsense and sense in schizophrenic language. *Schizophrenia Bulletin,* 1976, **2,** 286–301.

Freedman, B. J. The subjective experience of perceptual and cognitive disturbances in schizophrenia. *Archives of General Psychiatry,* 1974, **30,** 333–340.

Gerver, D. Linguistic rules and the perception and recall of speech by schizophrenic patients. *British Journal of Social and Clinical Psychology,* 1967, **6,** 204–211.

Goldman-Eisler, F. The predictability of words in context and the length of pauses in speech. *Language and Speech,* 1958, **1,** 226–231.

Goldman-Eisler, F. Pauses, clauses, sentences. *Language and Speech,* 1972, **15,** 103–113.

Hill, A. B. Validity and clinical utility of the grid test of schizophrenic thought disorder. *British Journal of Psychiatry,* 1976, **126,** 251–254.

Hoch, A. A review of some physiological and psychological experiments done in connection with the study of mental diseases. *Psychological Bulletin,* 1904, **1,** 241–257.

Huston, P. E., Shakow, D., & Riggs, L. A. Studies of motor function in schizophrenia: II. Reaction time. *Journal of General Psychology,* 1937, **16,** 39–82.

Joravsky, D. *The Lysenko Affair.* Cambridge, Mass.: Harvard Univ. Press, 1970.

Ladefoged, P., & Broadbent, D. E. Perception of sequence in auditory events. *Quarterly Journal of Experimental Psychology,* 1960, **12,** 162–170.

Laffal, J. *Normal and pathological language.* New York: Atherton, 1965.

Lang, P. J., & Buss, A. H. Psychological deficit in schizophrenia: II. Interference and activation. *Journal of Abnormal Psychology,* 1965, **70,** 77–106.

Lawson, J. S., McGhie, A., & Chapman, J. Perception of speech in schizophrenia. *British Journal of Psychology,* 1964, **110,** 375–380.

Lewinsohn, P. M., & Elwood, D. L. The role of contextual constraints in the learning of language samples in schizophrenia. *Journal of Nervous and Mental Diseases,* 1961, **133,** 79–81.

Lidz, T. *The origin and treatment of schizophrenic disorders.* New York: Basic Books, 1973.

Lisman, S. A., & Cohen, B. D. Self-editing deficits in schizophrenia: A word association analogue. *Journal of Abnormal Psychology,* 1972, **79,** 181–188.

MacGinitie, W. H. Contextual constraint in English prose paragraphs. *Journal of Psychology,* 1961, **51,** 121–130.

Maher, B. The shattered language of schizophrenia. *Psychology Today,* November 1968, pp. 30 ff.

Maher, B. The language of schizophrenia: A review and interpretation. *British Journal of Psychiatry,* 1972, **120,** 4–17.

Maher, B. Information, redundancy and Gestalt psychology: An historical note and translation. *Journal of the History of the Behavioral Sciences,* 1973, **9,** 76–85.

Maher, B. Delusional thinking and perceptual disorder. *Journal of Individual Psychology,* 1974, **30,** 98–113.

Maher, B., & Berman, W. Clause structure and intrusions in dichotic listening. *Language and Speech,* in press.

Maher, B., & Maher, W. B. Psychopathology. In E. Hearst (Ed.), *The first century of experimental psychology.* Hillsdale, N.J.: Erlbaum, 1979.

Maher, B., Manschreck, T. C., & Molino, M. Redundancy, pause distributions and thought disorder. *Language and Speech,* in press.

Maher, B., Manschreck, T. C., & Rucklos, M. Contextual constraint and the recall of verbal material in schizophrenia. *British Journal of Psychiatry,* 1980, **137,** 69–73.

Maher, B., McKean, K. O., & McLaughlin, B. Studies in psychotic language. In P. J. Stone, D. C. Dunphy, M. S. Smith & D. M. Ogilvie (Eds.), *The general inquirer: A computer approach to content analysis.* Cambridge, Mass.: MIT Press, 1966.

Maher, B., & Ross, J. Delusions. In H. Adams & P. Sutker (Eds.), *Comprehensive handbook of psychopathology.* New York: Plenum, 1983.

Manschreck, T. C., Maher, B., & Ader, D. N. Formal thought disorder, the type–token ratio, and disturbed voluntary motor-movement in schizophrenia. *British Journal of Psychiatry,* 1981, **139,** 7–15.

Manschreck, T. C., Maher, B., Rucklos, M. E., Vereen, D. R., & Ader, D. N. Deficient motor synchrony in schizophrenia. *Journal of Abnormal Psychology,* 1981, **90,** 321–328.

Matthysse, S. The biology of attention. *Schizophrenia Bulletin,* 1977, **3,** 370–372.

McGhie, A. Attention and perception in schizophrenia. In B. Maher (Ed.), *Progress in experimental personality research* (Vol. 5). New York: Academic Press, 1970.

McGhie, A., & Chapman, J. Disorders of attention and perception in early schizophrenia. *British Journal of Medical Psychology,* 1961, **34,** 103–116.

McGhie, A., Chapman, J., & Lawson, J. S. The effect of distraction on schizophrenic performance: 1. Psychomotor ability. *British Journal of Psychiatry,* 1965, **111,** 391. (a)

McGhie, A., Chapman, J., & Lawson, J. S. The effect of distraction on schizophrenic performance: 2. Perception and immediate memory. *British Journal of Psychiatry,* 1965, **111,** 383–390. (b)

McKean, K. O. An analysis of selected samples of normal and disorganized language productions of mental patients. Unpublished honors thesis, Radcliffe College, 1963.

Mednick, S. A., & Schulsinger, F. Some premorbid characteristics related to the breakdown of children with schizophrenic mothers. In D. Rosenthal & S. S. Kety (Eds.), *The transmission of schizophrenia.* New York: Pergamon, 1968.

Meyer, D. E., & Schvaneveldt, R. Facilitation in recognizing pairs of words: Evidence of a dependence between retrieval operations. *Journal of Experimental Psychology,* 1971, **90,** 227–234.

Miller, G., & Selfridge, J. Verbal context and the recall of meaningful material. *American Journal of Psychology,* 1950, **63**, 176–185.

Mittenecker, E. Eine neue quantitative methode in der sprachanalyse und ihre anwendung bei schizophrenen. *Monatsschrift für Psychiatrie und Neurologie,* 1951, **121**, 364–375.

Mittenecker, E. Perseveration und persönlichkeit. *Zeitschrift für Experimentelle und Angewandte Psychologie,* 1953, **1**, 5–31.

Moray, N. Attention in dichotic listening: Affective cues and the influence of instructions. *Quarterly Journal of Experimental Psychology,* 1959, **11**, 56–60.

Nickerson, R. S. (Ed.). *Attention and performance: VIII.* Hillsdale, N.J.: Erlbaum, 1980.

Nielsen, G. Om forstaaelighedsreserven og om overbestemthed. In G. Nielsen (Ed.), *Til minde om Edgar Rubin. Nordisk Psykologi,* 1956 (8), 28–37. (Monograph)

Oltmanns, T. F., Weintraub, S., Stone, A. F., & Neale, J. M. Cognitive slippage in children vulnerable to schizophrenia. *Journal of Abnormal Child Psychology,* 1978, **6**, 237–245.

Onifer, W. Associative intrusions in schizophrenic language. Unpublished doctoral thesis, Tufts University, 1980.

Posner, M. I. Orienting of attention. *Quarterly Journal of Experimental Psychology,* 1980, **32**, 3–25.

Posner, M. I., & Keele, S. W. Attention demands of movements. *Proceedings of the 17th Congress of Applied Psychology.* Amsterdam: Zeitlinger, 1969.

Raven, C. J. Verbal dysfunctions in mental illness. *Language and Speech,* 1958, **1**, 218–225.

Rochester, S. R., Harris, J., & Seeman, M. V. Sentence processing in schizophrenic listeners. *Journal of Abnormal Psychology,* 1973, **82**, 350–356.

Rochester, S. R., & Martin, J. *Crazy talk: A study of the discourse of schizophrenic speakers.* New York: Plenum, 1979.

Rochester, S. R., Thurston, S., & Rupp, J. Hesitations as clues to failures in coherence: A study of the thought-disordered speaker. In S. Rosenberg (Ed.), *Sentence production: Developments in research and theory.* Hillsdale, N.J.: Erlbaum, 1977.

Rosenbaum, D. A., & Patashnik, O. A metal clock-setting process revealed by reaction time. In G. Stelmach & J. Requin (Eds.), *Tutorials in motor behavior.* Amsterdam: North Holland, 1980.

Rosenberg, S., & Cohen, B. D. Referential processes in speakers and listeners. *Psychological Review,* 1966, **73**, 208–231.

Rutter, D. R. The reconstruction of schizophrenic speech. *British Journal of Psychiatry,* 1979, **134**, 356–359.

Salmoni, A. W., Sullivan, S. T., & Starkes, J. L. The attention demands of movements: A critique of the probe technique. *Journal of Motor Behavior,* 1976, **8**, 161–169.

Sandifer, M. G., Jr., Pettus, C., & Quade, D. A study of psychiatric diagnosis. *Journal of Nervous and Mental Disease,* 1964, **139**, 350–356.

Scheff, T. J. *Labeling madness.* Englewood Cliffs, N.J.: Prentice-Hall, 1975.

Schmidt, H., & Fonda, C. The reliability of psychiatric diagnosis: A new look. *Journal of Abnormal and Social Psychology,* 1956, **52**, 262–267.

Schneider, K. *Clinical psychopathology.* New York: Grune & Stratton, 1959.

Schwartz, S. Do schizophrenics give rare word associations? *Schizophrenia Bulletin,* 1978, **4**, 248–251.

Shakow, D. Segmental set. *Archives of General Psychiatry,* 1962, **6**, 1–17.

Shakow, D. Psychological deficit in schizophrenia. *Behavioral Science,* 1963, **8**, 275–305.

Shakow, D. Some observations on the psychology (and some fewer, on the biology) of schizophrenia. *Journal of Nervous and Mental Disease,* 1971, **153**, 300–316.

Simonini, R. C. Phonemic and analogic lapses in radio and television speech. *American Speech,* 1956, **51**, 252–263.

Spitzer, R., & Endicott, J. *Schedule for affective disorders and schizophrenia (SADS).* New York: New York State Psychiatric Institute, 1977.

Swinney, D. A. Lexical access during sentence comprehension. Reconsideration of context effects. *Journal of Verbal Learning and Verbal Behavior,* 1979, **18,** 214–241.

Swinney, D. A., Onifer, W., Prather, P., & Hirshkowitz, M. Semantic facilitation across sensory modalities in the processing of individual words and sentences. *Memory and Cognition,* 1979, **7,** 159–165.

Taylor, W. L. "Cloze Procedure": A new tool for measuring readability. *Journalism Quarterly,* 1953, **30,** 415–433.

Treisman, A. M. Contextual cues in selective listening. *Quarterly Journal of Experimental Psychology,* 1960, **12,** 242–248.

Ullman, L., & Krasner, L. *A psychological approach to abnormal behavior* (1st ed.). Englewood Cliffs, N.J.: Prentice-Hall, 1975.

World Health Organization, *International pilot study of schizophrenia* (Vol. 1). Geneva: W.H.O. Press, 1973.

PSYCHOPATHOLOGY OF MOTOR BEHAVIOR IN SCHIZOPHRENIA

Theo C. Manschreck

DEPARTMENT OF PSYCHIATRY
MASSACHUSETTS GENERAL HOSPITAL
HARVARD MEDICAL SCHOOL
BOSTON, MASSACHUSETTS

I. Introduction

Few students of schizophrenia have failed to note the remarkable changes in motor behavior associated with this disorder. Such dramatic features as catalepsy, posturing, and excitement as well as the more common occurrence of stereotypies, mannerisms, clumsiness, and incoordination have been observed repeatedly (Kleist, 1908; Kraepelin, 1919; Marsden, Tarsy,

& Baldessarini, 1975; Slater & Roth, 1969). Yet, there is only limited knowledge of the motor aspects of schizophrenia (Wulfeck, 1941; Yates, 1973). This circumstance contrasts sharply with the relative wealth of information concerning such schizophrenic features as disturbed perception, language, autonomic responses, and delusions.

Moreover, it is puzzling in view of the long history of clinical observations concerning abnormal motor features. Marsden and colleagues (1975) have reviewed this literature extensively, with particular reference to behavioral stereotypies and hypokinesia. However, possibly because of intermittent occurrence in individual patients (Jones & Hunter, 1968) and the confounding factor of antipsychotic drug treatment, intrinsic motor abnormalities have in recent years seldom been studied systematically. Yet their discovery clearly antedated the advent of neuroleptic therapy (Bleuler, 1950/1911; Kleist, 1908; Kraepelin, 1919).

The development of knowledge about motor behavior in schizophrenia is necessary for several reasons. First, despite extensive commentary on motor disturbance in schizophrenia, no systematic explanation has been put forward. Second, virtually no attempt has been made to determine the relationship of motor features with other classes of symptoms. Such an explanation is required for a detailed and satisfactory account of schizophrenic behavior. Third, the study of the natural history of motor features, still in its infancy, may provide critical insights regarding the pathogenesis of schizophrenia. For example, are motor features (and which ones) early or late manifestations of the disorder? Are they associated with cognitive impairments? Do they have prognostic significance? What factors, including neuroleptics and other treatments, modify their occurrence?

This chapter reviews the literature on these issues. Following the review, recent findings from clinical investigations of motor disturbance in schizophrenia are reported.

II. Motor Features of Schizophrenia

Although there is little specific knowledge about the motor features of schizophrenia, they have been consistently observed in remarkable variety over the years. Some are striking and easy to recognize, such as catalepsy. Others, such as mannerisms, may be more subtle. Attempts to classify them must, to some extent, be arbitrary. The scheme used here divides examples of abnormal behavior into those associated with increased movement (hyperkinesia) and those associated with decreased movement (hypokinesia) in relation to normal behavior (see Tables I and II). These categories are then

TABLE I

DISTURBANCES ASSOCIATED WITH DECREASED MOTOR ACTIVITY IN SCHIZOPHRENIA

Diffuse	
Retardation	Slowed in all activities, voluntary and vegetative, and often slowed in thinking and speech as well. Patients show little spontaneity, and goal-directed behavior is reported to be exhausting.
Poverty of movement	Reduction in the amount or quantity of motor activity, sometimes called hypokinesia.
Stupor	A severe form of decreased motor activity. There may be almost no animation, spontaneous movement, or locomotion at the extreme. In milder cases, only some movements may be transiently blocked (cf. below).
Patterned	
Motor blocking (obstruction)	A disorder of the execution of movement. Obstruction usually occurs episodically when movement suddenly is reduced or halted in the midst of normal or increased activity. Later the patient may be able to resume the movement. The patient may report the subjective experience of thought withdrawal or that the intended movement was forgotten following such episodes. Movement may appear stiff and awkward.
Cooperation	There are two forms: (1) *Mitmachen:* A displaced body part returns to its original position when released, after having passively acquiesced to movements made by the examiner. (2) *Mitgehen:* A more severe or extreme form of this disturbance in which the patient's body part continues to move in a given direction in response to light pressure.
Opposition (*Gegenhalten*)	Refers to the presence of muscular resistance to passive movement of the extremities. The opposite of cooperation.
Automatic obedience	The patient carries out all instruction, regardless of merit or propriety.
Negativism	A broad spectrum of motor behavior that is characterized by an apparently unmotivated failure to do what is suggested. This may lead to varying degrees of akinesia, or lack of movement. In its most severe form, it is also aptly described as stupor. Often it is called a disorder of volition.
Ambitendency	A form of negativism. In response to a request to carry out a voluntary action, the patient makes a series of tentative movements but does not reach the goal. For example, the patient may walk toward the examiner in response to a request to come forward and then halt halfway and return to his or her original position.
Echopraxia	The patient imitates the behavior of the examiner or other patients. (In *echolalia* speech is imitated.)
Last-minute responses	The patient (often mute) is unable to reply to questions or initiate conversation until the examiner is leaving the bedside. Then the patient may blurt out a response to a prior question.

TABLE II

DISTURBANCES ASSOCIATED WITH INCREASED MOTOR ACTIVITY IN SCHIZOPHRENIA

Diffuse	
Restlessness	A persistent or generalized increase in bodily movement.
Excitement	Prolonged bursts of energy, often chaotic, disorganized, and frenzied in character
Tremor	Involuntary, purposeless contractions of muscle groups that produce oscillating movements near a joint or of the head. They may occur at rest, with arms extended (postural), resting, or with movement (intentional). They may be described as fine or coarse, regular or irregular, rapid or slow.
Stereotyped movements (stereotypies)	Repeated performances of spontaneous non-goal-directed behavior in a uniform manner, often with some remnant of purposive behavior in the movement. Repeated gestures or actions (sometimes thought to have symbolic significance), including continuous movement in and out of a chair, crossing oneself, waving repeatedly in the air, touching objects over and over (*handling,* a form of stereotypy), and grasping one's hands or clothes continuously (*intertwining*). *Complex stereotypies* include eating a bite of food and closing the eyes five times.
Spasms	Involuntary contractions of muscles or groups of muscles, sometimes associated with pain, embarrassment, and fear. Examples include habit spasms and spasms of swallowing or of the tongue or the eyelids (*blepharospasm*).
Choreiform movements	Short, jerky movements that may affect the whole body. They may affect the periphery more than the trunk. They may be fine or coarse. Also, they may appear to be fragments of expression or gesture and are often disguised in this manner.
Athetoid movements	Spontaneous movements that are slow, writhing, and twisting (worm-like—hence athetoid), involving generally distal muscles, but possibly proximal also, and bringing strange postures to the body, especially to the hands.
Parakinesia	Spontaneous, continuous, irregular muscular movements—often jerky in character. Persistent grimacing, twitching, and jerking may be present. They may resemble tics superficially.
Myoclonic movements	Rapid contraction of either proximal or distal muscles, usually in an unrhythmic fashion but sometimes with bilaterally symmetrical presentation.
Perseverative movements (perseveration)	The involuntary continuation or recurrence of a movement more appropriate to a prior stimulus (e.g., request, command) whose purpose is already served, in response to a succeeding stimulus. Perseverative movement may be elicited by asking the patient to close the eyes, stick out the tongue, or write for the examiner, as well as by close observation of interview behavior.
Impulsive movements	Sudden, apparently purposeless, or involuntary acts, including screaming, biting, and exhibition of genitals.
Carphologic movements	These include picking at bedclothes, skin, or clothing in a purposeless manner.

(*continued*)

TABLE II—*Continued*

Agitation	The subjective report of anguish, psychic tension, or anxiety of very unpleasant proportions *and* one or more of the following: pacing, fidgetiness, inability to sit still, wringing of the hands, pulling at skin, hair, or clothing, shouting, or complaining in outbursts.
Tics	Short, sudden, repetitive, jerky movements of small groups of muscles of the face, neck, or upper trunk, often worsened by psychological circumstances. Most commonly affecting the face, tics may be part of an unusual blink or distortion of the forehead, nose, or mouth. Swallowing, grunting, coughing, or shoulder movements may also be tics.
Mannerisms	These consist in an unusual, frequently stilted variation in the performance of a normal, goal-directed movement. Examples include unusual movements in greeting, shaking hands, or writing, strange uses of words, and unusual verbal expressions out of keeping with the situation. Stereotypies are often difficult to distinguish from mannerisms. Stereotypies generally do not have a goal or form part of goal-directed behavior. Manneristic behavior may take the form of collecting or hoarding.

subdivided according to whether the feature is diffuse or patterned. This classification scheme is similar to that of Jaspers (1963), Marsden *et al.* (1975), and Manschreck and Keller (1979). Disorders of posture (Fish, 1967) are usually considered a form of motor disturbance, and these are also listed (see Table III). The features of catatonia, a classic syndrome of motor disturbance (see Table IV), overlap several of these categories. Although it is sometimes difficult in practice to distinguish drug-induced effects (see Table V) from those associated with psychiatric illness itself, both have rather distinct characteristics.

TABLE III
POSTURAL DISTURBANCES ASSOCIATED WITH SCHIZOPHRENIA

Increased muscle tonus in isolated area of the body	Parts of the body are held rigidly in one position. For example, there may be increased tension in the jaws (clenched tightly together), the eyes tightly shut, or the head held rigidly just above the pillow (*psychological pillow*).
Manneristic postures	Stilted often awkward postures that usually are not maintained. Such posture may be seen to express a turning away or withdrawal from surroundings.
Stereotyped postures	Bizarre postures often maintained for hours.
Waxy flexibility (catalepsy)	The patient allows him- or herself to be placed in any position and then maintains this position for at least several minutes.

TABLE IV
FEATURES OF CATATONIA

Excitement	Catalepsy
Stupor	Negativistic motor behavior
Stereotypies	Echopraxia
Mannerisms	Last-minute responses
Rigidity	

TABLE V
NEUROLEPTIC-INDUCED MOTOR BEHAVIORS

Tremor	As defined in Table II.
Dystonic movements	Usually acute. Bearing similarity to athetoid movements, but usually involving larger areas of the body musculature. Slowed hypertonic, occasionally grotesque movements with maintenance of peculiar postures.
Akathisia	Motor restlessness, often subjectively experienced as centered in the lower extremities and accompanied by muscular or somatic tension, a feeling of having to move, and an intolerance of sitting still. In milder states, shuffling or tapping movements, shifting, and rocking to and fro; in severer states, an inability to sit still at all and incessant movement.
Parkinsonian effects	Slowed movements (*bradykinesia*) with expressionless facies, slow initiation of movements, and loss of associated movements. A tremor at rest is often present as well as a "cog-wheel rigidity" of the limbs.
Tardive dyskinesia	Literally this is a late disorder of motility. There are choreiform movements of the extremities, orofacial movements (such as "flycatcher's tongue," unusual grimacing, and snouting), and dystonic postures. Younger patients appear more affected in the extremities and trunk, whereas in older patients, there is a greater restriction to the oral region.

III. Historical Contributions to the Psychopathology of Motor Behavior in Schizophrenia

A. KRAEPELIN

There are no better descriptions of the motor features of schizophrenia than those of Emil Kraepelin. Hence, it is fitting to begin this review with a survey of his contributions. Kraepelin's pioneering and influential classification of psychiatric disorders derived from two critical principles. The first is that virtually all mental disorders have biological causes. The second is that, in the absence of known causes, the best means of studying psychiatric disorders is to observe their course and to look for consistent patterns—hence, Kraepelin's strong emphasis on precise description and follow-up. Using these concepts, Kraepelin effectively revolutionized nineteenth-century thinking about psychiatric disorders and laid the groundwork for contemporary diagnostic categories. He investigated the psychopathology associated with diseases of established etiology, including trauma, infections, tumors, and metabolic disturbances. For those psychiatric disorders that could not be assigned a known cause, he proposed a new classification based on his longitudinal observations. Through his efforts, manic-depressive or circular insanity and dementia praecox (see Table VI) were put forth as distinct clinical disorders. Dementia praecox represented a disorder of will (e.g., loss of motivation), emotion (e.g., anhedonia), and judgment (e.g., bizarre behavior, inappropriate silliness or laughter) that had variable, subtle as well as dramatic and intermittent symptoms.

Among the patients who received the diagnosis of dementia praecox, Kraepelin noted multiple motor features, including echopraxia, catalepsy, forms of negativism, impulsiveness, excitement, stereotypies, mannerisms, perseveration, stupor, and reduced efficiency of fine movements. A marked clumsiness, jerkiness, or loss of smooth muscular coordination also characterized these patients. Kraepelin described the gait of the patient as having the appearance of walking through snow. Although the catatonic subtype of dementia praecox was dominated by motor disturbance features, Kraepelin observed similar features in the hebephrenic and paranoid forms of the disorder as well. Kraepelin investigated the productivity of these patients and discovered that their motor efficiency in a specific task deterio-

TABLE VI

EMIL KRAEPELIN'S DEMENTIA PRAECOX

(CIRCA 1896)

Onset
   Adolescence
Clinical Picture
   Always: Disturbance of emotion
                Disturbance of volition
                Weakening of judgment
   Usually: Hallucinations
                Delusions
                Motor behavior disturbance
Prognosis
   Complicated
   Generally deterioration (psychological
      enfeeblement or dementia)
   Temporary improvements

rated rapidly. In handiwork and crafts, particularly those involving fine work, he and others (Mailloux and Newberger, 1941; Wulfeck, 1941) noted a general decline in ability (work decrement).

Although Kraepelin viewed dementia praecox as a disease of unknown etiology, he offered a psychological explanation for many of its manifestations, including restricted and interrupted movements, such as last-minute responses and negativism. He considered the latter understandable on the basis of the psychic mechanisms of idea and counteridea, effort and countereffort. In dementia praecox, ideas evoke counterideas, efforts counterefforts. The effect of such experiences is to block action by interfering with its execution. When asked to do something, such as gesture with the arm, a patient wants to do so but does not want to do so as well. The arm may become rigidly immobile. Kraepelin also recognized that movement disorders suggestive of dementia praecox could be the consequence of other neurological diseases including encephalitis, syphilis, and epilepsy and he emphasized the value of differential diagnosis and careful follow-up to sort out such problems.

B. Bleuler

Eugen Bleuler (1950/1911) described many of the same motor features that Kraepelin had identified among dementia praecox patients, noting that motor anomalies were seldom absent. He also commented on "idiomuscular contractions," spasms, and a "will 'o the wisp" gait, with irregular timing and spacing of steps. He suggested that schizophrenia (the term he coined) was a group of disorders with a spectrum of prognoses and ages of onset. Common among this group of schizophrenic disorders were several fundamental symptoms: a marked disturbance of associations (disconnectedness or *Zerfahrenheit*), ambivalence, inappropriate affective responses, and excessive preoccupation with autistic thinking. Influenced by current faculty psychology, Bleuler believed the disorder was a consequence of disturbed will, emotion, and thinking. Of far-reaching importance was his decision to specify a pathogenetic mechanism—loosened associations—to explain the clinical features and private mental experiences of these patients. Bleuler hinted at a metabolic source(s) for these symptoms. However, his emphasis (1950/1911) on the mechanisms of disturbed associations and Kraepelin's views regarding the underlying disturbances of will, judgment, and emotion in dementia praecox set the stage for further attempts to elucidate the "psychic" origin of schizophrenia.

> The motor symptoms which we have been able to analyze could often be explained entirely on a psychic basis. However, the possibility must not be excluded that somewhere within the motor apparatus alterations take place which produce a portion of these symptoms or, at least, create the necessary predisposition to them. . . . there is no basis

for the assumption that the larger number of schizophrenic motor phenomena derive from innate mechanisms [Bleuler, 1950/1911, pp. 445–446].

C. JACKSON

James Hughlings Jackson, the English neurologist, contributed to the study of schizophrenic motor features through his major theoretical proposals concerning the hierarchical organization of the central nervous system. Although his ideas derived from the study of neurological disease, Jackson (1894/1958) considered his concepts applicable to mental disorders. In mental illness, he maintained, there is a dissolution of the highest cerebral centers. Complex functions normally under voluntary control are lost. Consequently, less complex and undamaged central nervous system components produce the striking manifestations of mental disorder.

> Disease only causes the negative element of the mental condition: the positive mental element, say a delusion, . . . however absurd it may be, signifies activities of healthy nervous arrangements, signifies evolution going on in what remains intact of the highest cerebral centres [Jackson, 1894/1958 p. 418].

Jackson proposed that, in psychosis, clinical features can be classified according to whether they result from dissolution (so-called negative symptoms) or from activity in the remaining undamaged nervous components (so-called positive symptoms). Negative symptoms of schizophrenia would include withdrawal, blocking, disturbances of identity, and passivity experiences. Positive symptoms would include hallucinations, delusions, stereotypies, mannerisms, and catalepsy. Jackson believed that the impact of mental illness in producing positive and negative symptoms was governed by (a) the depth of the dissolution; (b) the rate of the dissolution process; (c) the type of individual affected; and (d) the influence of bodily states and external environment.

Similar viewpoints were put forward by Carl Wernicke and Karl Kahlbaum (Jaspers, 1963), who argued that focal cerebral pathology was the basis for the motor features of psychotic disorders. The idea that subcortical mechanisms produce these features when deprived of the influence of higher centers has been popular. Kleist (1908), for example, felt that schizophrenic motor disturbances had a source identical to that of neurological diseases with similar motor manifestations. Other writers have echoed this theme (Arieti, 1945; Jelliffe, 1928; Marsden et al., 1975; Orton, 1930).

D. JASPERS

Karl Jaspers, building on earlier observations, noted certain remarkable characteristics of schizophrenic motor features. For instance, while there is increased muscle tone in certain limbs or areas, such as the face of a patient maintaining a catatonic posture, there is decreased or normal tone in other areas of the body, a kind of incoordination or fragmentation of motor function. Jaspers also observed that the "immobile" catatonic patient could initiate such basic activities as care of toileting, feeding, and dressing but was often unable to respond to verbal requests (Jaspers, 1963).

Jaspers argued that there are two ways to examine the grotesque and abnormal movements of mentally disordered individuals. The first, or neurological approach, is to become acquainted with the anatomy and physiology of the motor mechanism itself. The second, or psychological approach, is to get to know the "abnormal psychic life" and the patient's awareness as to what unusual and conspicuous movements reflect. Psychotic motor phenomena fall somewhere between the reaches of neurological and psychological approaches and are not comprehended satisfactorily by either alone.

For this reason, the term *psychomotor disturbance* was coined and applied to schizophrenia to suggest that the similarity between schizophrenic motor features and the features of certain neurological syndromes did not necessarily reflect a common set of causes or pathogenesis (Slater & Roth, 1969). In catatonic excitement, for example, patients may identify with their behavior and attempt to construct rationalizations for it. When outwardly similar behavior occurs in encephalitis lethargica, for example, patients tend to be distressed, bewildered, and occasionally confused by their motor symptoms.

E. Freeman

Thomas Freeman (1969) has elaborated an interesting framework for the evaluation of motor features in psychosis. His model encompasses both psychological and neurological dimensions and emphasizes description and diagnosis as well as theoretic interpretations of motor anomalies in various psychotic disorders.

Freeman also draws comparisons between the clinical motor phenomena characteristic of chronic schizophrenia and those characteristic of organic mental disorder. In schizophrenia, particularly the catatonic and hebephrenic subtypes, disturbances in such voluntary movements as blocking, overly repetitive activity, and difficulty in switching to new movements can be observed frequently in spontaneous behavior and elicited on examination (e.g., using Luria's tests, 1966, of motility). Freeman has noted that "normal motility," by implication movement free of the above disturbances, may appear in schizophrenia whenever the patient is interested in an object or is motivated by a need or anger. Disturbed movement is more likely to occur when the patient is inattentive, distractible, and generally unresponsive. The same characteristics are frequently found in organic mental states, although the appearance of normal motility is rare in progressive degenerative disease. Even in schizophrenia, Freeman argues, normal motility is transitory and uncommon. The movements that recur in so-called normal fashion in schizophrenia are those that could be described as highly practiced and those that usually develop early on in the patient's life; they are performed "automatically," as it were, apparently requiring little conscious coordination.

F. PSYCHOANALYTIC VIEWS

The motor features of schizophrenia have not been a major subject of psychoanalytic investigation. Some writers (e.g., Freeman, 1969) have claimed that this neglect is due to an almost exclusive focus on mental processes rather than bodily functions in psychoanalytic studies. Theorizing has tended to follow Kraepelin and Bleuler, hence to regard disturbances of posture and movement in schizophrenia as deficits secondary to more primary disturbances of thinking and emotion.

From Carl Jung onward, psychoanalytic writers have tended to view the motor manifestations of schizophrenia as the result of wishes and fantasies that find expression in movement. The symbolic nature of such expression and the meaning ascribed to the movements by patients have been taken as their actual cause. According to these writers, special themes and references to sexual and aggressive conflicts frequently appear in the verbalizations of patients who are exhibiting disordered movements. Some patients may endow their stereotypies with a magical significance. The concept of regression is used to account for this behavior by positing a reappearance of phenomena characteristic of the infantile phase of development wherein a quality of omnipotence may characterize both thinking and bodily movements.

No satisfactory answer exists as to why responses to these conflicts appear in the motor activity of the patient. Moreover, it is not clear whether psychic conflicts reflect the source or the response of the patient to changes in motor behavior.

The concept of regression that figures prominently as the theoretical basis for psychoanalytic explanation of motor anomalies bears some similarity to Jackson's evolution–dissolution themes on insanity. *Regression* as used by psychoanalytic writers implies the resurgence of infantile, childlike modes of mental functioning—in emotion, relationships, and even cognition. Dissolution appears nevertheless to be a broader concept than regression in that it encompasses all manifestations, both positive and negative, that ensue from the disorganization of mental processes (Freeman, 1969).

G. Summary

In spite of the promising quality of early contributions, there has been insufficient investigation of the motor features of schizophrenia beyond the stage of clinical description. This gap, we may speculate, has resulted from:

1. Implicit etiologic views regarding the nature of motor disturbance. The notion that bodily movement dysfunction is secondary to more primary psychological dysfunction was put forth by Kraepelin, Bleuler, and some psychoanalysts. Secondary features tend to assume secondary importance.
2. Absence of a model that possessed predictive and explanatory power concerning presumed relationships between thought, will, emotion, and motor activity.
3. A scarcity of performance measures capable of reliably defining the motor capacities of schizophrenic individuals.
4. The inconstant nature of motor disturbances; the fact that they occasionally, if temporarily, remit for no discernible reason, which may explain the popular notion that they are not essential characteristics of the disorder.

Since these initial contributions, knowledge has increased slowly. The following sections suggest the variety and complexity as well as the major gaps of present understandings of the clinical phenomena.

IV. Incidence, Prevalence, and Natural History

A. Catatonia and Catatonic Schizophrenia

In classic accounts particularly, catatonic schizophrenia has been associated with the most obvious and dramatic motor disturbances. Yet the motor anomalies of schizophrenia are not limited to this subtype. As Kraepelin and Bleuler both observed, motor disturbances occur in all subtypes of schizophrenia. When motor disturbances predominate, most cases are diagnosed catatonic. When motor disturbances are not detectable, or less striking, other characteristics (e.g., thought disturbance or paranoid thinking) determine subtype classification.

Matters are considerably less clear in contemporary clinical settings. Most schizophrenic patients manifest a mixture of catatonic, hebephrenic, and paranoid features, and relatively few qualify for the classic subtype labels. This circumstance has resulted in the increased use of the subtype diagnosis, undifferentiated schizophrenia. Indeed, there has been a reduction in the diagnosis of catatonic and hebephrenic subtypes over the last 50 years, although the overall incidence (about 1%) of schizophrenia appears to be stable (Morrison, 1973). For instance, it is increasingly uncommon to find obvious catatonic slowing, rigidity, or related classic features. When they do occur, they usually are short lived, often subtle, and frequently not associated with schizophrenic disorder (Andrews, 1981; Gelenberg, 1976). Over the years, the paranoid subtype has been diagnosed increasingly and has surpassed the frequency of the catatonic or hebephrenic subgroups of schizophrenic disorder. Yet even this observation should be viewed cautiously, because paranoid features may not indicate the presence of schizophrenia (Manschreck & Petri, 1978). Naturally, there has been speculation concerning the significance of such variation in clinical patterns. Some have argued that changes in patterns of treatment, particularly early intervention with antipsychotic drugs, may account for shifts in subtype characteristics (Lehmann, 1976). Others (e.g., Mahendra, 1981; Marsden, 1982) have suggested that certain neurological disorders with varied epidemiologic patterns (e.g., encephalitis or Parkinson's disease) may have contributed to such changes. Whatever the source, shifts in the incidence of symptoms and signs make more difficult the attempts to determine the frequency and nature of motor features in schizophrenia.

Not surprisingly, knowledge of incidence, prevalence, and natural history of motor features is sketchy because few reliable estimates appear in either the older or more recent literature (Jones & Hunter, 1968; Marsden et al., 1975). The only relevant information concerns either specific motor anomalies, such as stereotypies, or specific subtypes of schizophrenia, such as catatonia. Studies of catatonic schizophrenia have been complicated by serious diagnostic problems. Until recently, there have been no standard criteria for this diagnosis. Furthermore, the diagnosis of catatonic schizophrenia has been notoriously unreliable. In one study of diagnostic consistency in catatonic schizophrenia, a patient visiting multiple facilities and diagnosed as catatonic schizophrenic at one of them had less than a 10% chance of receiving the same diagnosis in a majority of contacts with other facilities (Guggenheim & Babigian, 1974). These authors implicated two sources for low diagnostic consistency. The first was the observation that catatonic symptoms in schizophrenia as well as in other types of mental and physical disorder are frequently transient. A second reason concerned the observation that diagnosis is frequently unreliable because it is hurried, imprecise, and considered lacking in practical importance.

Although Kahlbaum (1973/1874) and his successors, including Kraepelin and Bleuler, stressed that catatonic behavior has a number of different possible etiologies, there has been a tendency to regard catatonic behavior as signifying schizophrenia. It is, of course, well known now that fluorides, hyperparathyroidism, manic–depressive disorder, tuberculosis, and other diseases can be the source of catatonic behavior (Regenstein, Alpert, & Reich, 1977). Indeed, immobility, stupor, catalepsy, posturing, grimacing, stereotypic behavior, and negativism—that is, catatonia—constitute a symptom complex or syndrome that has been described in numerous psychiatric and medical disorders (see Table IV) (Gelenberg, 1976; Guggenheim & Babigian, 1974).

Classically, there are two extreme patterns of catatonic behavior—a retarded or withdrawn stupor and hyperkinetic occasionally aggressive excitement. Kraepelin believed that, when these patterns were persistent, not diagnosable as part of known disease, and associated with disturbances of will, judgment, and emotion, they formed a subtype of dementia praecox. Slater and Roth (1969) claim, as do others, that the more prevalent type of catatonic behavior in schizophrenia is retarded or withdrawn. Morrison (1973) categorized 250 patients as catatonic and subdivided them into excited, retarded, and mixed groups. This division revealed several features.

1. There was no difference among these three groups with respect to age, sex, education, race, or religion.
2. The excited patients were more likely to be married.
3. Mutism, negativism, posturing, staring into space, rigidity, and catalepsy were more characteristic of the retarded, whereas combativeness, impulsiveness, and nudism distinguished the excited.
4. The symptom pictures overlapped somewhat.
5. Excited patients tended to experience sudden onsets of illness and were more improved at discharge and at follow-up despite similar lengths of hospitalization.
6. Stereotypies occurred in 24% and mannerisms in 14% of the sample, indicating a rather high incidence for a less dramatic set of features.
7. Further examination of the excited subtype patients revealed that approximately 28% could be described as affectively disturbed according to research criteria (Feighner, Robins, Guze, Woodruff, Winokur, & Munoz, 1972).

B. SPECIFIC FORMS OF ABNORMAL MOVEMENTS

Descriptive studies of specific abnormal movements, such as stereotypies, are also complicated by problems of definition and interpretation. Lacking standard terminology, investigators have relied on their own concepts of these disturbances. Generally, only major or clinically obvious manifestations have been examined. Little work has attempted to explore more subtle features, such as clumsiness or incoordination, or the impact of motor disturbance on skilled performance. Most investigators have failed to assess these anomalies longitudinally. Without repeated observations, knowledge of natural history, response to treatment, and incidence and prevalence is difficult to obtain. Given the apparent reduced incidence of severe catatonic signs and symptoms in schizophrenia, the value of longitudinal studies utilizing sensitive, reliable measures of motor disturbance is especially great.

The incidence and prevalence of choreiform and athetoid movements in psychiatric patients remains somewhat controversial. Mettler and Crandell (1959) estimated that choreiform movements occurred frequently among schizophrenic patients and especially among chronic patients in psychiatric hospitals. Others (Marsden *et al.*, 1975), however, have claimed that these movements occur in neurological disease, especially basal ganglia disorders, and should not be considered part of the schizophrenic syndrome.

Jones and Hunter (1968) reported a 2-year longitudinal study of abnormal movements in a group of 127 (90 females, 37 males) chronic institutionalized psychiatric patients, one-third of whom had not received antipsychotic medication. Of the 127, 111 (87%) were diagnosed as schizophrenics. Approximately 25% of the entire sample had diagnosed brain disorder and/or subnormal intelligence. Unfortunately, this group was not separated from the larger group in reporting observations. These investigators looked at four kinds of movements: tremor, choreoathetosis, tics, and stereotypies (by which they meant any form of movement, apart from the other categories, that became abnormal because of repetition). Tremor, found in 30% of the sample, was equally common among men and women. Choreoathetoid movements were found in 18% of the women but only 5% (2) of the men. Tics were discovered in 21% of the females and 11% of the men. Stereotypies occurred in 47% of the women and 5% of the men. These included rocking (18 patients), hand movements (19 patients), and oral movements (19 patients). Thirty patients exhibited only one form of stereotypy, and 15 had two or more such movements. Other findings included the observation that choreoathetoid movements occurred primarily in the older age groups and particularly in the age group 71–80. Observations of patients never treated with antipsychotic medication were made on 21 women and 24 men; 62% of the women and 66% of the men had abnormal movements at some time during their illness. Examination of records showed that 75% of all patients had experienced catatonic posturing at least once previously, and all had records indicating "manneristic and grimacing" behavior.

The authors concluded that there is a high incidence and variability of pattern of abnormal movements among long-stay psychiatric patients. The pattern of such movements may escape notice in cross-sectional examinations. Tics, stereotypies, and choreoathetosis occurred more frequently in those who at some time had received antipsychotic medication. However, close examination of records disclosed abnormal movements of all types had been present in patients never treated with neuroleptics. In some patients, abnormal movements developed only after years of exposure to drugs; in others, only after drugs had been discontinued for months. Choreoathetosis, the least common type of abnormal movement, was the most persistent. Its occurrence in older patients as well as its association with neurological impairment suggest that it is not typically part of schizophrenia. Tics, tremors, and stereotypies tended to occur transiently, although established long-term patterns of stereotypy were also evident. Episodes of restlessness, nowadays usually associated with neuroleptic treatment, were common in the early stages of mental disorder and recurred in some patients over many years, independent of treatment.

This report is one of the few systematic attempts to evaluate the incidence and natural history of reported motor disturbances in schizophrenia. The inclusion of patients with known organic impairment makes interpretation difficult because motor anomalies are common in brain disease. Moreover, the study failed to examine the full range of motor abnormalities in schizophrenia. Nevertheless, the findings clearly indicate that motor disturbances occur frequently, variably, and usually subtly in schizophrenia. Certainly, attention to natural history, treatment, intercurrent organic disorder, as well as longitudinal and careful assessment appear necessary to properly classify and evaluate such anomalies.

A British study (Owens et al., 1982) has examined spontaneous involuntary disorders of movement in a sample of 411 hospitalized patients with chronic schizophrenia previously evaluated to determine only the presence or absence of such movements (Feighner et al., 1972). The findings, which were based on standardized recording techniques, the Abnormal Involuntary Movement Scale (AIMS) and the more detailed Rockland Scale, again indicate a high prevalence of involuntary movement abnormalities in the sample. With at least moderate degrees of severity, 50.6% of the patients had demonstrable anomalies on one or more of AIMS items; the corresponding Rockland Scale figure was 67.6%. The major component of abnormality was contributed by ratings of facial movements. Of particular interest was the opportunity to assess a subsample of 47 patients with no history of exposure to neuroleptic drugs. The authors found no differences in the prevalence and severity of movement disturbances and few differences in regional distribution of abnormality. They concluded that spontaneous involuntary movements can be a feature of chronic schizophrenia that is unmodified by drugs.

The study unfortunately did not report on disturbances in voluntary patterns of movement disorder. Assessment of neurological abnormalities of slight or gross degree was included and resulted in relatively few generally minor, peripheral findings. An important additional observation was that the movements considered in the study exhibited considerable stability in gross distribution and severity during a 12–18 month period of follow-up. Longitudinal stability seldom has been investigated. Although the evidence for stable prevalence was based on a rating of the presence or absence of motor anomaly 12–28 months prior to the detailed evaluation, it is an important contribution to the accumulating evidence of motor disturbance in schizophrenic disorders.

No one knows precisely when abnormal movements have their onset in schizophrenia. Typically, motor manifestations have been reported to occur after the appearance of other symptoms. Schneider (1959) offered an approach to diagnosis of schizophrenia in its early stages, in part because dramatic observable motor disturbances in acute cases are uncommon.

Schneider's symptoms reflect subjective experiences of an unusual and incomprehensible sort from the standpoint of normal human experience. Auditory hallucinations, delusional perception, and several forms of passivity experience constitute the first-rank symptoms that Schneider believed were pathognomonic for acute schizophrenia, if coarse brain disease was not present. Two of the passivity experiences (i.e., made impulses, made acts) suggest disturbances affecting motor functions. They reflect a sense of loss of control and coordination of movement not necessarily discernible to others. Like other first-rank symptoms, they tend to be reported by patients early in the course of illness, and they can become uncommon in fully established schizophrenia. Mellor (1970) found made impulses and made acts in 2.9% and 9.2%, respectively, of a group of 173 schizophrenics, independently diagnosed by two consultant psychiatrists. While the claim to pathognomonicity has been criticized (Carpenter, Strauss, & Muleh, 1973; Pope & Lipinski, 1978), there is general agreement that first-rank symptoms are highly discriminating symptoms for the diagnosis of schizophrenic disorder (World Health Organization, 1973).

Because objective motor abnormalities are uncommon early in the course of schizophrenia, Schneider's investigations suggest that subjective experiences may hold important keys to understanding motor disturbance in early schizophrenic disorder. Unfortunately, knowledge of the earliest stages of schizophrenic illness has been limited. The few studies attempted have tended to report nonspecific features: vague thinking, emotional blunting, incongruity of affect, lack of spontaneity in speech, preoccupation, perplexity, withdrawal, and changes in the experience of self (Chapman, 1966). Nevertheless, Chapman (1966) decided to evaluate changes in subjective experience among a group of schizophrenics early in the course of illness to learn specifically which features of behavior were altered. Subjective experiences of cognitive disturbances were strikingly common, often present well before overt signs of illness.

Chapman interviewed 40 patients, asking them to describe in detail any alteration of perceptual, motor, thinking, and speech experiences. In the motor realm, Chapman discovered frequent disturbances. Many of the patients (75%) reported difficulty coordinating the motor sequences necessary for simple specific activities, such as walking, eating, sitting down. Chapman named this disturbance ideokinetic apraxia. Movements seemed slow, required more deliberation and concentration, and felt more restricted than normal. Patients described a loss of automaticity of movements associated with heightened awareness of bodily processes. In 14 patients, motor and thought blocking characterized by transient immobility, blank expression, and fixed gaze were common. Echolalia and echopraxia also occurred in a number of these patients. Mutism was encountered at some point during the clinical illness in 16. In some patients, prolonged catatonic behavior and gross visual perceptual disturbances were associated with a deteriorating course.

The interesting findings reported by Chapman have been criticized on methodological grounds (Chapman & Chapman, 1973), and they provide only a limited idea of the longitudinal course of abnormal motor symptoms. However, they raise the possibility that objective assessment techniques, such as motor performance tests, might succeed in detecting early motor difficulties. Subjective accounts are helpful, but objective means would be more satisfactory and are essential if we are to extend our knowledge of the natural history of motor phenomena in schizophrenia.

Many have pondered the relationship between prognosis and motor anomalies as well as other symptoms in schizophrenia. Kraepelin (1919), of course, believed that dementia praecox has a poor outcome. The natural history of the disorder was variable in pattern if not result. Stereotypic movements, he (and Bleuler) noted, could persist for many years, to become progressively more simplified, possibly to occur independent of apparent expressive purpose, and to become preoccupying. They often were associated with verbigeration or thought disorder (Kleist, 1908). And many have held the view that motor disturbances such as stereotypies that may occur early in the course of schizophrenia portend a poor prognosis. The early onset of abnormal movements in the course of schizophrenia was thought to predict a catatonic form of the illness. Furthermore, the awkwardness, gracelessness, and clumsiness seen early on was felt to increase over the years. Arieti (1945) and Schilder (1931) have argued that there is a progressive deterioration in those patients who evidence stereotypic behavior from more complex stereotypies to more fragmented ones.

There have been few studies to confirm or refute such opinions. Jones (1965) found no relationship between complexity of stereotypies and age of onset, length of illness, or duration of hospitalization in 13 chronic schizophrenics with stereotypic behavior. He observed that such behavior increased depending on the degree of interpersonal contact that the patient engaged in and decreased during effort as in work, during periods of drowsiness, or during the initiation of volitional movements. For example, the stereotypies stopped entirely while patients shook hands, drank tea, or wrote their names. Occasionally, the stereotypic responses were somewhat understandable on the basis of associated delusions. In seven patients who came off medication during the study, there was some increase in frequency of stereotypic behavior. Jones also found that the distinction between mannerisms and stereotypies was arbitrary and difficult to apply.

In investigating the idea that an earlier onset of movement disorders is associated with poor prognosis, Yarden and Discipio (1971) did a follow-up study of 18 schizophrenic patients who exhibited abnormal movements. The movements were primarily choreiform and athetoid, but included tics, stereotypies, and mannerisms. The patients were described as free of neurological disease, retardation, or history of chronic hospitalization. These patients, compared to a control group of schizophrenics without abnormal movements, had an earlier age of onset of changes in mental state and longer hospitalizations. Patients with abnormal movements also showed significantly more severe thought disorder, purposeless activity, negativism, and neglect of personal hygiene. This group was less affected than the control group by pharmacologic interventions. Moreover, the presence of abnormal movements was associated with a significantly poorer prognosis for the period of study.

Perseveration is a well-known clinical sign of disturbed motor and speech behavior among neurologically and psychiatrically disordered individuals. Allison (1966 I, II) documented that perseveration occurs in a wide variety of medical, neurological, and psychiatric conditions, and especially in those associated with clouded consciousness. Focal brain disease, especially with symptoms of aphasia, is also associated with perseveration. And some perseverative behavior appears to be a normal feature of early human development.

There are few systematic studies of perseveration in schizophrenia. Freeman and Gathercole (1966) examined perseveration in chronic schizophrenia and dementia to determine whether there was something distinctive about the perseveration observed frequently in schizophrenia. These authors divided perseveration on the basis of previous accounts into three types:

1. Repeated actions, linked theoretically to subcortical lesions (e.g., Goldstein, 1943; Luria, 1966).

2. Elicited responses continuing after new stimuli have been presented. Goldstein referred to this form as secondary rigidity, and Luria called it switching. Both felt it to be due to cortical impairment.

3. Ideational or spontaneous perseveration.

Extensive testing using a number of methods to elicit forms of perseverative behavior was undertaken in a group of schizophrenic and demented patients. The results provided no evidence for a unitary trait of perseveration. Schizophrenics showed the repeated action form of perseveration felt to be related to subcortical disturbance more often than did demented patients. Senile dements showed the second or cortical impairment type. In testing of the ideational or spontaneous form of perseveration, there was no difference between schizophrenic and demented patients.

Knowledge of echopraxia and echolalia has progressed in limited ways. Stengel (1947) showed that echo reactions were common in a number of different conditions, although they have been considered a classic feature of catatonic disorder. Transcortical aphasia, mental deficiency, chronic epilepsy, delirium, early speech development in children, and states of fatigue and inattention in normals were the main disorders associated with echo phenomena. Echo phenomena tended to be associated in these conditions with an urge to act or speak, a tendency to repetition, and incomplete development or impairment in perception and expression of speech. Chapman and McGhie (1964) argue that breakdown in perceptual constancy in part precipitated by disturbed attentional focusing brings on echopractic phenomena. They note, interestingly, that delusions of influence occur in association with echopraxia in schizophrenia.

C. High-Risk Studies

Barbara Fish (1975) reports that motor symptoms are often found in children who suffer psychiatric disturbance at a later age. She cites research, such as Robins (1966; O'Neal & Robins, 1958), in which difficulty walking as a developmental symptom differentiated preschizophrenic children from others. Watt (1974) found that neurological disturbance and severe organic handicaps were more common at an earlier age among children who later developed schizophrenia than among classroom controls. Ricks and Nameche (1966) discovered slow motor development and nonspecific neurological symptoms twice as often in preschizophrenics as in controls, and more frequently in the group that became chronically disordered compared to that which experienced a more benign course of schizophrenia (Ricks & Berry, 1970). Such prominent symptoms as hyperactivity, rigidity, abnormal gait, poor coordination, and impaired attention were typical among those who later became chronically withdrawn schizophrenics. Marcus (1974) investigated so-called neurological soft signs in a group of 7–14-year-olds born of schizophrenic parents and a group of matched controls whose parents had no mental disease. He determined that facial asymmetry, fine motor coordination, left–right orientation, and evidence of disturbances of visual perception and auditory–visual integration were significantly more common among the high-risk sample. In the obstetric studies of high-risk individuals, conducted by Mednick, Mural, Schulsinger, and Mednick (1971), retarded motor development at 5 days and 1 year differentiated off-spring of schizophrenics from controls. Dozenko and Fatovi (Fish, 1975), using Ozeretski's method of studying motor maturity of children of schizo-phrenics, found that disturbances in speed, simultaneous movements, time, and rhythm were the maximally decreased skills of motor function that dis-tinguished the high-risk children. Fish's own work (1975) on infants at risk shows a spectrum of mild to severe irregularities and disruptions of physical growth as well as gross motor and visual-motor developmental ab-normalities. These anomalies are associated with the later development of a spectrum of psychiatric disturbances of varying severity. The presence of developmental disorders and complications thereof were significantly re-lated to being at genetic risk for schizophrenia and not to pregnancy and birth complication history.

Hanson, Gottesman, and Heston (1976) also completed a prospective study of children of schizophrenic parents. At age 4, 30% of these children demonstrated poor motor skills in hopping, walking a line, catching a ball, and finer tasks, such as stringing beads. Three variables—poor motor skills, the presence of large intraindividual inconsistency of performance in var-ious cognitive tasks, and observations of apathy, withdrawal, flatness, in-stability of relationships, irritability, and negativism—were chosen as predictors of vulnerability to schizophrenia on the basis of previous reports. These variables at extreme thresholds characterized 5 of 116 children, an incidence of about 10 times chance expectation. These 5 were all offspring of schizophrenic parents, and their case histories showed enduring forms of maladjustment of the types reported in the premorbid history of schizo-phrenia.

In sum, studies of high-risk populations suggest that motor disturbance may be detectable at an early age and may be associated with later devel-opment of chronic schizophrenia, possibly in its more severe forms.

V. Neuropsychiatric Investigations

Neuropsychiatric investigation of motor behavior has focused in four broad areas: electromyographic responses, neuromuscular studies, neuro-pharmacologic mechanisms, and the study of disordered ocular move-ments. The following reviews are included to point to general findings and are purposefully not exhaustive.

A. Electromyographic Studies

Practically since the development of electromyography, there has been interest in the relationship between motor tension levels and schizophrenia. Part of this interest has been based on psychological views of development and cognition that stress the close relationship between motor behavior and thinking (Jacobson, 1938). Whatmore and Ellis (1958) examined electromyographic activity in a group of schizophrenic patients at rest and compared these measures in a control population. Their findings disclosed that in all sites—forehead, jaw, forearm, and leg—significantly higher motor activity was present intermittently and/or continuously in the schizophrenic subjects. Malmo and Shagass (1949) and Malmo, Shagass, Belanger, and Smith (1951) showed similar high levels of responses in patients while under conditions of stress and while performing a specific activity. These findings have not been developed further.

A series of electromyographic studies of auditory hallucinations in schizophrenia may signal the advent of an important investigative area. These studies (Gould, 1948; McGuigan, 1966) have found evidence that electromyographic changes in the orofacial and laryngial regions occur in close temporal association with the report of hallucinatory activity. There is no evidence that this phenomenon can be accounted for on the basis of generalized arousal, since control sites for electromyographic activity remain stable during hallucinations.

B. Studies of Neuromuscular Mechanisms

For a number of years, Meltzer and colleagues have investigated the incidence of various types of neuromuscular dysfunction in patients with schizophrenic and affective disorders and in their first-degree relatives. In a review of his work, Meltzer (1976) points to the long-known association of neuromuscular dysfunction and central nervous system disease, an association that is common in a number of neurological illnesses. Studies have demonstrated a variety of pathological changes in the neuromuscular system of psychotic patients, including alterations in creatine kinase levels in acute psychotic states, morphological changes in muscle fibers and subterminal motor nerves, and physiological abnormalities in nerve conduction velocity and spinal cord (Hoffman) reflex mechanisms. According to Meltzer, these studies collectively support the view that there is an organic disorder in the major psychoses. Crayton, Stalberg, and Hilton-Brown (1977) have extended these observations to single-fiber electromyographic recordings; their data suggest that psychosis is associated with responses characteristic of denervation or reinnervation of single muscle fibers by collateral sprouting. Studies have shown that acute schizophrenics have decreased recovery of the Hoffman reflex and chronic schizophrenics have increased recovery (Goode, Meltzer, Crayton, & Mazura, 1977). These findings are consistent with increased dopaminergic influences on the alpha motor neuron system among acute schizophrenics and decreased dopaminergic influence on the same system among chronic schizophrenics. Hence, these findings may point to a link between neuromuscular dysfunction and the neurotransmitter theories of major psychoses (Meltzer, 1979).

C. Neuropharmacologic Studies

Neuropharmacologic studies have been extremely fruitful in developing hypotheses and increasing understanding of the relationship between motor functioning and central nervous system disturbance believed to be present in schizophrenia. One source of evidence linking the motor anomalies of schizophrenia with central nervous system mechanisms are observations of motor effects following neuroleptic administration. The term *neuroleptic* itself developed in response to the striking motor effects that resulted from administration of these drugs. In fact, early on in the history of treatment of psychotic illnesses with these medications, dosage decisions in part were based on the appearance of parkinsonian and other neuroleptic effects, as outlined in Table V. The fact that these drugs have such potent motor consequences raised interest in their neuropharmacologic mechanisms. Much of this research focused on the newly evolving knowledge of neurotransmitter brain chemistry, particularly as it affected the basal ganglia.

The dopamine hypothesis in schizophrenia, for example, is based in large part on the (blocking) effects of neuroleptic drugs on apomorphine- and amphetamine-induced stereotyped behaviors in laboratory animals (Matthysse, 1974; Snyder, Banerjee, Yammura, & Greenberg, 1974). In that these drugs interfere with the effects of dopamine, studies of the role of dopamine in psychomotor activity have flourished (Papeschi, 1972). It is clear that dopamine mechanisms are involved in spontaneous and purposeful motor activity. The anatomy relevant to this activity may be indicated by the high concentrations of dopamine found in the neo-striatum but particularly in nigro-striatal pathways. Physiological relationships are also interesting. The nigro-striatal pathway in primates seems to be necessary for spontaneous movements. Dopamine here may be an inhibitory neurotransmitter. It is also known that lesions in the neo-striatum lead to symptoms involving postural mechanisms and spontaneous motor activity. Ancillary evidence supporting the proposal that dopamine and motor behavior are closely linked comes from studies of Parkinson's disease, which is known to be associated with damage to the nigro-striatal pathways. Such disturbance or damage leads to reduction or delay of spontaneous motor activity. In a study of Sernyl (phencyclidine, a dopamine agonist) effects on normal subjects, Holzman (1972) reported the simultaneous occurrence of thought disturbance and a pronounced inability to coordinate movements. All subjects interviewed said that psychomotor integration and control were disrupted. Stevens (1978) has hypothesized that blink rate is modulated by central dopamine activity, and Karson, Fried, Kleinman, Bigelow, and Wyatt (1981) have found evidence in support of that view through the study of neuroleptic effects on blink rate. This area promises to provide useful data about central dopamine functions.

Work designed to elucidate the central nervous system mechanisms of motor behavior and their relationship to neuropharmacologic data remains at an early stage. However, evidence seems to be mounting to point to a close relationship between the neurotransmitters and basal ganglia and frontal lobe structures (Glassman, 1976; Munkvad, Pakkenberg, & Randrup, 1968). Among the pieces of evidence brought forward to establish this connection is the frequent association of schizophrenia-like disorders and basal ganglia disease. Such disorders as encephalitis and its sequelae, Huntington's disease, Wilson's disease, midbrain reticulosis, and essential hereditary tremor frequently result in psychotic manifestations.

A number of studies have demonstrated neurological impairment in psychiatric disorder (Hertzig & Birch, 1968; Larsen, 1964; Rochford, Detre, Tucker, & Harrow, 1970). These studies have usually examined the incidence of so-called soft or nonlocalizing neurological signs in hospitalized patients. Findings suggest that as many as three-quarters of schizophrenic patients demonstrate such disturbances on careful examination (Pincus & Tucker, 1974; Tucker, Campion, & Silberfarb, 1975). Longitudinal data are not available to determine whether such findings persist, remit, or become episodic. Tucker et al. (1975) showed that cognitive impairments, particularly thought disorder, occur more often in psychiatric patients with sensorimotor soft signs than in controls and that neurological impairment and schizophrenia have a strong if not exclusive association. Gur (1977) has suggested that findings of increased left-handedness in schizophrenics may reflect left-hemisphere dysfunction. Studies by Manschreck et al. (submitted for publication) of nonlocalizing signs, handedness, and laterality have also indicated left-hemisphere dysfunction in a significant purportion of schizophrenic patients. Those patients with greatest laterality impairments were also those manifesting the greatest motoric abnormalities.

D. STUDIES OF OCULAR MOVEMENT

In 1908, Diefendorf and Dodge reported that some schizophrenic patients exhibited ocular movement abnormalities, which they could photograph and which are detectable on careful neurological examination. Their work was extended only recently through a series of studies of oculomotor function in schizophrenia undertaken by Holzman and colleagues (1973, 1974, 1977, 1980). The results indicate that 65–80% of schizophrenic patients and about 45% of their first-degree relatives have disturbed horizontal pursuit eye movements; that the impairment is largely independent of voluntary efforts to improve performance; that it is stable and independent of clinical state or antipsychotic medication; and that it appears to have a strong genetic component. Less than 10% of normal subjects show similar abnormalities. An additional study (Latham, Holzman, Manschreck, & Tole, 1981) has demonstrated that pursuit impairments may be due to cortical dysfunction and that examination of specific optokinetic nystagmus responses (i.e., partial field optokinetic nystagmus, OKN) in schizophrenics also reveals disordered movements compared to normals. The full import of such findings remains unclear, although certainly the association between schizophrenic disorder and oculomotor dysfunction adds considerable interest to the study of other associated motor abnormalities likely to be present among schizophrenics. Moreover, the study of ocular movements is sufficiently precise to permit sensitive analyses of factors that might alter the movements, including drug treatment. Such study, exemplified by Latham et al.'s work (1981), promises progress in the anatomic localization of schizophrenic disturbances because of the body of knowledge and investigative methods concerning ocular system structures.

VI. Clinical and Experimental Studies of Disturbed Voluntary Motor Behavior in Schizophrenic Disorders

In order to address the questions raised by the renewed interest in motor disturbances in schizophrenic disorders, we investigated their occurrence and relationship to other features of this illness (Manschreck, Maher, Rucklos, & Vereen, 1982). Our study was guided by the attentional deficit hypothesis and by findings from prior examinations of language behavior in schizophrenia (Maher, 1972). Certainly there is an inadequate data base from which to derive hypotheses in a form sufficiently specific to be tested in the area of schizophrenic motor disturbance. However, we began to develop a rationale for such an investigation with the proposition that the most practical strategy in the formulation of any disease process is to employ the principle of parsimony—namely, to understand the largest number of components of the clinical picture through the assumption of the least number of primary pathologies.

A reasonable possibility for understanding the varied features of schizophrenic disorder is the attentional deficit hypothesis. This hypothesis has proved useful in understanding disturbances in language behavior, delusions, and dichotic listening as found among some schizophrenic patients. The role of attention in the control of motor skill (e.g., Coquery, 1978) and language (Maher, 1972) has already been developed, and it has been suggested that both processes may be characterized by an underlying grammar (Skvoretz & Fararo, 1980). It seems sensible to consider that a disorder in attentional processes is likely to lead to disturbances in both realms of activity. Speech is a behavioral activity that involves motor skills. Muscle activity is involved in the production of speech, and cognitive activity, including the deployment of attention, is involved in the construction of what is said. Likewise, other skilled motor movements may be presumed to require fine and continuous attentional monitoring similar to that in language utterance.

If these propositions are valid, they suggest that motor and thinking disturbances may be associated in schizophrenic disorder. Indeed, one cannot help but notice the striking similarities that exist between the incoordination, repetitiousness, and clumsiness of motor activity other than speech and the structural aspects of disordered language utterance found in some schizophrenic patients. It is unclear, however, to what extent disorganized motor and thinking behavior are present in the same individuals.

The aim of our study, then, was to examine disturbances in voluntary motor activity and to determine their relationship to a variety of relevant reliably assessed features of the disorder. We were particularly interested in the relationship with subtype diagnosis, affective blunting, neurological nonlocalizing signs, delusions, and formal disorders of thinking. Our specific hypothesis was that formal thought disorder and disturbances in voluntary motor behavior would be closely associated.

The method consisted of the selection of a carefully diagnosed group of schizophrenics and relevant psychiatric controls (i.e., affective psychosis) according to DSM-III criteria (American Psychiatric Association, 1980). Subjects were to be between 18 and 60 years of age, free of other illness, of average intelligence, and able to give informed consent. The plan of procedure consisted of an initial semistructured interview, administered to put the subject at ease and to gather basic demographic information. The interview also served to obtain sufficient samples of speech so that formal thought disorder ratings could be made according to criteria developed by Spitzer and Endicott (1977). The features assessed included understandability, derailment, logic, poverty of information conveyed, and neologisms. Delusional thinking was also evaluated as absent, suspected, or definitely present according to definitions provided by the same assessment tool. To reduce bias, the interview did not address the nature of the psychiatric illness.

There followed a series of behavioral ratings that required approximately 1 hr and were conducted by two independent raters whose interrater reliability was calculated for each procedure. Because neuroleptic drugs frequently induce motor effects, each subject was carefully examined for evidence of side effects to ensure that such effects were not being mistaken for disturbances associated with the schizophrenic disorder itself. Two rating scales summarized these observations: the Abnormal Involuntary Movement Scale (AIMS) (National Institute of Mental Health, 1974) and the Targeting of Abnormal Kinetic Effects (TAKE) (Wojcik, Gelenberg, LaBrie, & Berg, 1980). These scales rate the presence of defined motor effects as to the level of severity. The AIMS assesses evidence of tardive dyskinesia, and the TAKE assesses extrapyramidal effects and akathisia. After the behavioral ratings were completed, the research staff obtained information concerning current drug treatment and dosages. All dosages were then standardized according to chlorpromazine equivalents (Davis, 1976).

Motor disturbances not ascribable to medication were evaluated in two ways. First, each subject's spontaneous abnormal movements were observed and rated. Observed features included classic schizophrenic motor anomalies, repetitive movements (i.e., perseveration, mannerisms, and stereotypies), clumsiness, motor blocking, and forms of catatonic movement. Second, a series of examinations (DeJong, 1967; Freeman, 1969; Freeman & Gathercole, 1966) was undertaken to find disruptions in the orderly expression of skilled movements. We therefore tested general motility in several simple voluntary motor tasks, such as closing eyes and clapping and shaking hands, for evidence of disorganization, delayed response, lengthy completion, and postural persistence, according to the suggestions of Freeman (1969). The same assessments were made for complex motor tasks, namely Ozeretski's test, the fist-ring test, and the fist-edge-palm test (Luria, 1966). These tests, which were developed to assess problems in switching from one movement to another, have been used to elicit repetitive action, also associated with diffuse frontal-cortical lesions. We also examined coordination, station, and gait according to standard techniques.

Because of their reported frequency in schizophrenia, we evaluated subjects for the presence of agraphesthesia and astereognosis. Affective blunting was also assessed according to a modified scale devised and found reliable by Abrams and Taylor (1978). Such categories as shallow mood, unrelated affect, monotonous voice, and lack of social skills were rated.

Our results can be summarized as follows. The reliabilities of behavioral ratings were similar to those previously published and were within an acceptable range.

We examined 37 patients who met the criteria for the diagnosis of schizophrenic disorder, including 13 paranoid, 10 disorganized, 13 undifferentiated, and 1 catatonic. The affective disorder group totaled 16 and consisted of 3 manic subjects, 4 schizoaffective (manic subtype), 1 schizoaffective (depressed disorder), and 8 psychotic depressives. These groups did not differ by age, education, length of illness, or neuroleptic drug treatment. Thirty of the schizophrenic and 10 of the affective subjects were taking antipsychotic medication. Of the 7 unmedicated schizophrenics, 2 had never received drug treatment; of the 6 unmedicated affective controls, 3 had never been treated with antipsychotic drugs. All unmedicated subjects had been free of medication for at least 1 year, several for many years.

Evidence of drug-related extrapyramidal disturbance and/or tardive dyskinesia was found in 11 of the 30 schizophrenics and 4 of the 10 affective subjects on neuroleptics. The number and severity of the effects were in all cases minimal.

Disturbances in voluntary motor behavior were detectable in all but one schizophrenic (subtype paranoid) and were infrequent among affective subjects, except for the schizoaffective subtype. The most common form of spontaneous motor abnormality in schizophrenics was clumsiness or awkwardness, a postural disturbance. The second most common were stereotypic and manneristic movements followed by motor blocking. Not observed in this sample were ambitendency, catalepsy, automatic obedience, choreoathetoid movements, excitement, and stupor. Of the subtypes, a smaller proportion of the paranoid group exhibited spontaneous motor abnormalities (31%), whereas all of the disorganized (hebephrenic) subjects showed such anomalies.

An even greater proportion of the paranoid (92%) and undifferentiated subtypes (92%) showed deficits on examination than were present in the evaluation of spontaneous movements. The tests of Luria and Ozeretski detected the most frequent abnormalities, but there was widespread evidence of disturbances in the other tests as well. On the other hand, with the exception of the schizoaffective group, the performance of affective subjects was generally normal. The schizoaffective group displayed the major proportion of abnormalities among the affective controls. Indeed, four of the five schizoaffective subjects exhibited at least one feature of abnormal motor behavior on examination.

The effect of antipsychotic medication on motor movements was examined. The results suggest that neuroleptics tended to reduce the number and/or severity of such abnormalities. Moreover, a comparison of scores for medicated affective psychotic controls (10) with dosage-matched schizophrenic subjects showed a significant difference ($t = 2.8$, $df = 9$, $p < .02$), suggesting that motor impairments are related primarily to schizophrenic illness and not to medication. Furthermore, there was no relationship between neuroleptic dosage and ratings of formal thought disorder, nor was hospitalization status a discriminating characteristic. Because parkinsonian features may be associated with changes in movements, emotional expression, and reduced thought content, comparisons of the impact of such features and the impact of treatment for those features were undertaken. Schizophrenics under antiparkinsonian treatment did not differ from those not under such treatment with respect to ratings of voluntary motor disturbance, affective blunting, or formal thought disorder. Also, schizophrenics (11) with evidence of extrapyramidal effects were no different from those without these effects with respect to the same comparisons.

The relationship of disturbance of voluntary motor activity to other features was also quite interesting. There was a positive and significant association between schizophrenic motor features and affective blunting and between nonlocalizing neurological signs and intrinsic motor features. But the most striking association was the one between totaled abnormal intrinsic motor features and formal disturbances of thinking ($r = .62, p < .0005$, one tailed). A separate examination of the association between spontaneous motor features and formal thought disorder was also significant and was analyzed to determine the specific connection between readily observed motor features and disturbed thinking. The association between formal thought disorder and nonlocalizing signs was in a positive, possibly significant direction. There was no evidence of a relationship between voluntary motor disturbances and delusional thinking.

In summary, our first major finding was that disturbances in voluntary motor behavior (i.e., those that were not attributable to drug effects or known neurological disorder) occur in virtually all cases of conservatively defined schizophrenic disorder. The observed abnormalities were generally short-lived phenomena that might easily be missed if they were not carefully scrutinized. The fact that additional procedures for eliciting motor disturbance increased the number of observed abnormalities indicates that routine examination or occasional observation may not detect their presence. Indeed, the optimal method for discovering motor disturbances is clinical observation of patients over extended periods. Nevertheless, this study demonstrated that, failing the capacity to undertake longitudinal investigations, it is possible to appreciate a variety and relatively high frequency of motor changes associated with this disorder.

It is also worthwhile noting that certain dramatic features were not in evidence (e.g., automatic obedience, catalepsy, or excitement). And only 1 of the 37 schizophrenics qualified for the subtype diagnosis of catatonia. These observations are consistent with current reports of reduced incidence of catatonic schizophrenia. Yet abnormal movements were ubiquitous among the schizophrenic subjects regardless of subtype, tempting the suggestion that they have been neglected largely because the search for motor manifestations has been focused on fairly uncommon and unusual features to the exclusion of more common ones (McGhie, 1969).

The relative absence of motor disturbances in affective subjects suggests that while these features are certainly not pathognomonic for schizophrenia they tend to be significantly concentrated among individuals bearing that diagnosis. Of considerable interest is the fact that it was among the schizoaffective subgroup of affective subjects (a grouping that is controversial based on the presence of both schizophrenic and affective features) that most of the voluntary motor disturbances occurred. The sample ($N = 5$) was, however, too small to justify conclusions, and additional studies of this group would be worthwhile.

The fact that affective blunting and nonlocalizing neurological signs also were associated with disturbed motor features points to interesting implications. The latter features have been considered evidence for subtle neurological impairment in schizophrenia. The frequency of affective blunting and soft sign incidence is also consistent with published reports (Tucker & Silberfarb, 1978) and indicate that the sample of schizophrenics in this study is not atypical.

The second major finding of the study was the significant, positive association of motor abnormality and disturbance in the form of thinking, a finding that is congruent with the attentional deficit hypothesis. The coincidence among schizophrenics of features from both these dimensions of behavioral functioning suggests that they may have a common pathogenetic basis.

It would be possible, of course, to interpret these findings, which are necessarily of a correlational variety, in other theoretical frameworks. Thus, this study cannot be seen as providing crucial support for the attentional deficit hypothesis in contrast to other hypotheses. Nevertheless, given the established role of attentional efficiency in both normal language and motor behavior, and strong evidence of an attentional deficit in schizophrenic patients and at least some of their relatives, the interpretation of the data in attentional deficit terms is clearly plausible.

The potentially difficult problem of neuroleptic drug effects was dealt with by the careful measurement of drug-induced motor activity and its exclusion from the computation of the motor behavior abnormality that was related to thought disorder. The incidence of neuroleptic side effects was consistent with previous reports and thus argues against a systematic underestimation of such effects. Moreover, we found significant differences between disturbed voluntary movement scores of medicated and nonmedicated schizophrenics, suggesting that drugs tend to reduce those anomalies. On the other hand, in the paired comparisons of medicated schizophrenic and affective subjects, schizophrenic patients had significàntly more voluntary motor disturbances, suggesting that motor impairment is more closely associated with the latter disorder.

It is naturally possible that some drug effects not detected by the rating scale methods we employed might be present (while other dramatic extrapyramidal features were absent), which could interfere with the programmed sequence of motor acts and the initiation of voluntary motor activity. The elicited motor activity assessments would be most susceptible to such effects; a separate analysis of the schizophrenic motor features observed in spontaneous behavior and formal thought disorder proved consistent with the hypothesized relationship between language and motor disturbance.

A. ADDITIONAL INVESTIGATIONS

The findings of this survey of motor abnormalities in schizophrenic disorder led to two additional investigations (Manschreck et al., 1981a; Manschreck, Maher, Rucklos, Vereen, & Ader, 1981b). In the first, we examined the relationship between formal thought disorder and clinical motor disturbance with more objective measures of language disorganization. In the second, we developed a laboratory measure of motor function, to compare disorganization in motor performance among schizophrenic and control subjects with assessments of thinking and motor behavior.

Reliable measures for formal thought disorder have developed slowly. Clinical rating scales, such as those of Andreasen (1979) or Spitzer and Endicott (1977), have helped standardize the evaluation of thought disturbance and have provided a foundation for further clinical and epidemiologic study. But laboratory assessments of formal thought disorder (e.g., object sorting) have not been as useful as hoped for and have seldom been used routinely in clinical settings. Generally, such testing has focused on particular dimensions of thought disorder, such as abstraction deficit, lack of logical consistency, or unusual associative intrusions; such approaches have derived from specific theoretical concepts of the nature of schizophrenia (Chapman & Chapman, 1973).

Moreover, in view of the traditional emphasis on disturbed thinking in the diagnosis of schizophrenia, it is striking how little work has addressed the formal features of actual utterances and written language of schizophrenic subjects. The number of relevant measures is large—for example, Cloze analysis (Manschreck, Maher, Rucklos, & White, 1979), frequency indices of words, and hesitation characteristics (Maher, Manschreck, & Molino, 1983).

In the first study, we decided to measure the type–token ratio (TTR) because it is a simple, reliable, and quantifiable index of language deviance, unbiased by clinical judgment, and because in prior reports the TTR as an index of spoken language disorganization is statistically lower for formal thought-disordered schizophrenics compared to non-thought-disordered schizophrenics and psychiatric controls (Manschreck *et al.*, 1981a). Also age, education, and medication status do not appear to substantially influence this difference. The TTR is a measure of variability (or repetitiousness) in lexicon usage and is computed by dividing the total number of words (tokens) into the number of different words (types) in samples of uniform length. The ratio between thought-disordered speech and the TTR, in our prior work, was analyzed with reference to specific features of thought disturbance. Poverty of content ($r = .54$, $p < .01$, point biserial correlation coefficient) and disturbed understandability ($r = .43$, $p < .05$) were significantly associated, although both logic and loosening of associations (derailment) bordered on significant associations as well.

Thus, the first study extending the survey examined the hypothesis that disruptions in language behavior, as indicated by the TTR, would be associated with clinical evidence of disruptions in motor movement. Samples of language (at least 100 words) were obtained in response to requests to describe "The Wedding Feast," a painting by Brueghel; they were tape-recorded, transcribed, and assessed using the mean segmental type-token ratio (MSTTR) measure, which represents the average of TTRs for consecutive segments of 100 words. The motor response testing was the same as described in the survey study.

The subjects included 21 schizophrenics (10 with evidence of formal thought disorder—5 disorganized and 5 undifferentiated phenomenological subtypes). The 11 non-thought-disordered schizophrenics included 8 paranoid and 3 undifferentiated subtypes. There were 12 affective subjects (6 major depressives, 3 manics, and 3 schizoaffectives, manic type) and 12 normals. None of the affective or normal controls had clinical evidence of formal thought disorder.

Each schizophrenic subject and several affective (schizoaffective types, in particular) showed evidence of disruption of skilled motor performance in the testing procedure. In order of frequency, clumsiness, stereotypic, manneristic, and motor blocking responses were found commonly in spontaneous behavior, and among the testing procedures, the tests of Luria and Ozeretski were most likely to elicit disturbance.

Analysis of covariance revealed negligible impact of education and age on motor summary scores and on the TTR characteristic.

The relationship between scores summarizing evidence of disruption in skilled motor movements and MSTTRs was examined, using the Pearson product–moment correlation procedure. Because six of the affective subjects showed evidence of motor disturbance, the affective group was included in this analysis. The results indicated a very strong negative association ($r = -.59$, $df = 32$, $p < .001$). These results appear to confirm the relationship between disturbed sequential behavior in the speech and motor spheres.

Following this analysis, we examined the relationship between motor disturbance and the dimensions of formal thought disorder in the schizophrenic group. The results showed a strong relationship between the poverty of content feature and motor disruption ($r = .78$, $df = 20$, $p < .001$), impaired understandability ($r = .71$, $df = 20$, $p < .001$), and disturbed logic ($r = .61$, $df = 20$, $p < .01$). Loosened associations and motor disturbance were associated, but not significantly so ($r = .37$).

The effects of medication status were examined through the following comparisons. First, summary scores of motor disturbances of schizophrenics not taking neuroleptics (5) were compared to those motor disturbances not attributable to drugs of medicated schizophrenics (16). Nonmedicated and medicated schizophrenics were not statistically distinguishable ($t = -1.75$, $df = 19$, nonsignificant). Second, because 4 of the 5 nonmedicated schizophrenics were thought disordered, a further comparison between their scores and those of 6 medicated thought-disordered individuals was done. This comparison, which would appear to be more informative because of the shared thought disorder status, again revealed no significant difference ($t = 0.72$, $df = 8$, nonsignificant).

The main finding of the first study, then, was that indices of disorganized motor behavior and language are strongly associated. Age and education appear to have little impact on the basic correlation. The evidence is too limited to draw definitive conclusions about the relationship between drug status and measures investigated; nonetheless, the data provide no evidence of significant differences between medicated and drug-free subjects. A longitudinal study of initially drug-free subjects tested serially while off and then on medication would be one means of examining this issue.

The results point to a potentially important relationship between disruptions in speech and movements behavior especially in, but not limited to, schizophrenics, particularly among the thought-disordered subgroup. The use of an index of language disturbance, the TTR, that is more reliable than the clinical ratings usually made represents an extension of and further support for the association between formal thought disorder and disrupted movements, a feature of schizophrenia not confounded by language.

The first study also pointed to the need for assessments of motor behavior that would be free of the inherent bias of clinical evaluation techniques in order to complement the greater reliability of language measures, such as the TTR. Hence, the conduct of laboratory studies of motor disturbance is essential to confirm the presence of the relationships between motor and language anomalies and to provide greater precision in quantifying them.

The laboratory study of motor deficit (Manschreck *et al.*, 1981b) in schizophrenic disorders poses two problems: One is to establish that a reliable relationship exists between clinically observed motor phenomena and laboratory measures of the deficit; the second is to establish that the motor anomalies have a reliable relationship with some other important aspect of the psychopathological syndrome.

Workers investigating the components of skilled motor performance have made extensive use of the concept of redundancy. From the standpoint of information theory, any event can be regarded as redundant to the extent that it is predictable from observation of a chain of immediately prior events. An object moving through space with fixed course and velocity is moving with high redundancy, whereas an insect flitting unpredictably from one point to another is moving with low redundancy. Simple rhythmic movements, such as are seen in the repeated hammering of a nail or the polishing of a surface, are examples of high-redundancy activities. Such patterns of motor activity permit adaptive responsiveness to other stimuli in the environment. Where an individual is deficient in the adaptive use of redundancies, we should expect rhythmic performance to be impaired. Indeed, some investigations reported elsewhere (Breil, 1953; Kneutgen, 1976) suggest that this is the case.

There is substantial evidence that schizophrenic patients fail to make use of redundancy (Cromwell, 1968) and that this is associated with the presence of thought disorder in these patients (Maher, Manschreck, & Rucklos, 1980; Manschreck *et al.*, 1979). On this basis it seems reasonable to study rhythmic behavior in schizophrenic patients. We predicted that the schizophrenic would be less able than nonschizophrenic controls to synchronize a motor movement with rhythmic stimuli. However, defective performance among schizophrenic patients on almost any task is practically axiomatic. Hence, we needed to be sure that by varying the difficulty of the rhythm task we could detect a differential deficit in the performance of schizophrenic subjects and not a uniform depression of adequacy of response across all conditions. We also expected that those patients who showed the most marked deficit would show deficits in the nonmotor sphere (i.e., in thought disorder).

If we find that, at levels of task difficulty that are neither at the floor nor ceiling of performance accuracy, schizophrenic patients do as well as other psychiatric patients at some but less well at other levels, we would have a prima facie reason to doubt the general deficit explanation of the poor performance. The general deficit hypothesis demands that the schizophrenic patients be below the level of comparison groups at all levels of the task other than at the floor or ceiling. If we adduce general deficit to account for poor performance but assume that it disappears, by definition, whenever there is adequate performance, we would encounter the usual risks attached to post hoc explanations. However, there remains the possibility that accumulating deficit (fatigue, declining motivation, etc.) operates systematically over time on a sequence of tasks and does so particularly in schizophrenic patients. This is, of course, handled by presenting the various levels of difficulty in a confounded sequence.

There is no prior literature to inform us as to the ranges of task difficulty likely to be operative for schizophrenics in this situation. Hence, we decided to select rates of response that ranged from too low to permit accuracy to too high to do so. In this respect the investigation offered the possibility of establishing the task limits that would serve to detect differential deficit in schizophrenic and other psychiatric patients.

For this study, we hypothesized that (a) schizophrenic performance on a rhythm synchronization task would reflect a relative incapacity to automate a motor performance (i.e., to rhythmize repetitive motor behavior) and would not be explainable by task difficulty; (b) clinical evidence of motor disturbance would be associated with evidence of poorer relative performance on the laboratory rhythmic tasks; and (c) laboratory motor abnormality would be associated with severity of formal thought disorder.

Subjects were selected in a manner similar to that of the survey investigation that is, by strict diagnostic criteria (Feighner et al., 1972) and by Research Diagnostic Criteria (RDC) (Spitzer, Endicott, & Robins, 1975). Phenomenological subtype diagnoses were made according to RDC definitions. Sixteen schizophrenics were studied, including 5 paranoid, 7 disorganized, and 4 undifferentiated subtypes. Eight psychiatric (affective psychosis) controls were studied, including 5 major depressives and 3 schizoaffectives. Eleven of 16 schizophrenic subjects and 6 of 8 affective controls were taking neuroleptic medication. Dosages were matched according to chlorpromazine equivalents. Eight normal controls were also studied and were required to meet both the "currently not mentally ill" and "never mentally ill" categories of the RDC.

The procedure for clinical assessments of motor, thinking, and neuroleptic effects followed that of the survey investigation. Language samples were also obtained for TTR assessment of language disorganization according to the method described earlier. The synchronization task took place in a quiet, windowless laboratory. An Esterline Angus variable speed signal generator was used to produce rhythmic stimuli—uniform acoustic clicks. Acoustic stimuli were used instead of visual ones, for example, because of the greater assurance that the acoustic stimuli would be perceived. Unaccented (i.e., uniform) clicks create what is called a *tremolo rhythmic pattern* (Lundin, 1967). For each trial, a randomly ordered series of standard-volume acoustic clicks of one rate (8, 12, 20, 40, 80, 120, 200, or 400 beats per minute) was presented. A wide range of rates was employed because it was not clear at which one the predictability of clicks would influence performance; although it was thought likely that at extremely slow and fast rates, this factor would exert less influence on accuracy than on the ability to estimate intervals and tapping speed, respectively. To ensure that the effects of change in the rate were not confounded by changes in the pattern of rhythm, only the rate of clicks varied across trials. Durations of trial presentations were 8 beats per minute for 60 sec; 12 beats per minute for 60 sec; 20 beats per minute for 30 sec; 40 beats per minute for 20 sec; 80 and 120 beats per minute for 15 sec each; and 200 and 400 beats per minute for 10 sec each. Subjects were instructed to tap a telegraph key along with the acoustic clicks. Prior to the subjects' responses, the clicks were presented for 5 sec (for rates 400 beats per minute to 40 beats per minute) or for 3 beats (for rates 20 beats per minute to 8 beats per minute). A polygraph recorded stimuli and subject responses at a constant feed of 30 cm per minute. Synchronization was defined as simultaneous stimulus and subject response. Because of the possibility of random correct responses, rates of 80–400 beats per minute required at least three successive synchronization responses in order to be given a score above 0.

To determine the extent of the relationship between clinical and laboratory findings, the following strategy was applied. Disturbed motor activity scores (sum of ratings of spontaneous and elicited features), formal thought disturbance (sum of ratings of understandability, derailment, logic, poverty of information conveyed, and neologisms), and type–token ratios were compared among all subjects, using the Pearson product–moment correlation statistic, with synchronization accuracy at the rate that most distinguished the subject groups. Because the schizophrenic sample size was small, analysis of performance on the laboratory measure was made without respect to subtype diagnosis. The same strategy was applied to the affective control sample.

The results of this study can be summarized as follows. First, 15 of 16 schizophrenic subjects manifested one or more of the features of formal thought disorder (mean rating = 9.1, SD = 5.6), while 3 of the psychiatric controls showed such disturbance (mean rating = 1.0, SD = 1.7). Second, clinical motor disturbances (mean = 6.8, SD = 4.8) were evident among all but 2 schizophrenics, whereas only 3 psychiatric controls showed such evidence (mean = 0.5, SD = 0.7). Normal controls showed no evidence of thought or motor abnormality. Third, evidence of neuroleptic side effects occurred in 2 of the 8 (25%) affective psychotic controls and in 5 of the 11 (45%) schizophrenic subjects taking neuroleptics. Within each group, subjects with neuroleptic side effects did not differ from those without side effects on ratings of other disturbed motor behavior. Medicated (11) and nonmedicated (5) schizophrenic subjects did not differ in clinical motor ratings ($t(14) = .97$, nonsignificant). On the other hand, medicated schizophrenic subjects and medicated affective controls were significantly different in clinical motor ratings ($t(14) = 3.05$, $p < .005$).

Fourth, synchronization accuracy was very poor at 8, 12, and 20 beats per minute for all groups (see Fig. 1). At 40 beats per minute, accuracy improved substantially among all groups, with no significant group differences. At 80 beats per minute, normal subjects performed almost flawlessly. The affective and schizophrenic groups also improved, but notably, normal and affective group's accuracy was significantly better than that of the schizophrenic group (normal versus schizophrenic, $t(22) = 2.11$, $p < .025$). At 120 beats per minute, differences among the groups were less, and at 200 beats per minute, accuracy among groups was relatively similar and again indistinguishable. Our first hypothesis—that schizophrenic group performance would be distinctive and not explained by task difficulty—was supported. The schizophrenic group was significantly less able than normal or psychiatric control groups to rhythmize (or synchronize) performance at the slower rates (i.e., at 40 or slower) and at the faster rate of 200. This suggests that difficulty cannot account for these results and that other factors can operate to distinguish performance at the intermediate rates.

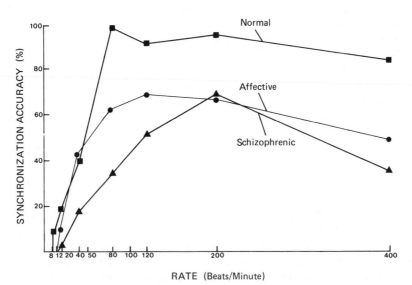

FIGURE 1.   Synchronization accuracy versus rhythm rate.

Fifth, comparisons between clinical and laboratory measures were examined. Specifically, the relationship between clinical (i.e., summed score of spontaneous and elicited voluntary motor activity disturbances) and laboratory evidence of motor deficiency was assessed using the synchronization response at 80 beats per minute as the laboratory measure. This measure was selected because it was the most sensitive indicator of group differences. Clinical and laboratory measures of motor features were inversely related at a significant level, indicating that anomalous motor behavior is associated with reduced synchronization accuracy ($r = -.53, p < .005$).

Hence, our second hypothesis—that clinical measures of motor abnormality would be associated with evidence of lower laboratory performance in motor tasks was also supported.

The relationship between clinical evidence of formal thought disorder, as defined in this report, and laboratory measures was also analyzed. Synchronization at 80 beats per minute, the rate showing the greatest spread among groups, was correlated highly with formal thought disorder ($r = .50, p < .005$). Because of the impact of the normals' lack of formal thought disorder, a second comparison between the third of the psychiatric subjects with the highest thought disorder scores independent of diagnosis (eight schizophrenic subjects) and the third with the lowest scores (seven affective subjects and one schizophrenic) was made, using accuracy at 80 beats per minute as the dependent variable. The difference again was significant ($t(14) = 2.12, p < .03$).

The relationship between formal thought disorder and synchronization at the other rates was also calculated and indicated generally the same relationship—namely, that formal thought disorder was related to poorer synchronization.

Hence, our third hypothesis—that performance on the laboratory task is associated with degree of formal thought disorder—was also supported. The relationship is negative and significant.

The MSTTR was compared to synchronization accuracy at 80 beats per minute across all subjects, because all subjects had a specific index on this measure. These features were correlated at a significant level ($r = .35, .025 < p > .05$), indicating that reduced accuracy on the motor task is associated with evidence of language impairment and providing further confirmation of the third hypothesis.

The major finding of this study is that measures of synchronization with auditory stimuli appear to distinguish the performance of schizophrenics and controls. Because schizophrenic performance overlaps with that of controls at some rates and diverges markedly at others, neither low motivation, the effect of general psychosis, difficulty of the procedure, motor dexterity, drug effects, nor tapping speed ability satisfactorily accounts for the observed differences. The plausibility of these explanations depends fundamentally on their ability to operate consistently across the experimental procedures. Failing that, other explanations must be considered.

These results are, however, consistent with predictions based on the hypothesis that schizophrenics are less able than controls to take advantage of the redundancy (in the information-processing sense of the term) of the auditory stimuli in order to synchronize tapping efficiently and accurately, a process similar to that required to automate any skilled motor activity (Posner & Keele, 1969; Schmidt, 1968). The ability to be aware of and make use of the redundancy or predictability of the clicks has the effect of decreasing the need to attend to estimating click occurrence and selecting and coordinating the tapping response. Prior work summarized by Maher (1972) has suggested that a disturbance in attentional focusing operates to impair the production of comprehensible speech in schizophrenics. In the synchronization procedure, a similar difficulty may disrupt performance. Specifically, we might expect that schizophrenics fail to adapt their attentional processes to the redundancies intrinsic to the task and hence exhibit relatively inefficient tapping and inaccurate synchronization. Indeed, schizophrenic performance, like that of controls, is aided by the redundancy of the stimuli, but to a significantly lesser degree.

An additional finding is that synchronization responses correlate with clinical measures of disturbed thinking and motor behavior and with the TTR measure of language disorganization. These results lend support to the accumulating evidence for an association between motor and thinking disturbance in schizophrenia, but they suggest that this association is not unique to schizophrenic disorder. Because this new laboratory measure is more objective than clinical motor evaluations, it may provide a means for further experimental analysis of these potentially important relationships.

B. COMMENT

The results of the survey investigation of motor abnormalities in schizophrenic disorder and those of the additional studies just discussed can be interpreted in different ways. This writer favors an interpretation that points to the central role of attentional deficiency in mediating the observed relationships between motor and language features of schizophrenia.

Many investigators have indicated the probable attentional deficit in the pathogenesis of symptom features of this illness (Allan & Kristofferson, 1974; McGhie, 1969; Shakow, 1962). A specific emphasis to the association between attentional deficit and schizophrenic language disorder has been given by Maher (1972), Cromwell and Dockecki (1968), and Neale and Oltmanns (1980).

Much work in experimental psychology has also shown that the performance of motor responses depends critically upon the operation of attentional processes (Ells, 1973; Rosenbaum, 1980; Stelmach, 1978). Particular importance has been attached to the effects of attention on the timing of sequential movements (Rosenbaum & Patashnik, 1980). Moreover, in view of the work of Sternberg, Monsell, Knoll, & Wright (1978), who demonstrated a connection between language and motor control in an investigation of speech and typewriting, and Barlett's observations about the connections between language, thought, and motor movement, and their elaboration by Posner (1980) into a sophisticated model pointing to the processes of attention involved in the sequencing and shifting of motor acts and thoughts, the results of the present investigation, which demonstrate a strong association between motor and language disorders that clinically have certain similarities (e.g., repetition in speech and movement) in schizophrenia, can reasonably be considered within an attentional deficit frame of reference. Yet other views may be appropriate as well and a skeptical attitude toward this as well as other explanatory models is warranted until it is better supported.

On the other hand, given the current lack of a neuropathology for schizophrenic disorder, a model based on the attentional deficit approach can stimulate further research through the development of more precise experimental analyses of schizophrenic behavior and perhaps through greater differentiation of the group of schizophrenic disorders into specific types.

VII. Conclusions

The clinical and experimental literature on psychopathology of motor behavior and schizophrenia is sketchy at best. Nevertheless, important observations have been made that suggest avenues for further investigation.

1. The incidence of motor anomalies intrinsic to schizophrenic disorder is much higher than generally believed and is not limited to the catatonic schizophrenia. A long history of clinical observations, high-risk studies, and cross-sectional surveys such as that reported here attest to this. Yet dramatic and unusual motor anomalies, such as catalepsy, are not common currently, and this fact may contribute to the widespread belief in low incidence. On the other hand, more subtle features, such as clumsiness and repetitive movements (e.g., stereotypies, perseveration, as well as disorganization, delayed response, postural persistence, and lengthy completion of movements), are frequent, occurring to varying extents in virtually all conservatively diagnosed cases. However, such features require either longi-

tudinal and frequent assessment or examination techniques designed especially to elicit them in a systematic manner.

2. Certain movement abnormalities, such as choreiform and athetoid movements, are probably not a part of schizophrenic disorder. Other basal ganglia diseases and drug effects are more likely sources for these motor abnormalities.

3. Antipsychotic medications produce many motor side effects, but they tend to reduce voluntary motor anomalies intrinsic to schizophrenic disorder and apparently do not modify the occurrence of spontaneous involuntary disordered movements, at least among chronic cases. Further research, preferably in drug-free patients, could be an important step to clarification and extension of knowledge on this matter.

4. Schizophrenic motor disturbances, as currently understood, are not pathognomonic for schizophrenic disorder. Indeed, most schizophrenic motor abnormalities occur in a variety of diseases involving basal ganglia and other subcortical structures. Nevertheless, the concentration of motor abnormalities, both voluntary and involuntary, among schizophrenic patients compared to affective patients suggests that certain specific relationships between motor disturbance and schizophrenic disorder exist. The coincidence of motor features, psychotic features, and cognitive impairment in schizophrenic disorder is also characteristic of some cases of hepatolenticular degeneration (Wilson's disease), Huntington's chorea, Parkinson's disease, and related disorders. Comparative studies involving schizophrenic patients might generate useful information about the pathogenesis, anatomy, and treatment of such disorders.

5. Schizophrenic motor disturbances are associated with formal thought disorder, certain neurological nonlocalizing signs, and affective blunting. The connection between formal thought disorder and motor disturbances is especially interesting because of its congruency with predictions based on the attentional deficit hypothesis in schizophrenia.

6. The exact relationship of motor features to prognosis is unclear. It appears, however, that the more severe the profile of motor disturbance, the more grave the illness. Observations of motor developmental difficulty in high-risk children also suggests that motor abnormalities detectable at an early age and prior to the onset of illness may portend a more severe and serious outcome.

7. Studies attempting to examine the motor and language deficits with laboratory techniques—more reliable than clinical evaluation—confirm the association between the two dimensions of behavior in schizophrenic disorder.

8. The relationships of motor and other features described occur predominantly, but not exclusively, in the schizophrenic patient groups, sug-

gesting that further investigation of these findings may lead to knowledge applicable to a broader range of psychopathologic disorders.

9. A broad range of neuropsychiatric studies have centered on motor disturbances. The results, however preliminary, provide important support for the view that investigations attempting to integrate clinical and laboratory dimensions of motor abnormality may significantly extend our understanding of schizophrenic disorders.

References

Abrams, R., & Taylor, M. S. A rating scale for emotional blunting. *American Journal of Psychiatry*, 1978, **135**, 226–229.

Allan, L. G., & Kristofferson, A. B., Successive discrimination: Two models. *Perception and Psychophysics*, 1974, **15**, 37–46.

Allison, R. Perseveration as a sign of diffuse and focal brain damage. I and II. *British Medical Journal,* **1966**, 1027–1032; 1095–1101.

American Psychiatric Association. *Diagnostic and statistical manual of mental disorders,* third edition (DSM III). Washington, D.C.: American Psychiatric Association, 1980.

Andreasen, N. Thought, language, and communication disorders, evaluation of their reliability. *Archives of General Psychiatry*, 1979, **36**, 1315–1321.

Andrews, E. Catatonic behavior: recognition, differential diagnosis, and management. In T. C. Manschreck (Ed.) *Psychiatric Medicine Update: Massachusetts General Hospital Revisions for Physicians.* New York: Elsevier North Holland, 1981.

Arieti, S. Primitive habits and perceptual alterations. *Archives of Neurology and Psychology*, 1945, **53**, 378.

Asarnow, R. F., Steffy, R. A., MacCrimmon, D. J., & Cleghorn, J. M. An attentional assessment of foster children at risk for schizophrenia. *Journal of Abnormal Psychology*, 1977, **86**, 267–276.

Bartlett, F. C. *Thinking.* New York: Basic Books, 1958.

Bleuler, E. *Dementia praecox or the group of schizophrenias.* New York: International Universities Press, 1950. (Originally published 1911).

Breil, M. S. Graphologische Untersuchungen über die Psychomotorik in den Handschriften Schizophrenen. *Monatschrift fur Psychiatrie und Neurologie*, 1953, **125**, 193–238.

Carpenter, W. T., Jr., Strauss, J. S., & Muleh, S. Are there pathognomonic symptoms in schizophrenia? An empiric investigation of Kurt Schneider's first rank symptoms. *Archives of General Psychiatry*, 1973, **28**, 847–852.

Chapman, J. The early symptoms of schizophrenia. *British Journal of Psychiatry*, 1966, **112**, 225–251.

Chapman, J., & McGhie, A. Echopraxia in schizophrenia. *British Journal of Psychiatry*, 1964, **119**, 365–374.

Chapman, L., & Chapman J. *Disordered thought in schizophrenia.* Englewood Cliffs, N.J.: Prentice-Hall, 1973.

Coquery, J. M. Selective attention: a motor program. In J. Requin (Ed.), *Attention and Performance.* Hillsdale, N.J.: Erlbaum, 1978.

Crayton, J., Stalberg, E., & Hilton-Brown, P. The motor unit in psychotic patients: A single fiber EMG study. *Journal of Neurology, Neurosurgery, and Psychiatry*, 1977, **40**, 455–463.

Cromwell, R. L. Stimulus redundancy in schizophrenia. *Journal of Nervous and Mental Disease*, 1968, **146**, 360–375.

Cromwell, R. L., & Dockecki, P. Schizophrenic language: A disattention interpretation. In S. Rosenberg & J. H. Kaplan (Eds.), *Developments in applied psycholinguistics research.* New York: Macmillan, 1968.

Davis, J. M. Comparative dose and costs of antipsychotic medication. *Archives of General Psychiatry*, 1976, **33**, 858–861.

DeJong, R. *The neurological examination.* New York: Harper, 1967.

Diefendorf, A. R., & Dodge, R. An experimental study of the ocular reactions of the insane from photographic records. *Brain*, 1908, **31**, 451–489.

Ells, J. G. Analysis of attentional and temporal aspects of movement control. *Journal of Experimental Psychology*, 1973, **99**, 10–21.

Feighner, J., Robins, E., Guze, S., Woodruff, R. A., Winokur, G., & Munoz, R. Diagnostic criteria for use in psychiatric research. *Archives of General Psychiatry*, 1972, **26**, 57–63.

Fish, B. Biological antecedents of psychosis in children. In D. X. Freedman (Ed.), *Biology of the Major Psychoses.* New York: Raven, 1975.

Fish, F. *Clinical psychopathology.* Bristol: John Wright, 1967.

Freeman, T. *Psychopathology of the psychoses.* New York: International and University Press, 1969.

Freeman, T., & Gathercole, C. Perseveration the clinical symptom in chronic schizophrenia. *British Journal of Psychiatry*, 1966, **112**, 27–32.

Gelenberg, A. The catatonic syndrome. *Lancet II*, 1976, 1339–1341.

Glassman, R. A neural systems theory of schizophrenia and tardive dyskinesia. *Behavioral Sciences*, 1976, **21**, 274–288.

Goldstein, K. *After effects of brain injuries in war.* London: Heinemann, 1942,

Goode, D. J., Meltzer, H. Y., Crayton, J. W., & Mazura, T. A. Physiologic abnormalities of the neuromuscular system in schizophrenia. *Schizophrenia Bulletin*, 1977, **3**, 121–139.

Gould, L. N. Verbal hallucinations and activity of vocal musculature: An electromyographic study. *American Journal of Psychiatry*, 1948, **105**, 367.

Guggenheim, F. & Babigian, H. Diagnostic consistency in catatonic schizophrenia. *Schizophrenia Bulletin,* 1974, **11**, 103–108.

Gur, R. Motoric laterality imbalance in schizophrenia. *Archives of General Psychiatry*, 1977, **34**, 33–37.

Hanson, D., Gottesman, I., & Heston, L. Some possible childhood indicators of adult schizophrenia inferred from children of schizophrenics. *British Journal of Psychiatry.* 1976, **129**, 142–154.

Hertzig, M. A., & Birch, H. C. Neurologic organization in psychiatrically disturbed adolescent girls. *Archives of General Psychiatry*, 1968, **19**, 528–537.

Holzman, P. Assessment of perceptual functioning in schizophrenia. *Psychopharmacology*, 1972, **25**, 29–41.

Holzman, P., Kringlen, E., Levy, D., & Haberman, S. Deviant eye tracking in twins discordant for psychoses: A replication. *Archives of General Psychiatry*, 1980, **37**, 627–631.

Holzman, P., & Levy, D. Smooth pursuit eye movements and functional psychoses: A review. *Schizophrenia Bulletin*, 1977, **3**, 15–27.

Holzman, P., Proctor, L., & Hughes, D. Eye-tracking patterns in schizophrenia. *Science*, 1973, **181**, 179–181.

Holzman, P., Proctor, L., Levy, D., Yasillo, N., Meltzer, H., & Hurt, S. Eye-tracking dysfunctions in schizophrenic patients and their relatives. *Archives of General Psychiatry*, 1974, **31**, 143–151.

Jacobson, E. *Progressive relaxation*. Chicago: Univ. of Chicago Press, 1938.

Jackson, J. The factors of insanities. In *Selected writings of James Hughlings Jackson* (Vol. 2). New York: Basic Books, 1958. (Originally published, 1894.)

Jaspers, K. *General psychopathology*. Chicago: Univ. of Chicago Press, 1963.

Jelliffe, S. The mental pictures in schizophrenia and in epidemic encephalitis. *Research Publication of the Association of Nervous and Mental Diseases*, 1928, **5**, 204.

Jones, I. H. Observations on schizophrenic stereotypies. *Comprehensive Psychiatry*, 1965, **6**, 323–335.

Jones, M. Measurement of spontaneous movements in adult psychotic patients. *Journal of Psychology*, 1941, **11**, 285–295.

Jones, M., & Hunter, R. Abnormal movements in patients with chronic psychiatric illness. In G. Crane & R. Gardner (Eds.), *USPHS Pub. #1936*, 1968.

Kahlbaum, K. *Catatonia*. Baltimore: Johns Hopkins Press, 1973. (Originally published, 1874.)

Karson, C., Fried, W. J., Kleinman, J. E., Bigelow, L. B., & Watt, R. J. Neuroleptics decrease blinking in schizophrenic subjects. *Biological Psychiatry*, 1981, **16**, 679–682.

Kleist, K. *Untersuchungen zur Kenntnis der psychomotorischen Bewegungstoerungen bei Geisteskranken*. Leipzig: W. Klinkhart, 1908.

Kneutgen, J. Experimentelle Analyse einer Wahrnehmungsstorung bei Schizophrenie: Desynchronisation von Handbewgungen mit einer gleich-formigen akutischen Frequenz. *Fortschrift Neurologische Psychiatrie*, 1976, **44**, 182–191.

Kraepelin, E. *Dementia praecox*. Edinburgh: Livingstone, 1919.

Larson, V. Physical characteristics of disturbed adolescents. *Archives of General Psychiatry*, 1964, **10**, 55–64.

Latham, C., Holzman, P., Manschreck, T. C., & Tole, J. Optokinetic nystagmus and pursuit eye movements in schizophrenia. *Archives of General Psychiatry*, 1981, **38**, 997–1003.

Lehmann, H. Clinical features in schizophrenia. In A. M. Freedman, I. Kaplan, B. Sadock, (Eds.), *Comprehension of psychiatry*. Baltimore: Williams & Wilkins, 1976.

Lundin, R. *An objective psychology of music*. New York: Ronald Press, 1967.

Luria, A. R. *Higher cortical functions in man*. New York: Basic Books, 1966.

Mahendra, B. Where have all the catatonics gone? *Psychological Medicine*, 1981, **11**, 669–671.

Maher, B. A. The language of schizophrenia: A review and interpretation. *British Journal of Psychiatry,* 1972, **120**, 3–17.

Maher, B. A., Manschreck, T. C., & Rucklos, M. Contextual constraint and the recall of verbal material in schizophrenia: The effect of thought disorder. *British Journal of Psychiatry*, 1980, **137**, 69–73.

Maher, B. A., Manschreck, T. C., & Molino, M. Redundancy, pause distributions and thought disorder in schizophrenia. *Language and Speech*, 1983, **26**, 191–199.

Mailloux, N. M., & Newberger, M. The work curves of psychotic individuals. *Journal of Abnormal and Social Psychology*, 1941, **36**, 110–114.

Malmo, R., & Shagass, C. Physiologic studies of reaction to stress in anxiety and early schizophrenia. *Psychosomatic Medicine*, 1949, **11**, 9–24.

Malmo, R., Shagass, C., & Davis, J. A method for the investigation of somatic response mechanisms in psychoneurosis. *Science*, 1948, **112**, 325–328.

Manschreck, T. C., & Keller, M. Biological mental status examination: General appearance and behavior. In A. Lazare (Ed.), *Diagnosis and treatment in outpatient psychiatry*. Baltimore: Williams and Wilkins, 1979.

Manschreck, T. C., Maher, B. A., & Ader, D. N. Formal thought disorder, the type-token ratio, and disturbed voluntary motor movement in schizophrenia. *British Journal of Psychiatry*, 1981, **139**, 7–15. (a)

Manschreck, T. C., Maher, B. A., Rucklos, M. E., & Vereen, D. E. Disturbed voluntary motor activity in schizophrenic disorders. *Psychological Medicine*, 1982, **12**, 73-84.

Manschreck, T. C., Maher, B. A., Rucklos, M. E., Vereen, D. R., & Ader, D. N. Deficient motor synchrony in schizophrenia. *Journal of Abnormal Psychology*, 1981, 90(4) 321-328. (b)

Manschreck, T. C., Maher, B. A., Rucklos, M. E., & White, M. The predictability of thought-disordered speech in schizophrenic patients. *British Journal of Psychiatry*, 1979, **134**, 595-601.

Manschreck, T. C., & Petri, M. The paranoid syndrome. *Lancet,* 1978, *II,* 251-253.

Marcus, J. Cerebral functioning in offspring of schizophrenics. *International Journal of Mental Health*, 1974, **3**, 57-73.

Marsden, C. D. Motor disorders in schizophrenia. *Psychological Medicine*, 1982, **12**, 13-15.

Marsden, C., Tarsy, D., & Baldessarini, R. Spontaneous and drug induced movement disorders in psychotic patients. In D. Benson & D. Blumer (Eds.), *Psychiatric aspects of neurological disease*. New York: Grune & Stratton, 1975.

Matthysse, S. Dopamine and the pharmacology of schizophrenia. *Journal of Psychological Research*, 1974, **11**, 107-113.

McGhie, A. *Pathology of attention*. Baltimore: Penguin, 1969.

McGuigan, F. J. Covert oral behavior and auditory hallucinations. *Psychophysiology*, 1966, **3**, 73-80.

Mednick, S. A., Mural, M., Schulsinger, F., & Mednick, B. Perinatal conditions and infant development in children with schizophrenic parents. *Social Biology*, 1971, **18** (Suppl.), 108-118.

Mellor, C. S. First rank symptoms of schizophrenia. *British Journal of Psychiatry*, 1970, **117**, 15-23.

Meltzer, H. Neuromuscular dysfunction in schizophrenia. *Schizophrenia Bulletin*, 1976, **2**, 106-135.

Meltzer, H. Biochemical studies in schizophrenia. In L. Bellak (Ed.), *Disorders of the schizophrenic syndrome*. New York: Basic Books, 1979. Pp. 45-135.

Morrison, J. R. Catatonia. Retarded and excited types. *Archives of General Psychiatry*, 1973, **28**, 39-41.

Munkvad, I., Pakkenberg, H., & Randrup, A. Aminergic systems in basal ganglia associated with stereotyped hyperactive behavior and catalepsy. *Brain Behavior Evolution,* 1968, **1**, 89-100.

National Institute of Mental Health. *Abnormal involuntary movements scale*. Bethesda, Md.: U.S. Government Printing Office. 1974.

Neale, J., & Oltmanns, T. F. *Schizophrenia*. New York: John Wiley, 1980.

O'Neal, P., & Robins, L. Childhood patterns predictive of adult schizophrenia. *American Journal of Psychiatry*, 1958, **115**, 385-391.

Orton, S. T. Some neurologic concepts applied to catatonia. *Archives of Neurology and Psychiatry*, 1930, **23**, 114-129.

Owens, D. G. C., Johnstone, E. C., & Frith, C. D. Spontaneous involuntary disorders of movement. *Archives of General Psychiatry*, 1982, **39**, 452-461.

Papeschi, R. Dopamine, extrapyramidal system and psychomotor function. *Psyneur Neruochirurgia*, 1972, **75**, 13-48.

Pincus, J., & Tucker, G. *Behavioral neurology*. New York: Oxford Univ. Press, 1974.

Pope, H. G., & Lipinski, J. F. Manic depressive disorders and schizophrenia. *Archives of General Psychiatry*, 1978, **35**, 1-22.

Posner, M. I. Orienting of attention. *Quarterly Journal of Experimental Psychology*, 1980, **32**, 3-25.

Posner, M., & Keele, S. W. Attention demands of movements. In *Proceedings of the 17th Congress of Applied Psychology*. Amsterdam, The Netherlands: Zeitlinger, 1969.

Regenstein, Q., Alpert, J., & Reich, P. Sudden catatonic stupor with disastrous outcome. *Journal of the American Medical Association*, 1977, **238**, 618-620.

Ricks, D., & Nameche, G. Symbiosis, sacrifice, and schizophrenia. *Mental Hygiene*, 1966, **50**, 541-555.

Ricks, D., & Berry, J. Family and symptom patterns that precede schizophrenia. In M. Roff & D. Ricks (Eds.), *Life history research in psychopathology* (Vol. 1). Minneapolis: Univ. of Minnesota Press, 1970.

Robins, L. *Deviant children grow up*. Baltimore: Williams & Wilkins, 1966.

Rochford, J., Detre, T., Tucker, G., & Harrow, M. Neuropsychological impairments in functional psychiatric diseases. *Archives of General Psychiatry*, 1970, **22**, 114-119.

Rosenbaum, D. A. Human movement initiation: Specification of arm, direction, and extent. *Journal of Experimental Psychology*, 1980, **109**, 444-474.

Rosenbaum, D. A., & Pastashnik, D. A mental clock setting process revealed by reaction time. In G. E. Stelmach & J. Requin (Eds.), *Tutorials in motor behavior*. Amsterdam: North-Holland, 1980.

Schilder, P. Brain and personality: Studies in the psychological aspects of cerebral neuropathy and the neuropsychiatric aspects of the motility of schizophrenia. *Nervous and Mental Disease Monograph*, 1931, **53**, 92-135.

Schmidt, R. A. Anticipation and timing in human motor performance. *Psychological Bulletin*, 1968, **70**, 631-646.

Schneider, K. *Clinical psychopathology*. New York: Grune & Stratton, 1959.

Shakow, D. Segmental set. *Archives of General Psychiatry*, 1962, **6**, 1-17.

Skvoretz, J., & Fararo, T. J. Languages and grammars of action and interaction: A contribution to the formal theory of action. *Behavioral Science*, 1980, **25**, 9-22.

Slater, E., & Roth, M. *Clinical psychiatry*. London: Ballere, 1969.

Snyder, S., Banerjee, S., Yammura, A., & Greenberg, D. Drugs, neurotransmitters, and schizophrenia. *Science*, 1974, **21**, 1243-1253.

Spitzer, R., & Endicott, J. *Schedule for Affective Disorders and Schizophrenia (SADS)*. New York: Biometrics Research, New York State Psychiatric Institute, 1977.

Spitzer, R., Endicott, J., & Robins, E. *Research diagnostic criteria for a selected group of functional disorders (RDC)*. New York: Biometrics Research, 1975.

Stelmach, G. F. (Ed.). *Information processing in motor control and learning*. New York: Academic Press, 1978.

Stengel, E. A clinical and psychological study of echo reactions. *Journal of Mental Science*, 1947, **93**, 598.

Sternberg, S., Monsell, S., Knoll, T. L., & Wright, C. E. The latency and duration of rapid movement sequences: Comparisons of speech and typewriting. In G. F. Stelmach (Ed.), *Information processing in motor control and learning*. New York: Academic Press, 1978.

Stevens, J. R. Eye blink and schizophrenia: Psychosis or tardive dyskinesia. *American Journal of Psychiatry*, 1978, **135**, 223-227.

Strauss, J., & Carpenter, W. Characteristic symptoms and outcome in schizophrenia. *Archives of General Psychiatry*, 1974, **30**, 429-434.

Tucker, G., Campion, E., & Silberfarb, P. Sensorimotor functions and cognitive disturbance in psychiatric patients. *American Journal of Psychiatry*, 1975, **132**, 17-21.

Tucker, G., & Silberfarb, P. Neurologic dysfunction in schizophrenia. In H Akiskal & W. Webb (Eds.), *Psychiatric diagnosis*. New York: Spectrum, 1978.

Watt, N. Childhood and adolescent routes to schizophrenia. In D. Ricks, A. Thomas, & M. Roff (Eds.), *Life history research in psychopathology* (Vol. 3). Minneapolis: Univ. of Minnesota Press, 1974.

Whatmore, G. B., & Ellis, R. M., Jr. Some motor aspects of schizophrenia: EMG study. *Journal of Psychiatry*, 1958, **114**, 882–889.

Wojcik, J. D., Genelenberg, A. J., LaBrie, R., & Berg, M. Prevalence of tardive dyskinesia in an outpatient population. *Comprehensive Psychiatry*, 1980, **21**, 370–379.

Wood, R. L., & Cook, M. Attentional deficit in the siblings of schizophrenics. *Psychological Medicine*, 1977, **9**, 465–467.

World Health Organization. *Schizophrenia, an international pilot study*. New York: Wiley, 1973.

Wulfeck, W. Motor function in the mentally disordered. *Psychological Record*, 1941, **4**, 271–323.

Yates, A. J. Abnormalities of psychomotor function. In H. J. Eysenck (Ed.), *Handbook of abnormal psychology*. San Diego: Robert Knapp, 1973.

Yarden, P. E., & Discipio, W. J. Abnormal movements and prognosis in schizophrenia. *American Journal of Psychiatry*, 1971, **128**, 317–323.

PROGRESS IN EXPERIMENTAL PERSONALITY RESEARCH, VOLUME 12

THE ORAL AND WRITTEN PRODUCTIONS OF SCHIZOPHRENIC PATIENTS

Louis J. Cozolino

DEPARTMENT OF PSYCHOLOGY
UNIVERSITY OF CALIFORNIA, LOS ANGELES
LOS ANGELES, CALIFORNIA

I. Introduction

A. Ideas Concerning Schizophrenic Language

And now her present condition depends wholly on what Dr. J. M. plans for the future, who wishes to make himself acquainted with what is in connection with it, and of whose condition she wished to be again acquainted with, which he wished on his own

101

desire. Now he has nothing at all but what was yours, which seems to lose what was his, but he himself tried to lose it, the fortune which for him was trying to be acquainted [Kraepelin, 1919/1971, p. 20].

For more than a century, the enigma of schizophrenic language has baffled clinicians and researchers while at the same time sparking the imaginations of writers, ethnologists, and religionists. The richly descriptive reports of Eugen Bleuler and Emil Kraepelin have inspired a multitude of theories and studies concerning the nature, cause, and objectives of the language of schizophrenic patients.

It seems likely that one reason for the vast number of studies examining schizophrenic language lies in the nature of the data. The amazing diversity and complexity of language production has served as fertile ground for countless theories of thought disorder. Schizophrenic language and thought have been described as derailed, convoluted, and involuted; archaic, regressed, and primitive; overgeneralized and idiosyncratic; and for dessert, word salad—all this in the absence of any solid knowledge concerning the relationship between language production and thought.

In fact, schizophrenic language seems to have served as a kind of projective test for many psychologists, linguists, and a host of global thinkers. Research has consequently been based upon a morass of conflicting and diverse assumptions, undefined terminology, and undemonstrated logical leaps. Thus, it is difficult to separate what we "know" from what we feel should be true.

B. THE SCOPE OF LANGUAGE STUDY IN SCHIZOPHRENIA

The nature of an individual's language results from an interaction of cultural and personal histories with verbal capacity, intellectual ability, and personality. Theories concerning the etiology of aberrant thought and language production have ranged from those that are primarily biological and physiological, such as neurotransmitter imbalances (Snyder, Banerjie, Yamamura, & Greenberg, 1974), to those that posit psychogenic causes of deficient ego development (Hartman, 1964).

Whether the perceived problem is learned or innate, environmental, chemical, or an interaction of many factors, the investigator's first responsibility is to examine the relationship between what is being uttered by the patient and the investigator's perception of it. Those who see schizophrenic language as being everything from poesis to overconcrete do so, to a large extent, because this is what they are looking for. Colorful terms may capture the imagination, but they interfere with our understanding of the formal structure of the language of schizophrenic patients as well as with our ability to understand the patient's attempt to communicate her or his experience of the illness.

Clinicians have come to trust their "praecox feeling" in diagnosis, as researchers trust their theories of overinclusion, filter defect, dyslogia, etc. All of these assumptions need to be reexamined not only in relation to explicit theorizing but also in their implicit effects on the design and analysis of research, the utility and success of diagnosis, and the methods and outcome of therapeutic intervention.

That schizophrenic patients often produce language that we consider to be "aberrant" or "abnormal" is assumed. What is usually forgotten in this labeling process is the active role of the perceiver in making her or his judgment. When there is a speaker, an assumption is made that there is a listener; they both need to be examined. In the quantification of verbal data, analysis must remain true to the reciprocal nature of communication and not be evaluated in a vacuum. The analysis of verbal behavior has, for the most part, treated language as if it were easily quantifiable without taking into account its ultimately social and interactive nature. Monologue and interview situations are more socially oriented than test situations, even with the consideration that tests are usually administered in the presence of the experimenter. They are also more relevant to the patient's experience of his or her illness, as they more often relate to matters pertinent to the patient's life and specifically to the illness. The additional structure provided by laboratory tests may complicate the data with other difficulties of attention, and a stage of processing a decision that may make data from structured to unstructured settings incomparable.

C. A Schizophrenic Language?

A popular notion among some writers has been that there is a shared language among schizophrenic patients (Sommer, Dewar, & Osmond, 1960). The possibility of such a shared language may be a function of the patients' need to believe they can communicate with their peers as well as the tendency of observers to seek order in chaos. The beginnings of this notion may well be based on ward observations where researchers or doctors did not comprehend patient interchange while the patients seemed to understand one another. There is also an anecdotal report in the literature of a patient developing a private language with his nurse (Caudill, 1959) and empirical evidence that suggests some internal consistency in the associations of individual patients (Laffal, 1960, 1961, 1965, 1979). However, there is still no evidence for a shared language. Norma McDonald, a former schizophrenic patient who describes her experiences in the article "Living with

Schizophrenia'' (1960) states that "there is no common meeting ground between schizophrenics [p. 220]." Her experience mirrors the autobiographical reports of many schizophrenics who describe themselves as engulfed in isolation, distrust, and fear (Sechehaye, 1951; Vonnegut, 1975).

Using the Kent–Rosanoff Word Association Test (Kent & Rosanoff, 1910), Sommer and his colleagues investigated the possibility of a common schizophrenic language by examining the associations of schizophrenics, with the assumption that language is the product of shared associations. It was felt that a shared language would be accompanied by shared relationships between words. If there is a common language among schizophrenics, then their associations would be shared but seem unusual to normal listeners. They found that the associations of a group of schizophrenics were more uncommon, variable, and individually idiosyncratic than those of a group of normals. From this data it seems that, if a shared language is based on common associations within a group, schizophrenics move away from this mutual verbal ground.

Research with the Cloze procedure (a measure of predictability and communicability) indicates that schizophrenic subjects predict the language of other schizophrenics less well than they do for normal subjects (Deckner & Blanton, 1969; Moroz & Fosmire, 1966; Rutter, Wishner, & Callaghan, 1975). Honigfeld (1963) demonstrated that schizophrenics were unable to Cloze (discern missing words deleted from a text) a speech passage uttered by a schizophrenic with any more success than they could a passage from a normal subject on psilocybin.

Thus, it appears that, although patients or any group of people can develop shared meanings and speech habits that are not shared by the broader society, schizophrenics do not possess a language of their own and in fact seem to be less well understood by each other than by normal subjects. The inference that schizophrenics have a shared language seems to be a function of the perspective of the observer. It does not appear to be subjectively experienced by the patient, nor has it been empirically verified.

D. VERBAL BEHAVIOR

The term *verbal behavior* has become a catchall in schizophrenia research for any experimentation involving verbal responses. Research involving testing in memory, personality, intelligence, differential deficit, and information processing most often relies upon verbal and/or written responses as their data and have been subsumed under the category of verbal behavior. The focus of this review will be primarily on those studies that have used as their data either free spoken and written samples or continuous verbal production in an interview context. The difference in demand characteristics between a free speech sample and a test response led to this decision, as did the possible confusion that may arise when comparing data collected by research based on such disparate methodological practices. Methods for collecting the data presented here range from using 3-minute samples of uninterrupted speech during interviews to requesting hospital staffs to gather examples of written works of the patients on their wards. Thus, the studies reviewed here are not without differences in demand characteristics. It does seem, however, that more legitimate generalizations can be arrived at by looking at this group of studies than can be attained by attempting to encompass all aspects of research involving the communication patterns of schizophrenic patients. Such a broad overview would risk the impression that research in the area has been a united effort, guided by common theoretical and methodological principles.

This chapter shall discuss a variety of research methodologies, along with the abundant confounds present in any research in psychopathology. Suggestions for further research are also considered in light of our most promising findings to date.

E. The Importance of Language Analysis for Diagnosis

While detailed linguistic analysis of the language content of schizophrenic patients may at times appear detached from the clinical realities and treatment needs of the patient, this is far from true. The language of a schizophrenic patient is our only real link to an understanding of what that individual experiences during a psychotic episode and how these sensations and perceptions change as the patient goes into remission. Careful attention to the phenomenological reports of patients (Chapman, 1966; Chapman & McGhie, 1962; McGhie & Chapman, 1961) also led to the development of the "filter defect" theory of attention, which stands as a forerunner of current theories of information-processing deficits in schizophrenia. Simply asking the patients about their experiences has served as a valuable source of information in psychopathology.

Psychopharmacological advances in the treatment of schizophrenia and the affective disorders have recently brought to the fore an emphasis on proper differential diagnosis. With most diagnoses made by interview, a large part of the decision is based on direct verbal interchange between patient and staff. Thus, to understand the distinguishing features of "schizophrenic language" and to discriminate it reliably from the language of other types of patients is a crucial task for diagnosis.

Clinical textbooks abound with examples of schizophrenic language from which each generation of clinicians, in turn, learns to recognize and diagnose schizophrenia. While there are certainly other parameters for a diagnosis of schizophrenia, few would disagree that the majority of schizophrenic diagnoses are based on a thought disorder inferred from communication that is deemed aberrant in either form or content.

While clinicians and lay raters seem to be able to distinguish "normal" from "pathological" speech with good reliability (Hunt & Jones, 1958), they are most often unable to define the criteria on which their judgments are based. A good deal of research has been directed at distinguishing which aspects of schizophrenic language prompt both clinicians and lay raters to a decision of thought disorder.

Wide clinical acceptance of the validity of the "praecox feeling" in diagnosis and therapy emphasizes the importance of a clinician's subjective impressions. The sort of "uncomfortable, confused feeling" that a clinician experiences is certainly not a measure of observed symptomology but rather a gut reaction in the context of the interaction. In George Kelly's terms (1963), the anxiety experienced by the clinicians can be understood as a function of their inability to match their experiences with their constructs of logical communication. This incongruence is experienced as a threat and leads to a subjective experience of anxiety. Rochester and Martin (1979) describe a "double inference" involved in diagnosing thought disorder:

> The clinician proceeded from a personal experience of confusion to infer that the patient is confused. The inference is made to account for the listener's experience. Next, from the conclusion that the patient's speech is confusing, the clinician infers that the patient's thought must be confused. This inference is an effort to account for the speaker's behavior [p. 169].

As listeners we are constantly attempting to comprehend the meaning of what we hear. We depend a great deal on surveying, synthesizing, and digesting the constant flood of input from the environment, rendering it intelligible, categorizable, and masterable. We do this automatically in conversation, at work, or in simply observing our surroundings. The schizophrenic patient, exhibiting what we call "thought disorder" eludes our attempts at categorization and is thus outside of our cognitive mastery. The patient's affects and associations are often unpredictable and many of his or her experiences are beyond our immediate understanding. As Kelly pointed out, there is a degree to which our survival is threatened by the unknown or at least the unpredictable. An awareness of the source of this anxiety and an understanding of the active role of the listener in judging communication to be aberrant may assist the clinician in a more careful evaluation and diagnosis of a patient who makes them uncomfortable. The impetus and goal of many studies into schizophrenic language has been to operationalize theories relating to the cause of this "praecox feeling" and to quantify and explain this phenomenon in linguistic and psychological terms.

F. APPROACHES TO ANALYSIS

1. Analysis Based on Linguistic Features

The systematic analysis of schizophrenic language was launched in 1944 with the work of Fairbanks and Mann in an entire psychological monograph devoted to the topic. In that same year, Kasanin's book on *Language and Thought in Schizophrenia* was published. These two camps were represented by "quantifiers" of language data on the one hand and those with more of a penchant for theorizing on the other. While this chapter follows empirical studies over the past four decades, many of the empirical paradigms have their genesis in psychodynamic and psychoanalytic concepts. Because of this, the research using free speech and written samples followed two main paths into the mid-1960s: One quantified the formal characteristics of speech (e.g., grammar, diversity of vocabulary, adjective–verb ratios), whereas the other analyzed the content of schizophrenic speech and writing (e.g., examining categories derived from the inferences of raters or computer programs that code and categorize topic areas). In both cases researchers hoped to identify what was unique to the communication of schizophrenics.

A change in perspective came in the 1960s with the use of the Cloze analysis that reflected a shift in emphasis from treating the data as isolated bits of information to an appreciation of the interactive effect between the language data and the raters. This expanded the scope of analysis of schizophrenic language by including the receiver in the process of communication. The most recent work by Rochester and Martin (1979) examining the cohesive links between clauses has firmly established the study of language in schizophrenia on an interactive and communication-based model.

2. Analysis Based on Motor Features

Relatively little research has been done in the area of motor features of schizophrenic speech. Analyses such as rate of speech and the ratio of pause to speech time have been included in a few studies over the past 20 years. However, just as in the measurement of linguistic features, there has been a gradual progression from simple quantification of rate of speech to an exploration of the interaction between motor movements and speech abilities. Recently, investigations have expanded to examine hesitations in speech in relation to their grammatical location within the structure of a sentence. Most recently, measures of verbal behavior have been found to relate to clinical ratings of symptomatology, prognosis, and performance on motor tasks. Thus, the temporal and visceral components of speech offer another perspective for evaluation of the complex processes of language and may offer new understanding into the diagnosis and treatment of schizophrenia.

II. Analysis of Linguistic Features

A. Grammatical Components

> Not infrequently the tendency toward stereotypy is a further cause for the derailment of the patient's associational activity. The patients are caught in and remain fixed to the same circle of ideas, the same words, the same sentence structures, or, at any rate, return to them again and again without any logical need [Bleuler, 1950, p. 27].

Clinicians and researchers often describe schizophrenic language as redundant and repetitive. The phenomenon of stereotypy in speech, writing, and motor behavior is reported by both Kraepelin and Bleuler. Schizophrenic patients often exhibit perseveration on certain themes and particular words that seems to disrupt the flow of communication.

> I am of I-Building in B _____State hospital. With my nostrils clogged and Winter here, I chanced to be reading the magazine that Mentholatum advertised from. Kindly send it to me at the hospital. Send it to me Joseph Nemo in care of Joseph Nemo and me who answers by the name of Joseph Nemo and will care for it myself. Thanks everlasting and Merry New Year to Mentholatum Company for my nose for my nose for my nose for my nose for my nose [Maher, 1968, p. 30].

Mittenecker (1951) suggests that the utterance of a word or syllable establishes a "submental" activation of that word or syllable, which results in an increased probability that it will be repeated. If this is the case, schizophrenic patients may either have a heightened activation of this process or be less able than normal speakers to filter out these internal distractions. Other theories concerning the repetitiveness of schizophrenic speech have focused on psychological defenses (Bobon, 1967, as cited in Maher, 1972), short-term memory, and other information-processing deficits (Venables, 1964).

1. Type-Token Ratio

The type–token ratio (TTR) was developed as a measure of the heterogeneity of the language used. Its creator, Wendell Johnson (1944), describes it as "a measure of language flexibility or variability, designed to indicate certain aspects of language adequacy [p. 1]." It is computed by taking the ratio of different words (types) to the total number of words used (tokens). For example, the sentence *I went, I went, I was going to the doctor* has a total of 10 words (tokens) and 7 different words (types). The TTR for this particular sentence is .70.

The 14 studies since 1944 using the TTR with schizophrenic patients have produced mixed results (see Table I). These data are difficult to summarize because of differences in techniques, orientations, and analyses. Generally, the data show that schizophrenic patients seem to have a lower TTR than do normal subjects. The differences are small but consistent. Pavy, Grinspoon, and Shader (1969) found a strong negative correlation between chronicity and TTR, which the Silverman (1973) study did not replicate.

2. The Adjective–Verb Quotient

The adjective–verb quotient (AVQ) as used by Boder (1940) and subsequent researchers is the ratio of adjectives (which come before nouns and main verbs) to the number of verbs. Used in this way, a high AVQ would be indicative of a lack of action in the presence of description and clarification, whereas a low AVQ denotes little description and much action. Table II briefly outlines research with the AVQ. These studies suggest that schizophrenics may have a lower AVQ than do normal subjects. The lack of description in the language of schizophrenics concurs with studies that indicate that they tend to use shorter clauses and fewer ties between clauses (Rochester & Martin, 1979). Adjectives should decrease with shorter clauses, while the number of verbs would increase due to a greater number of clauses in collecting a language sample of a set length.

3. Parts of Speech

More extensive formal analysis (see Table III) reveals a trend toward the use of fewer nouns by schizophrenic patients and the omission of prepositions. For an exhaustive review of research into the formal characteristics of schizophrenic speech, see Maher's (1966) textbook chapter on language and thought disorder in schizophrenia.

4. Self-Reference

The egocentric nature of much schizophrenic speech and writing often reflects a preoccupation with unshared subjective relalities. Delusions, especially those of a paranoid nature, are often filled with ideas of reference and the patient's concerns about his or her own safety. On the basis of these clinical observations, researchers have examined the number of personal pronouns in schizophrenic communication to see whether increased self-reference can reliably distinguish the speech and writing of schizophrenics from the communication of normals. In direct contradiction to this hypothesis, the psychoanalytic theory of poor ego structure in the psychoses suggests that there may be a decrease in the number of personal pronouns due to negative or vacuous self-perception.

TABLE I

Results of Fourteen Studies Using Type-Token Ratio, 1944-1981

Study	Subjects	No.	TTR	Context	Sample length	Results
Fairbanks (1944)	Schizophrenics	10	.57	Spoken responses to proverbs	3000	Significantly lower TTR for schizophrenics.
	Freshmen	10	.64		3000 30/100 passages	Only one freshman scored below highest schizophrenic.
Mann (1944)	Schizophrenics	24	.66	Written story of "your life"	2800	Significantly lower TTR for schizophrenics.
	Freshmen	24	.71		2800 28/100 passages	
Baker (1951)	Female schizophrenic	1	.67	Written	40,000 400/100 passages	No control; data consisted of letters written to a newspaper editor.
Lorenz & Cobb (1954)	Paranoid schizophrenics	10	.32	Spontaneous speech in an interview	1000	No significant differences between schizophrenics and other groups.
	Manics	10	.32		1000	
	Obsessive-compulsives	10	.28		1000	
	Hysterics	10	.29		1000	
	Normals	10	.34		1000	
Seth & Beloff (1959)	Schizophrenics	20	.56	Verbal conversation	1000	TTR significantly differentiated TB patients from schizophrenics.
	TB patients	—	.59		1000 10/100 passages	
Feldstein & Jaffe (1962)	Male schizophrenics	30	—	Narratives on five pictures	Mean of an unreported number of 25 word pass.	No significant differences between groups.
	Male patients (medical)	30	—			
Salzinger, Portnoy, & Feldman (1964)	Schizophrenics First 100 words	13	.60	Uninterrupted portions of speech from monologues in interview setting	2/100 word passages	No significant differences between nonpatients and schizophrenics. Rank order correlation between TTR and Cloze scores was not significant.
	Second 100 words		.62			

110

Study	Group	N	TTR	Sample	No. of words	Comments
	Nonpatients First 100 words	12	.61			
	Second 100 words		.67			
Hammer & Salzinger (1964)	Schizophrenics	9	.32	Monologue, speaking on any topic of interest	900	Overall higher TTR for normals in matched pairs. Ethnic background thought to make a difference.
	Normals	7	.34		900	
Critchley (1964)	"Schizophrene"	1	.26	Letters	1241	Anecdotal study—no general conclusions. Note wide variability.
	"Schizophrene"	1	.65		79	
	Aphasic	1	.28		39	
	Aphasic	1	.50		42	
	Aphasic	1	.50		89	
Maher, McKean, & McLaughlin (1966)	TD schizophrenics	30	.71	Written samples obtained from hospital staff	50	No significant differences.
	NTD schizophrenics	23	.74		50	
Replication						
	TD schizophrenics	53	.72		100	No significant differences.
	NTD schizophrenics	27	.74		100	
Pavy, Grinspoon, & Shader (1969)	Acute schizophrenics	9	.69	Diary excerpts "please write about your thoughts"	100	Strong negative correlation between TTR and chronicity. TTR higher in acute than in chronic schizophrenic patients.
	Chronic schizophrenics	6	.48		100	
Hart & Payne (1973)	Paranoid schizophrenics	26	.33	Verbal responses to the question: "How did you happen to come to the hospital?"	500	Disordered thinking, defined as over inclusiveness, was not related to TTR. Analyses comparing populations were not performed.
	Other schizophrenics	14	.32		500	
	Manics	5	.36		500	
	Neurotics	8	.33		500	

(continued)

TABLE 1—Continued

Study	Subjects	No.	TTR	Context	Sample length	Results
	Pathological personality	10	.32		500	TTR and fourth-word Cloze scores were significantly correlated for first and second 100-word sets, and fifth-word Cloze for the second 100-word set.
Silverman (1973)	Depressed	9	.32		500	
	Acute schizophrenics	4	.40	Verbal responses to prompting; topics of speech encouraged were ones relevant to psychological issues	200	
	Chronic schizophrenics	2	.42		200	
	Schizoaffective	2	.52		200	
	Remitted schizophrenics	2	.51		200	
	Endogenous depression	1	.51		200	
	Nonpatients	2	.48		200	
	Anorexia nervosa	1	.46		200	
Manschreck, Maher, & Ader (1981)	I TD schizophrenics	15	.58	Subjects asked to describe Brueghel's "Wedding Feast."	100 Mean TTR across sets.	TD schizophrenics were found to have a significantly lower TTR than NTD schizophrenics. TTR found to negatively correlate with measures of understandability, poverty of content, and disturbed logic as measured by the SADS/RDC system.
	NTD schizophrenics	12	.65		100	
	Affective disorders	12	.65		100 Number not reported.	
	Normal controls	12	.68		100	
	II TD schizophrenics	10	—	Same as Part I	100	Disturbances in voluntary motor movements were found to have a significant negative correlation with TTR.
	NTD schizophrenics	11	—		100	
	Affective disorders	12	—		100	
	Normal controls	12	—		100	

TABLE II
STUDIES USING ADJECTIVE–VERB QUOTIENT, 1940–1966[a]

Study	Context	Adjective–verb quotient
Boder (1940)[b]	Conversational (drama)	11
	Normative (legal statutes)	20
	Narrative (fiction)	35
	Journals (Emerson's)	47
	Descriptive (science)	76
Fairbanks (1944)[c]	Schizophrenics	20
	Freshman	29
Mann (1944)[a]	Schizophrenics	43
	Freshmen	51
Lorenz & Cobb	Manics	60
(1954)[b]	Obsessive–compulsives	60
	Hysterics	69
	Schizophrenics	75
	Normals	94
Mahler, McKean, &	Schizophrenics	
McLaughlin (1966)[b]	reactive	39
	process	31
	Nonschizophrenics	35

[a] From *Principles of Psychopathology: An Experimental Approach* by Brendan A. Maher. Copyright © 1966, Brendan A. Maher. Used with the permission of the McGraw-Hill Book Company.

[b] Written samples.

[c] Spoken samples.

An overview of these results outlined in Table IV reveals scattered and contradictory findings that may reflect variations in subject populations. Also, operationalizing ego strength on the basis of specific verbal output is highly inferential and would require initial verification in relating the construct of ego strength to verbal content.

Recent studies suggest that acute schizophrenics and those actively thought disordered use a higher frequency of personal pronouns. This seems to reflect the findings in broader content studies that suggest a general egocentric perspective and an agitated effort at self-orientation. A lower number of self-referents may exist in chronic and/or thought-disordered subjects. The type and context of the task may also affect the use of personal pronouns.

B. CONTENT ANALYSIS

Blocking, poverty of ideas, incoherence, clouding, delusions, and emotional anomalies are expressed in the language of the patients. However, the abnormality does not lie in the language itself, but rather in its content. . . . Their thoughts are transformed

TABLE III
STUDIES USING GRAMMATICAL ANALYSIS, 1944–1968

Study	Results
Fairbanks (1944)[a]	Significantly fewer nouns, conjunctions, prepositions, adjectives, and articles in schizophrenic speech samples than in normals.
Mann (1944)[b]	Significantly fewer nouns in schizophrenic writing samples than in normals.
Mayers & Mayers (1946)[a]	Omission of articles and pronouns. Confusion of sexes through pronoun switches. Lack of prepositions.
Lorenz & Cobb (1954)[b]	Substantives down for all patients. Paranoids closest to normals in use of modifiers. All patients showed a higher use of verbs. Conjunctions and prepositions lower for all patients. Articles used less frequently by all patients. Psychotics used more conjunctions than did neurotics.
Salzinger, Portnoy, & Feldman (1964)[a]	No significant differences between lexical and functional words used by schizophrenics and matched controls. Slightly more lexical words for schizophrenics than normals over second 100 words. Normals were constant.
Maher, McKean, & McLaughlin (1966)[b]	Normal documents contained more qualifiers per verb than those judged pathological. This result was not significant.
Cheek & Amarel (1968)[a]	Schizophrenic speech contained more content than function words plus pronouns than the speech of alcoholics.

[a] Spoken samples.
[b] Written samples.

into speech without relation to the environment. . . . Speech may also be the only function which remains entirely normal or which may be inhibited or blocked [Bleuler, 1950, p. 147].

1. Content Categories

Distinctive characteristics of the content of schizophrenic communication have been noted since the earliest clinical observations. Delusional content most often seemed to be related to global issues of politics and religion about which the patient had some special insight (see Table V). Perhaps the most obvious clue to the diagnosis of schizophrenia relates to the content of the patients verbiage upon admittance. Talk of God, the Apocalypse, or plots by the Communists are strong predictors for a diagnosis of schizophrenia.

Three of the studies in Table V used the General Inquirer computer program (Stone, Dunphy, Smith, & Ogilvie, 1966) or an adaptation for their content analysis. Each content category is called a "tag," and the program

TABLE IV
STUDIES OF SELF-REFERENCE THEMES, 1940–1979[a]

Study	Results
Balkan & Masserman (1940)	Hysterics used fewer personal pronouns than did anxiety state or obsessive–compulsive patients.
Fairbanks (1944)	Schizophrenics used more first-person singular pronouns than did freshman controls in spoken language.
Mann (1944)	No difference in self-reference frequency between schizophrenics and freshman controls in written language.
White (1949)	Schizophrenics avoided reference to personal themes.
Ellsworth (1951)	Schizophrenics and children used more pronouns (especially "I") than normal adults did.
Lorenz & Cobb (1954)	Hysterics and obsessive–compulsives used "I" more often than did manic, paranoid schizophrenic, and normal adult groups; no differences between these latter three groups.
Maher, McKean, & McLaughlin (1966)	No reliable differences between good-premorbid and poor-premorbid schizophrenics.
Tucker & Rosenberg (1975)	Schizophrenics used 3 times as many personal pronouns as did other patients and 10 times as many as normal subjects.
Rochester & Martin (1979)	In an interview context, all speakers, thought-disordered, non-thought-disordered, and normals, used the same proportion of personal reference. Non-thought-disordered schizophrenics did not differ from normals in the use of personal reference in interview, narrative, or cartoon description, whereas thought-disordered schizophrenics used more personal references than did normals in the context of explaining a cartoon.

[a] Studies from 1940–1966 from *Principles of Psychopathology: An Experimental Approach* by Brendan A. Maher. Copyright © 1966, Brendan A. Maher. Used with the permission of the McGraw-Hill Book Company.

functions such that it "reads" the text with reference to a predesignated set of categories and tabulates their frequency. Those tags that seem to differentiate between schizophrenic and control subjects are reported.

Recent studies using tag systems depict schizophrenic patients as concerned with inadequate intrapsychic and interpersonal orientation in the presence of a good deal of confusion and hostility. This lends depth to the previous content studies that emphasized overvalent universal themes and inappropriate institutional concerns. Tucker and Rosenberg (1975) summarize their findings thus: "In general, the language content of the schizophrenic patient mirrored an almost agitated attempt to locate oneself in time and space and to defend against internal discomfort and confusion [p. 611]."

TABLE V
STUDIES OF THEME TOPICS, 1949–1979

Study	Results
White (1949)	Schizophrenics tended to speak more of universal themes (e.g., science, religion, politics) than did normal subjects.
Maher, McKean, & McLaughlin (1966)[a]	Universal themes were more prevalent in thought-disordered schizophrenics. Non-thought disordered schizophrenics used more personal, domestic, and family themes.
Reilly, Harrow, & Tucker (1973)	Between the first and seventh week after an acute break, schizophrenics decreased in: Overdetailed verbalizations. Vividness of verbalizations. Delusional verbalizations. Overall significant events. Concern with the past. Self-immersion. Unable to follow directions. Unable to follow train of thought. The rating on which schizophrenics increased was concern with future.
Tucker & Rosenberg (1975)[a]	From a factor analytic study, a set of 12 tags were found that were used 3 times more often by schizophrenics than by other patients and 10 times more often than by normals: Other; non-sex-specific pronouns for other. Think; cognitive processes. Overstate; emphatic or exaggerated words. Time reference. Get; obtaining, achieving action. Distress; states of despair, fear, guilt. Move. Peer; status. Avoid; movement away from. Space reference. Attack; destructive, hostile action. Self; pronoun reference to the self.
Rosenberg & Tucker (1979)[a]	Found that general themes related to schizophrenic were: Negativism and hostility (not attack). Somatic concerns; body, parts of the body. Processes of thought and communication. Males tended to show impractical institutional concerns (artistic, academic) but to follow cultural expectations in regards to guidance themes. Females seemed to behave in a semantically masculine manner as measured by guidance themes. Between first and seventh week after hospitalization, the utterances of schizophrenic patients become more like those of other patients.

[a] Used General Inquirer computer program (Stone, Dunphy, Smith, & Ogilvie, 1966).

2. Contextual Associates

The work of Laffal (1960, 1961, 1965, 1979) has been concerned with patterns of interrelationships between the verbal associations of individual patients. His method of contextual associates explores the complex maze of personal and cultural history embodied in an individual's language production.

> Words appearing in proximity with each other in an individual's language are, by this fact, psychologically associated with each other. Words are related also by synonymy or similarity of reference. These two aspects of association, contiguity and similarity . . . have a direct application in the exploration of meaning in the disturbed language of the schizophrenic patient [Laffal, 1965, p. 126].

Through his method of "contiguity and similarity," he has developed a 100-category, 5000-word dictionary of contextual associates. Decisions concerning categorization are based partly on shared meaning and partly on psychological theory. Laffal's assumptions are threefold:

1. For all people, some associations are stronger than others.
2. In the absence of pathology, patients will tend to give associations of the highest general frequency.
3. All people, given a unique set of motivations (i.e., anxiety, high drive state, overvalent ideas, etc.) will give unique responses.

Thus, a patient with unique motivation due to either delusional beliefs or unusual experiences will have a certain consistency to her or his speech that becomes predictable and will change with modifications in symptoms. Laffal has demonstrated that category frequencies change during therapy (1961) and that there is internal consistency in the utterances produced by disturbed individuals (1960, 1965).

The obvious weakness of this method is that it is steeped in theoretical interpretation and subjective judgment concerning the significance and membership of words within the category structure. It also takes a great deal of time and is incompatable with a cross-sectional design, thus, telling us little about schizophrenic language in general. However, besides its contribution as another perspective to therapeutic process, it raises question as to the validity of cross-sectional research with something as complex and varied as schizophrenic language.

3. Social Alienation and Personal Disorganization

Over the last three decades, Gottschalk and his associates (1958; Gottschalk & Gleser, 1964, 1979) have worked extensively on the analysis of verbal content in various populations and disorders. They began with the premise that certain thematic content can be correlated with and predictive of the presence and extent of pathology.

> We have entertained the hypothesis that, perhaps, the degree of personal and social disorganization of an individual can be quantitatively assessed, at any one time, from the frequency of occurance of a cluster of speech habits and themata which have pertinence to the individual's subjective experience [Gottschalk, 1958, p. 141].

Based on psychodynamic notions and clinical experience, a scale was developed that was judged to contain those categories most representative of the schizophrenic syndrome. The original goals were to test for a relationship between the frequency of occurrence of different themata and the degree of isolation, alienation, and disorganization of the patient. The continuing focus of the project was to continue reanalyzing and reweighing items in relation to the empirical evidence collected. Table VI indicates the various content categories and their relative weightings.

TABLE VI

VERBAL ANALYSIS SYSTEM FOR RATING SEVERITY OF SCHIZOPHRENIC DISORGANIZATION
AND SOCIAL ALIENATION[a]

Scores (weights)	Categories and scoring symbols
	I. Interpersonal references (including fauna and flora)
	A. To thoughts, feelings or reported actions of avoidance, leaving, deserting, spurning, not understanding of others
0	1. Self avoiding others
+1	2. Others avoiding self
	B. To unfriendly, hostile, destructive thoughts, feelings, or actions
+1	1. Self unfriendly to others
+1/3	2. Others unfriendly to self
	C. To congenial and constructive thoughts, feelings, or actions
−2	1. Others helping, being friendly toward others
−2	2. Self-helping, being friendly toward others
−2	3. Others helping, being friendly toward self
	D. To others (including fauna, flora, things, and places)
0	1. Bad, dangerous, low value or worth, strange, ill, malfunctioning
−1	2. Intact, satisfied, healthy, well
	II. Intrapersonal references
	A. To disorientation—orientation, past, present, or future. (Do not include all references to time, place, or person, but only those in which it is reasonably clear the subject is trying to orient himself or is expressing disorientation with respect to these. Also, do not score more than one item per clause under this category.)
+2	1. Indicating disorientation for time, place, person, or other distortion of reality
0	2. Indicating orientation in time, place, person
0	3. Indicating attempts to identify time, place, or person without clearly revealing orientation or disorientation

(continued)

TABLE VI—*Continued*

Scores (weights)	Categories and scoring symbols
	B. To self
0	1. a. Physical illness, malfunctioning (references to illness or symptoms due primarily to cellular or tissue damage)
+1	b. Psychological malfunctioning (references to illness or symptoms due primarily to emotions or psychological reactions *not secondary* to cellular or tissue damage)
0	c. Malfunctioning of indeterminate origin (references to illness or symptoms not definitely attributable either to emotions or cellular damage)
−2	2. Getting better
−1	3. Intact, satisfied, healthy, well
+1/2	4. Not being prepared or able to produce, perform, act, not knowing, not sure
+1/2	5. To being controlled, feeling controlled, wanting control, asking for control or permission, being obliged or having to do, think, or experience something
+3	C. Denial of feelings, attitudes, or mental state of the self
	D. To food
0	1. Bad, dangerous, unpleasant, or otherwise negative; interferences or delays in eating; too much and wish to have less; too little and wish to have more
0	2. Good or neutral
	E. To weather
−1	1. Bad, dangerous, unpleasant, or otherwise negative (not sunny, not clear, uncomfortable, etc.)
−1	2. Good, pleasant, or neutral
	F. To sleep
0	1. Bad, dangerous, unpleasant, or otherwise negative; too much; too little
0	2. Good, pleasant, or neutral
	III. Miscellaneous
	A. Signs of disorganization
+1	1. Remarks or words that are not understandable or audible
0	2. Incomplete sentences, clauses, phrases; blocking
+2	3. Obviously erroneous or fallacious remarks or conclusions; illogical or bizarre statements
	B. Repetition of ideas in sequence
0	1. Words separated only by a word (excluding instances due to grammatical and syntactical convention, where words are repeated, e.g., "as far as," "by and by," and so forth. Also, excluding instances where words as "I" and "the" are separated by a word)
+1	2. Phrases, clauses (separated only by a phrase or clause)
+1	IV. A. Questions directed to the inverviewer
+1/2	B. Other references to the interviewer
+1	V. Religious and Biblical references

^a From Gottschalk and Gleser (1964). Used with the permission of the Association for Research in Nervous and Mental Disorders, Inc.

The schizophrenic target group was chronic hospitalized patients. Free speech samples are tape-recorded via a telephone in response to the following instructions:

> While you are here in the hospital and getting treatment, there are certain examinations that I will be doing every week. I'd like to explain one of these. I would like you to pick up this "telephone" and talk into it for three minutes. It doesn't matter what you say; anything that comes to your mind. The important thing is to say everything that comes into your mind. I will tell you when three minutes are up. You probably wonder where this phone goes to. It goes to a dictating machine so that one of our secretaries can type up what you say. In this way we will have a weekly record which will be kept confidential in your hospital chart. Do you have any questions [Gottschalk & Gleser, 1979, p. 187]?

Gottschalk and his associates have run many validation studies with schizophrenics over the last two decades. Their cross-sectional and longitudinal studies seem to show that schizophrenics can be reliably distinguished from other patients (except for brain-damaged patients) based on themes focused around social alienation and personal disorganization and that changes in symptomatology in a patient can be measured by their system of verbal analysis.

4. Discomfort–Relief Quotient

In an attempt to empirically measure the relative degree of subjectively experienced tension or discomfort in a written document, Dollard and Mower (1947) developed the discomfort–relief quotient (DRQ).

> In order to determine the D.R.Q. for any given sample of written material the first step is to read the material and as you do so make a list of all words which indicate discomfort (suffering, tension, pain, unhappiness) and another list of words which indicate relief (comfort, satisfaction, enjoyment) [Dollard & Mowrer, 1949, p. 22].

The actual DRQ is the number of discomfort words divided by the total of discomfort and relief words. On an individual case, Dollard and Mowrer found that DRQ rating correlated with the case worker's impression and the "objective" movement in the case.

Maher, McKean, and McLaughlin (1966), in analyzing written documents, found that:

1. The DRQ of pathological documents was lower than for nonpathological documents.
2. The process group had a lower DRQ than the reactive group.
3. A high DRQ was not necessarily a cue to thought disorder.

C. PREDICTABILITY AND COHESION ANALYSIS

Early measures of readability involved a descriptive analysis of the written sample based on a general notion of complexity. The Flesch method (Flesch, 1951) combined a ratio of words per sentence and one for syllables per word to attain its readability rating. The method of Dale and Chall (1948) also included a count of words as rated by frequency of general usage.

1. The Cloze Procedure

The Cloze procedure was described by its originator Wilson Taylor in the fall 1953 issue of *Journalism Quarterly*. He defined it as:

> A method of intercepting a message from a "transmitter" (writer or speaker), mutilating its language patterns by deleting parts, and so administering it to receivers (readers or listeners) that their attempts to make the patterns whole again potentially yield a considerable number of Cloze units [p. 416].

The Cloze method seemed simple enough—take a continuous sample of speech or writing, delete words (each word is referred to as a Cloze unit) according to some schedule or formula, and give it to raters to be restored. The theory is that readability or the ability to understand a text depends upon a certain amount of redundancy and predictability. The more accurately a rater can fill in the missing words, the more "understandable" the passage. Taylor saw the Cloze method as "a new psychological tool for measuring the effectiveness of communication. The method is straightforward: the data are easily quantifiable; the findings seem to stand up [p. 415]." This seeming simplicity and straightforwardness made the Cloze procedure an attractive laboratory test for psychopathologists. Only after many years of utilization in research with schizophrenic subjects have some of its numerous complexities been recognized.

There is obviously more to readability than the length, kind, and number of words used. Contexts are created and interwoven in communication, so also are affective qualities, properties of redundancy, and transitional probabilities. These elements seem infinite and too complex to analyze given our present knowledge of linguistics and communication. Taylor's hope for the Cloze procedure was that, although it failed to define exactly what it was measuring, it appeared to be: "a measure of the aggregate influences of *all factors* which interact to affect the degree of correspondence between the language patterns of transmitter and receiver [Taylor, 1953, p. 432]."

When examining Cloze data, it becomes immediately obvious that any small portion of the passage does not sample a significant number of different parts of speech, syntactical location in a sentence, and contextual cues. It is easy to find extremely unpredictable sentences with high Cloze scores because of the positioning of the blanks. These problems led Aborn, Rubinstein, and Sterling (1959) to study significant contextual variables involved with controlled deletion. They found that:

1. "The length, distribution, and grammatical structure of context are all independently effective sources of constraint on words in sentences."

2. "The predictability of words belonging to a given class is, in general, inversely related to the size of that class."
3. "Increasing the context beyond 10 words does not increase predictability [p. 179]."

MacGinitie (1961) found that regular omission of every twenty-fourth, twelfth, or sixth word made little difference to predictability but omitting every third word made prediction more difficult. These findings seem to parallel Taylor's position as to adequate sampling when he said: "The answer is that if *enough* words are struck out at random the blanks will come to represent proportionally all kinds of words to the extent that they occur. The matter boils down 'How many are enough?'—a problem to be settled by experiment [Taylor, 1953, p. 419]."

His position seems intuitively correct when dealing with literature or any long, *consistent* written sample. In fact, his initial work confirmed the hypothesis that the longer the passage, the better the Cloze procedure would be able to discriminate between passages by different writers. But does this apply to a study of the predictability of pathological speech, which is often not continuous and seldom consistent? Even after thought disorder and clinical ratings of abnormal speech production are controlled for, this speech is seldom constantly "abnormal." The question remains, how is a sample passage to be chosen?

Taylor found that the Cloze could distinguish between passages of writing from Caldwell, Stein, and Joyce with the same success as did the two other measures of readability (Dale & Chall, 1948; Flesch, 1951). From these data he found that it was a simple step to generalize the value of the procedure to verbal communication that could be either mutilated on tape or transcribed and prepared for written "Clozure." The primary method of research with the Cloze has been to transcribe, mutilate, and rate in writing what were originally oral communications. A fundamental question is whether any conclusions about spoken messages can be made by means of such a procedure.

To this shift in modality, add a shift in the focus of analysis. The previous measures of readability were based on an hypothesis of complexity that was operationalized on the basis of the actual content of the communication. In the Cloze procedure, this focus of analysis shifts from the stimulus materials to their interaction with the rater. Thus, the raters become as significant a part of the analysis as the subjects or the stimulus materials rendering the analysis of the Cloze data as complex as that of its predecessors.

In his early article, Taylor (1953) hinted that there was a correlation between the ability to successfully Cloze a mutilated passage of writing or speech and intelligence as rated on general ability tests. He later (Taylor, 1956) found a .74 correlation between Air Force Qualification Test scores and the ability to successfully rate Cloze passages. This was supported first by Rankin (1959) and later by Amarel, Cheek, and Stierhem (1966), who found a high correlation between scores on the School and College Ability Test and scores in rating speech patterns of schizophrenic and alcoholic subjects. Silverman (1972) found a significant difference between raters using an analysis of variance in both fourth- and fifth-word deletion schedules. Despite these findings, the Cloze procedure continued to gain popularity, with little note taken of the influence of the raters on the data.

Encouraged by the success of the Cloze procedure in distinguishing between real and sham suicide notes (Osgood & Walker, 1959) and between speech emitted by aphasics and normals (Fillenbaum & Jones, 1962), Salzinger, Portnoy, and Feldman (1964) used it in an analysis of the language of schizophrenic patients (see Table VII). Salzinger et al. report finding a positive difference in 12 of 13 matched pairs of schizophrenics and normals (no data are given concerning the raters). They found that the predictability of schizophrenic speech decreased markedly over the second 100 words of a monologue as compared to the first 100, whereas the passages of normals seemed to increase in comprehensibility. One could hypothesize that a context is established by a normal subject over the first 100 words that aids in the prediction of later Cloze units. These contextual cues may not be offered by schizophrenic subjects. It is further hypothesized that the schizophrenic decreases in comprehensibility because he or she is getting further away from the original stimulus and has to depend on his or her own message for reference. Salzinger calls this "response produced stimuli" as opposed to externally produced stimuli, which are most common in conversation. Schizophrenics seem to extinguish more rapidly—that is, the original stimulus exerts influence over the behavior of normals for longer periods of time than for schizophrenics. This is of particular interest in light of the results of Cheek and Amarel (1968), who found that, although they could find no significant differences between the verbal Cloze passages of schizophrenics and alcoholics, the alcoholic passages were predicted with slightly more accuracy after the first 100 words, whereas the speech passages of schizophrenics became more difficult to predict. However, using only acute schizophrenic subjects, Rutter, Draffan, and Davies (1977) found no significant difference in predictability between the first and second 100 words of speech patterns as measured by the Cloze.

Salzinger's productive start provided an exciting lead into using the Cloze with schizophrenic patients.

The fact that the technique differentiates speech samples not only of chronic schizophrenic patients but also—and this is probably more important—of schizophrenics who

TABLE VII

Cloze Analyses, 1964–1980

Study	Subjects	No.	Diagnosis	Raters	No.	Sample length	Deletion	Results
Salzinger, Portnoy, & Feldman (1964)	Acute schizophrenics Chronic schizophrenics Nonpatients	11 2 12	Hospital	College students	—	200 words	Every fifth word	In 12 out of 13 matched pairs, nonpatients were more predictable than schizophrenics. Predictability of normal speech increased over the second 100 words, whereas it decreased markedly for the schizophrenic patients. No significant correlation between Cloze and TTR.
Moroz & Fosmire (1966)	Newly admitted schizophrenics	10	Hospital	Schizophrenic patients Normals	6 6	235–470 words	Every fifth word	Significant variation between passages, but no difference between schizophrenic and normal raters. Modified Cloze procedure where only nouns, pronouns, and adjectives were deleted.
Cheek & Amarel (1968)	Chronic schizophrenics Alcoholics	10 15	Research hospital	College students	279	50 words	Every fifth word	Correct Cloze scores were 7.6 for alcoholics and 7.4 for schizophrenics. No significant difference. Very small speech samples.

124

Reference	Patients	n	Setting	Comparison	n	Text length	Deletion schedule	Findings
Silverman (1972)	TD schizophrenics / Other patients without schizophrenic behavior	7 / 7	Hospital	Nonpatients / Anorexic	3 / 1	200 words	Every fourth and fifth word	Both fourth- and fifth-word deletion schedules distinguished schizophrenics from controls. An important study in the separation of TD and NTD subjects.
Silverman (1973)	TD schizophrenics / Other patients without schizophrenic behavior	8 / 7	Hospital	Nonpatients / Anorexic	3 / 1	200 words	Every fourth and fifth word	Actively schizophrenic patients significantly less predictable than "other" group for both fourth- and fifth-word deletion schedules.
Hart & Payne (1973)	Overinclusive patients / Nonoverinclusive patients	12 / 10	Hospital	College students	20	500 words	Every fifth word	Overinclusive subjects had significantly lower scores in 10 of 12 matched pairs. Overinclusive patients also decreased in predictability between first and last 100-word segments.
Rutter, Wishner, & Callaghan (1975)	Nonparanoid schizophrenics / Medical patients	2 / 2	Hospital	Schizophrenics / Medical patients	12 / 12	200 words	Every fourth and fifth word	Schizophrenics were more difficult to predict, and schizophrenic raters rated less well than medical patients.

(continued)

125

TABLE VII—*Continued*

Study	Subjects	No.	Diagnosis	Raters	No.	Sample length	Deletion	Results
Rutter, Draftan, & Davies (1977)	Acute schizophrenics	25	Hospital	College students	—	2/200 word passages	Every fourth and fifth word	No correlation between predictability and ratings of thought disorder. No differences found between fourth and fifth-word deletion schedules, stress and neutral monologues, or first and second 100-word sections.
Rutter, Wishner, Kopytynska, & Button (1978)	I. Nonparanoid schizophrenics Medical patients	10 10	Hospital	College students	6	203 words	Every fourth and fifth word	With entire test visible to raters, no significant differences between schizophrenics and normals. No difference between first and second 100-word sections.
	II. Nonparanoid schizophrenics Medical patients	10 10	Hospital	College students	20	203 words	Every fourth and fifth word	With some raters not able to see entire document, no significant differences between schizophrenics and medical patients, between fourth- and fifth-word deletion schedules, and between raters seeing and those not seeing the entire document.

126

Study	Subjects	N	Diagnosis	Sample	N	Passages	Deletion	Results
Manschreck, Maher, Rucklos, & White (1979)	TD schizophrenics NTD schizophrenics Normal controls	5 5 8	SADS/RDC	2/male 3/female	5	—	Every fourth and fifth word	TD speech found to be significantly less predictable than NTD and normal speech in fifth-word but not fourth-word deletion.
Manschreck, Maher, & Rucklos (1980)	TD schizophrenics NTD schizophrenics Normal controls	5 5 8	SADS/RDC	2 male 3/female	5	—	Every fourth and fifth word	No significant differences between schizophrenics and normals using written materials.
Spring, Briggs, Cozolino, & Manuzza (1982)	Schizophrenics Major depressive disorders Siblings of schizophrenics Normal controls	18 13 13 19	SADS/RDC PSE	College students	18	2/100 word passages	Every fifth word	Schizophrenic subjects found to be the most predictable of the four groups for the neutral monologue but the least for the stress monologue. Schizophrenics decreased in predictability under stress, whereas all other groups became more predictable. Siblings of patients were less predictable than normal controls.

do not have the obvious symptoms by which almost anybody can recognize a chronic patient. We will most likely investigate the usefulness of the C score as a prognostic and diagnostic index, since it provides a great deal of information on the basis of a very short speech sample [Salzinger *et al.*, 1964, p. 858].

Amarel and Cheek (1965) and Honigfeld (1963) showed the effects of psychomimetic drugs on language predictability using the Cloze procedure. Silverman (1972) was the first to make some important methodological advances. First, he reported the range and average age of his raters, noting that there were four in all—three normal and one outpatient with anorexia nervosa. While these are not all of the important demographics, the inclusion of a description of the raters suggests concern with the nature of the raters' impact on data collected in this study. Silverman divided his subjects into two categories: those who were actively schizophrenic (showing obvious schizophrenic symptomatology, with some degree of thought disorder) and others who showed no schizophrenic symptomatology at the time of the experiment. While he does not report his criteria for these two categories, his results show a highly significant difference for both groups using fourth- and fifth-word deletion schedules. The validity of this distinction is supported by Hart and Payne (1973), who found a difference between "overinclusive" and "nonoverinclusive" schizophrenics.

Rutter *et al.* (1975) found that schizophrenic speech was less predictable than normal speech, using two nonparanoid schizophrenics and two hospitalized controls. Rutter, Wishner, Kopytynska, and Button (1978) increased their sample size to 10 schizophrenics and 10 controls but failed to replicate their previously positive findings. A major problem with this study, as with most other studies until this point, is the absence of an adequate set of diagnostic criteria for schizophrenia. In both studies, Rutter and his colleagues used intake diagnoses from hospital records to identify schizophrenic subjects, a method subject to a multitude of confounding variables. Rutter and his colleagues lamented these inconsistent findings and postulated that, "despite the discrepancies in the existing literature, future research may yet identify some group of schizophrenic patients who do reliably produce speech which is less predictable than normal speech [Rutter *et al.*, 1968, p. 231]."

In what seemed like an answer to this prediction, Manschreck, Maher, Rucklos, and White (1979) used consistent diagnostic criteria as outlined by the Research Diagnostic Criteria (RDC) (Spitzer, Endicott, & Robins, 1975) and divided schizophrenic subjects into thought-disordered (TD) and non-thought-disordered groups (NTD). While thought-disordered speakers were significantly different from non-thought-disordered and normal speakers, Manschreck *et al.* found no difference in the predictability of speech from non-thought-disordered schizophrenics and normal controls.

Taking a positive stance toward the use of the Cloze procedure, Manschreck and his associates point to the lack of methodological rigor as a cause of previously conflicting results. They emphasize the transitory nature of schizophrenic symtomatology and the erroneous assumption that "the diagnosis of schizophrenia implies the presence of disordered speech [p. 599]."

In their 1980 study, Manschreck, Maher, and Rucklos found no significant differences between schizophrenic and control subjects when using the Cloze procedure on written samples gathered using the same stimulus materials as in their previous study of verbal output. This suggests a greater discrimination between the speech of normals and thought-disordered patients, not readily discernable in their written productions.

Recent findings by Spring, Briggs, Cozolino, and Manuzza (Note 1) indicate that under stress conditions (having subjects speak about how it was they came to be in the hospital) the speech of schizophrenic patients is less predictable than that of normals. Under neutral conditions, however, schizophrenic speech was more predictable than the passages obtained from normal subjects. The authors offer these findings as a possible reason for the conflicting results of past research that used a variety of eliciting stimuli for verbal responses. In pursuing the data gathered thus far using the Cloze procedure with schizophrenic patients, Manschreck and his associates cite four main points of methodological weakness:

1. The lack of rigorous and explicit criteria for the diagnosis of schizophrenia.
2. A mistaken assumption that schizophrenics exhibit relevant symptom disturbance (e.g., disordered thought) every waking hour of the day.
3. The lack of standardized techniques for using the Cloze procedure.
4. The lack of data regarding the sensitivity of the Cloze procedure to various modes of language response.

Utilization of the Cloze procedure has pointed to a dearth of information regarding normal communication and the primitive nature of the methodological controls in selecting subject groups. This research also emphasizes that there is no simple way to operationalize theories concerning the role of a theorized cognitive deficit specific to schizophrenia in general language and communication. While the value of the actual data is often questionable, many positive insights have been gained in the process of data collection. The progress and development of the Cloze procedure has exemplified the evolution of an interactive notion of communication and has illustrated a multitude of parameters that need to be addressed in future studies.

2. Paragraph Reconstruction

The conflicting findings in experiments using the Cloze procedure done by Rutter and his associates (1975, 1977, & 1978) led them to postulate that the unpredictability of schizophrenic speech was to be found at the level of intersentence construction rather than in individual words (Rutter, 1979). Taking the same continuous speech samples obtained in their Cloze study from 1978, where no significant differences were found using the Cloze procedure, Rutter had them punctuated by a "graduate" and arranged by sentences on separate cards. Five judges attempted to rearrange these sentences into the order in which they had been originally spoken. The two hypotheses were:

1. The passages of schizophrenics would be reconstructed with less accuracy than normal passages.
2. The differences between the two groups would be most pronounced as the number of sentences increased.

The results showed that, while there was no significant difference between groups for the two sentence strings, a significantly greater number of three-sentence strings were reconstructed from the normal group than from the schizophrenic group.

> If the findings are confirmed we shall have good evidence that there is a detectable abnormality in schizophrenic speech which affects its comprehensibility but that it stems from the relationship between sentences rather than the content of the individual sentence [Rutter, 1979, p. 359].

While these are hopeful findings, this study suffers from the same methodological difficulties as does research with the Cloze procedure. No account was taken for the rater's input or the confounding effect of the transcriber's subjective judgment on sentence division. The continuing problems associated with the use of written stimulus materials from verbal productions were ignored and the diagnostic criteria were inadequate.

3. Cohesion Analysis

In their book *Crazy Talk* (1979), Rochester and Martin apply Halliday and Hasan's (1976) method of cohesion analysis to samples of schizophrenic and normal speech. They summarize their goals to be to "build a model of language use and not formal structures or machine processes or philosophical theories about speech acts [p. 49]." In general, *cohesion* is a term used to refer to the semantic bonding between the different elements of a text that make it a unit. There are many benefits in using this sort of analysis over paragraph reconstruction; the primary advantages are:

1. An analysis of schizophrenic language is tied to a more sophisticated linguistic theory.
2. Paragraph construction reveals how the rater's "restring" yields no information concerning the type of anomaly present.
3. Cohesion analysis has established rules for rating that minimize the confounding effect produced by the rater's subjective input.

Cohesion categories and examples are presented in Table VIII.

TABLE VIII
CATEGORIES OF COHESION[a]

Category	Subcategory	Examples[b]
Reference	1. Pronominal:	*We met Joy Adamson and had dinner with HER in Nairobi.*
	2. Demonstrative:	*We went to a **hostel** and oh THAT was a dreadful place.*
	3. Comparative:	*Six **guys** approach me. The LAST guy pulled a knife on me in the park.*
Substition	1. Nominal:	*The oldest **girl** is 25 and the next ONE'S 22.*
	2. Verbal:	*Eastern people **take it seriously**, at least some of them DO.*
	3. Clausal:	*I'm **making it worse for myself**. I would think SO.*
Ellipsis	1. Nominal:	*He's got **energy** too. He's got a lot more ∅ than I do.*
	2. Verbal:	*I could **go to university** all my life, ∅ keep going to school.*
	3. Clausal:	*Have you ever **been to Israel?**—No, my brother has ∅ .[c]*
Conjunction	1. Additive:	*I read a book in the past few days AND I like it.*
	2. Adversative:	*They started out to England BUT got captured on the way.*
	3. Causal:	*It was a beautiful tree SO I left it alone.*
	4. Temporal:	*My mother was in Ireland. THEN she came over here.*
	5. Continuative:	*What kind of degree?—WELL, in one of the professions.*
Lexical	1. Same root:	*Mother needed **independence**. She was always DEPENDENT on my father.*
	2. Synonym:	*I got **angry** at M. but I don't often GET MAD.[c]*
	3. Superordinate:	*I love catching **fish**. I caught a BASS last time.*
	4. General item:	*The **plane** hit some air pockets and the BLOODY THING went up and down.*

[a] Adapted from Halliday and Hasan (1976). Reprinted from Rochester and Martin (1979).
[b] The PRESUMING ITEM *is set in italic caps; the **referent** is set in bold italic.*
[c] Constructed example.

Rochester and Martin analyzed free speech samples taken from interviews and speech samples obtained from a narrative task (subjects were asked to paraphrase a short story). Their subjects were 20 schizophrenic patients (diagnosed according to the criteria outlined by the New Haven Schizophrenia Index, Astrachan, Harrow, Adler, Brauer, Schwartz, Schwartz, & Tucker, 1972) and 10 normal controls. Half of the schizophrenic subjects were judged to the thought disordered using Cancro's Index of Formal Signs of Thought-Disorder (Cancro & Sugarman, 1969). The data obtained from these subjects comprise a subset of the data from a previous paper (Rochester, Thurston, & Rupp, 1977) that examined hesitation patterns (discussed later). The initial hypotheses of this study were:

1. Schizophrenics will use less cohesive ties.
2. Different ties will be used across groups.
3. Thought-disordered subjects will use more lexical ties.

The results are outlined in Table IX.

Analyses revealed that all schizophrenic speakers produced shorter clauses and used fewer cohesive ties than did normal subjects in the interview task. The use of lexical (lexis column in Table IX) cohesive linkages were found to be significantly greater for thought-disordered schizophrenics than for normals and non-thought-disordered schizophrenics. While this was not true for all thought-disordered subjects, it was peculiar to the thought-disordered group.

> This means, roughly, that schizophrenic speakers are more likely to focus on lexical meanings in their discourse than on the meaning of whole clauses or the way in which clauses are related. And it indicates that schizophrenic listeners are more likely to be biased by the "strong" or "preferred" meaning of a word than the meaning of a word in its sentence or discourse context. In addition, there is a suggestion that schizophrenic speakers and listeners are more likely than normals to attend to the sound character of an individual word [Rochester & Martin, 1979, p. 91].

These results also indicate that speakers rely more on cohesive ties while narrating than while talking freely in an interview setting. These findings also suggest that schizophrenics respond to the demand characteristics of these varying contexts in generally the same way as normal subjects. These results mirror findings obtained by Fairbanks (1944) and Mann (1944) that suggest that the types of grammatical and lexical changes that occur in normal speech from spoken to written productions also hold for schizophrenic patients.

4. Reference and Phoricity

"The phoricity systems are those systems in English which structure utterances on the basis of what speakers assume their listeners know [Rochester & Martin, 1979, p. 103]." Developed by Martin (1978), the reference

TABLE IX
DISTRIBUTION OF COHESIVE TIES[a]

	Narrative			
	Percentage of ties per category			
Group	Reference	Conjunction	Lexis	Ellipsis
Thought disordered	52.0	21.7	24.9	0.7
Non-thought disordered	49.9	24.1	22.8	3.2
Normal	46.5	21.1	30.3	2.0
Mean	49.5	22.3	26.0	2.0
	Interview			
Thought disordered	28.6	20.2	45.8[b]	4.0
Non-thought disordered	33.8	25.9	31.3	8.1
Normal	29.9	28.1	36.0	5.8
Mean	30.8	24.8	37.8	6.0

ANOVA

		Groups	Contexts	Groups × Contexts
	df	2,27	2,54	4,57
Reference	F	1	60**	<1
	w^2	0	.47	0
Conjunction	F	<1	<1	<1
Lexis	F	3.79*	17.5**	2.8
	w^2	.07	.20	0
Ellipsis	F	1.98	5.3	<1
	w^2	0	.06	0

[a] From Rochester and Martin (1979).
[b] One-way ANOVA yields $F(2,27) = .3.83$; f < .05; Scheffé tests indicate NTD ⊕ TD.
* $p < .05$.
** $p < .001$.

system (part of the broader category of phoricity) is a system for mapping the directions given by a speaker to a listener as to how to go about understanding what is being said. Basically, a phoric group says "to understand me look elsewhere," whereas a nonphoric group does not assume information from elsewhere in the text (see Fig. 1). Both phoric and nonphoric groups can be further divided into subclasses that define their roles in the communication (see Table X).

The method was to take the same speech samples used in the cohesion study and divide them into nominal groups. From this point each was categorized as phoric or nonphoric and then further subdivided into the various levels of reference. In the area of general reference, Rochester and

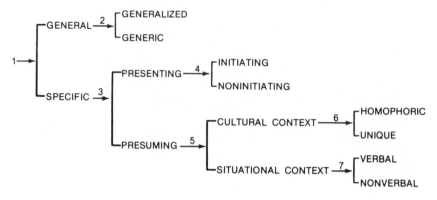

FIG. 1   Reference network. (From Rochester & Martin, 1979.)

TABLE X

REFERENCE CATEGORIES AND THEIR INSTRUCTIONS TO THE LISTENER[a]

Category	Instruction	Examples
Nonphoric nominal groups		
General reference	"You don't need to know my particular identity."	(a) *You* say a prayer and *you* cut the egg-bread.
		(b) There's a lot of information about *drugs* in the school.
Specific reference	"My identity is important."	
PRESENTING nominal groups	"To understand me, stay here."	(a) The lift consisted of *a cable* coming down.
		(b) *Some of my friends* stopped in for tea.
Phoric nominal groups		
PRESUMING nominal groups	"To understand me, search elsewhere."	
Cultural context		(a) *The full moon* always makes me romantic.[b]
		(b) *Pierre Elliot Trudeau* wants to stay out of Canadian bedrooms.
Situational context		(a) Mary slapped Sam. I hope *she* doesn't hit *him* again.[b]
		(b) *This*[c] is simply outrageous!

[a] From Rochester and Martin (1979).

[b] Constructed example.

[c] This example assumes that "this" is exophoric to the situation.

Martin found that, in the context of an interview, thought-disordered speakers seem to rely on the use of simple generic items, whereas non-thought-disordered speakers did not. Thus, it seems that non-thought-disordered speakers are appropriately specific to the given context, whereas thought-disordered speakers are more apt to use general categories during descriptions. In the narrative context, thought-disordered speakers were the only subjects to introduce new generics into their retelling of the original text. All normal speakers and most non-thought-disordered speakers used only those generic items that were given.

In a cartoon task (subjects were asked to describe the contents of pictures and to explain why they were supposed to be funny), the texts given by non-thought-disordered speakers were lacking in descriptive detail, but they introduced participants in much the same way as did normal speakers. Thought-disordered speakers, however, were distinguishable from other subjects in a few important ways. First, it appeared that they failed to distinguish between characters of major and minor importance and that they relied less than normals on items that initiated chains of reference. More importantly, while both thought-disordered speakers and normals depended on a large number of implicit references, the referents of the thought-disordered speakers were less frequently accessible to the listener than the referents of the normal speakers. Between 33% and 50% of the implicit references of the thought-disordered speakers were obscure to the listener in this study. Using demonstratives and pronouns, thought-disordered speakers will "point" with their words but do not include the specific item that would clarify their communications.

5. Stratal Slips

On the basis of their research on cohesion, phoricity, and hesitations, Rochester and Martin (1979) have outlined a general theory regarding schizophrenic language, which they refer to as *stratal slips*. This theory presumes that, from normal to thought-disordered speakers, there exists a continuum in the ability to successfully use the various components of language during communication. Furthermore, it states that the speech of individuals under stress will begin to fail in certain predictable patterns. Finally, it is claimed that, as a person loses control over language processing, "he or she begins to fail in certain orderly ways to produce coherent discourse [p. 177]."

The first level of language breakdown is expected to be related to a lack of cohesion between sentences and clauses: This would be experienced by the listener as rambling or a lack of topic direction. Speakers at this level might also fail to distinguish between major and minor characters when describing a story or be unable to establish clear lines between events. At the second level, which includes the first, speakers would also exhibit syntactical breakdown, improper use of words, and the more indicative signs of schizophrenic language, such as neologisms and clang associations. The third and final level is presumed to be a complete linguistic breakdown "signaled by the speaker's inability to match intonation patterns or select rhyming words when asked [p. 178]."

Despite its title, *Crazy Talk* is as sophisticated a study of schizophrenic language as is offered in the literature. Rochester and Martin's methodological rigor in group selection, testing, and analysis can serve as a model for future studies, not only in the analysis of language, but in other areas of schizophrenic cognition, communication, and interaction. Their methods afford an empirical window to examine such theories of thought-disordered language as broken associative threads, overinclusion, and loss of major set that have, until recently, been the domain of clinical intuition. Their work is consistent with recent findings concerning the value of separating thought-disordered from non-thought-disordered speakers and of using well-defined diagnostic criteria determined by the researchers rather than relying on a hospital diagnosis.

Most importantly, cohesion analysis has a high explanatory power because of its development in the context of "normal" language study. The high reliability of its scoring system and its freedom from the multiplicity of problems encountered by using raters and broad inferential leaps (as seen in the Cloze and paragraph reconstruction tasks) also adds to its impressiveness.

Finally, cohesion analysis is a system based on a view of language as an interactive communication; it seems to tap the three-dimensional nature of verbal intercourse. If we are diagnosing schizophrenia on the basis of samples of interpersonal interactions, then this is the level at which we need to understand schizophrenic language production. A systematic understanding of language breakdown may aid in determining not only diagnosis but severity of symptoms.

III. Analysis Based on Motor Features

Thus far, we have reviewed research that has used the written or transcribed word as data. Analyses of grammatical types, word meanings, and predictability all focus on the content, not the process of written and verbal communication. Spoken language, however, is a temporal, sequential process that allows us other means of analysis, such as rate of speech, the ratio of pause to speech time, and hesitations. Spoken language is not identical to thought; it needs to be viscerally enacted utilizing the organs of respiration and ingestion as well as the vocal chords, larynx, and pharynx. Speech represents the coodination of a variety of cognitive and motor functions, many of which are possible points of disruption to the physiological and psychological abnormalities of the schizophrenias. When measured in relation to the various grammatical components within a sentence, a temporal analysis can also yield suggestions concerning abnormalities in information processing.

A. RATE OF SPEECH

Due to the diversity of symptomatology among the various schizophrenic syndromes and lack of diagnostic rigor, results from studies of simple rates of speech depend largely on the experimenter's particular definition of schizophrenia or her or his available subject population. From Seth and Beloff (1959): "In general, our group consisted of ten male and ten female schizophrenics selected on the basis of psychiatric diagnosis. . . . No further breakdown into subtypes of schizophrenia was made [p. 228]."

No doubt the prototypical back ward schizophrenic will speak more slowly than a normal control or the average adolescent schizophrenic. The speech of a paranoid will differ from that of a catatonic. In light of the numerous variables effecting rate of speech (e.g., transitory mood, subject matter, experimental context), it is not surprising that the findings of such studies should be random and contradictory. Thus, while Seth and Beloff (1959) found significant differences in rate of speech between schizophrenics and controls, Weintraub and Aronson (1965) and Hart and Payne (1973) found no significant differences between schizophrenics, other psychiatric patients, and neurotics.

As just stated, Hart and Payne (1973) found no difference in rate of speech when comparing free speech samples from 40 schizophrenic patients with those from a variety of patients with other diagnoses. Verbal samples were collected on tape in response to the question of how they happened to come to the hospital. They did, however, find strong negative correlations between speech rate and ratings of symptoms associated with motor activity ($r = -.51$), speed of thought ($r = -.43$), drive ($r = -.38$), elevation–depression of feelings ($r = -.28$), and grandiose–depreciative delusions ($r = -.24$). It was also found that high initial speech rate was correlated with improvement in the categories of drive ($r = .34$), speech activity ($r = .33$), and depreciative delusions ($r = .27$). Thus, speech rate may be a quantifiable correlate of internal processes and a prognostic indicator associated with thought, affect, and motivation, suggesting that objective measures of speech may be found to be of assistance in decisions of diagnosis and treatment. It is conceivable that rate of speech may be one of many variables involved in an equation for differential diagnosis between schizophrenia and the affective disorders as well as among the subcategories of schizophrenia.

B. PAUSE TO SPEECH RATIO

Goldman-Eisler (1968), in her studies of normal speech, found that the ratio of pauses to speech time increases with the cognitive complexity of the verbal materials. Silverman (1973) analyzed free speech samples of patients (some of whom were actively symptomatic, while others were not) and normals. He calculated "pause time" by dividing the sum of the length of pauses greater than .25 sec by the total time involved in vocalization. His assumption was that a lower pause to speech ratio would be related to lower cognitive complexity of the verbal production and a more severe level of disturbance. The naive nature of this assumption is reflected in data that suggest, on the basis of their higher pause to speech ratios, that chronic schizophrenics deal with issues of more cognitive complexity than do nonpatients. Weintraub and Aronson (1965) defined a pause–speech ratio as the total number of words divided by the number of nonsilent minutes to the nearest 15 sec and found no significant differences between a mostly schizophrenic delusional group of patients and a group of controls.

A lack of awareness of the multitude of variables in language study is reflected here and led Silverman (1973) to conclude: "Perhaps the most important finding to emerge from the present study is the rarity of careful psycholinguistic analyses of schizophrenic speech and that methodology in this field is still open to refinement [p. 413]."

Clearly, speech production is dependent upon factors of social learning, intelligence, characterological, and personality variables as well as transitory moods, situational factors, and symptomatology. Chronic schizophrenics pause longer than normals for a completely different set of reasons than would a great scientist pondering the secrets of the universe. Still, pause to speech ratio, when tested in more controlled situations, may yield clues of the nature of information-processing differences between schizophrenics and normals.

C. HESITATIONS

In the course of her extensive research on spontaneous speech in normal populations, Goldman-Eisler (1968) found that duration of pauses in speech were highly variable across subjects. She also found that the length of hesitations changed as a function of the pressure of social interaction, spontaneity, and (as mentioned earlier) the complexity of the verbal task. She divided pauses in speech into two main categories:

1. Grammatical—pauses representing natural punctuation points, such as at the end of a sentence, between clauses, after an interrogative, or when parenthetical references are made.
2. Nongrammatical—pauses in the middle of phrases or clauses or a disruption due to a false start where the speaker stops midsentence and begins anew.

Applying this framework to the investigation of schizophrenic speech, grammatical and nongrammatical pauses may have differing diagnostic implications as well as offer insight into the nature of attentional dysfunction in schizophrenia. The research of Rochester and her colleagues (1977) seems to point toward the fact that the incoherence in schizophrenic speech is not created by inadequate lexical or syntactic components within clauses but rather by ties between propositions. While schizophrenics seem to be able to string words together to form clauses, they seem less able to string clauses together to form sentences or paragraphs that are accessible to the listener.

Based on the notion that between- and within-clause hesitations could offer some clues concerning verbal processing, Rochester et al. quantified hesitations in the verbal production of 10 schizophrenics with thought disorder, 10 schizophrenics without thought disorder, and 10 normal controls. Diagnosis was done by two clinicians, and all schizophrenics met the New Haven criteria (Astrachan et al., 1972). The 10 thought-disordered patients were diagnosed using the Cancro Index of Formal Signs of Thought Disorder (Cancro & Sugarman, 1969).

A clausal unit was defined as any combination of a noun–verb phrase. The data came from (a) 3-min speech sections of uninterrupted monologue during a half-hour interview; and (b) descriptions of a series of 10 cartoons. The dependent measures were:

Latency: for the cartoon task only—the time between the end of the question and the subject's initiating a response.
Pauses: silent pauses longer than 250 msec.
Initial pauses: pauses preceding or following the first word of a clausal unit.
Within pause: pauses occuring at any location.
Hesitations: Filled pauses   1. (*a*ah) - (e*rr*) - (*m*mm)
                                       2. exact word and phrase repetitions
                                       3. stutters
                                       4. word connections
                                       5. tongue slips

While the general trends pointed toward slower processing (i.e., longer hesitations for schizophrenics than for normals), only initial silent pauses tended to differentiate thought-disordered speakers from non-thought-disordered schizophrenics and normals. A relative hesitancy rate was computed, which took rate of speech into account; the results were the same. The data point toward an attentional explanation for disordered language as opposed to a specific linguistic dysfunction. Rochester *et al.* hypothesize that, during these long initial pauses, subjects may either (*a*) efficiently plan ahead; (*b*) be distracted from the production of the subsequent clause; or (*c*) still be occupied with the clause just uttered. Thought-disordered speakers are thought to be either perseverating on past content or distracted from the communication task by unfilterable internal or external stimuli. Research into the cognitive processes during interclausal pauses may offer supportive evidence for one or more of the many theories of information-processing deficiencies thought to be operating in thought-disordered patients.

D. Voluntary Motor Movement and Language

A study by Manschreck, Maher, Rucklos, Vereen, and Ader (1981) indicates a relationship between voluntary motor movement, as measured by the accuracy of synchronization in a finger tapping task, and verbal impairment, as measured by the type–token ratio (described earlier). Schizophrenic subjects are distinguished from normal and affective controls at a tapping rate of 80 beats per minute but are statistically indistinguishable from these two groups at either lower or higher rates. This is thought to rule out factors related to dexterity, drugs, or motivation. It is reasoned that, at 80 beats per minute, the normal and affective control subjects could benefit from the redundancy of the auditory information, whereas the schizophrenic subjects were unable to do so.

A subsequent investigation (Manschreck, Maher, & Ader, 1981) found a highly significant correlation between type–token ratio and ratings of disturbed motor movements as measured by the Abnormal Involuntary Movement Scale (AIMS) (National Institute of Mental Health, 1974) and the Targeting of Abnormal Kinetic Effects (TAKE) (Wojcik, Gelenberg, La Brie, & Mieske, 1980). Ratings of disturbed motor movements were also significantly correlated with poverty of content, impaired understandability, and disturbed logic as rated by the Schedule of Affective Disorders and Schizophrenia (SADS).

Maher (1972) suggests a parallel process for both speech and motor impairment, which he refers to as "associate intrusions and attentional deficit." Stated briefly, attentional deficits "affect the processing of sensory input" as well as the "failure to inhibit associations from intruding into language [p. 12].'' Thus, in both speech and motor movement, the schizophrenic patient suffers from a deficiency in discerning the nature and relevance of both internal and environmental input. This common attentional deficit is thought to be causally related to both language production and motor movement, thus accounting for the correlation between performance on language and motor tasks. One can further speculate as to the importance of internal dialogue in concentrating on a motor task as well as the need for proper motor coordination for speaking and writing. Thus, interrelationships may exist that would offer interesting new insights into the interdependence of cognitive and visceral processes. It can be hoped that changes in modifiable aspects of language behavior can generalize to other types of behavior, such as motor movement. Looked at another way, if behavioral therapy directed at physical movement can help focus a schizophrenic's attention, perhaps there would be a generalizing effect that would reach language production. This is, of course, very speculative and will only be approachable with an increase in our knowledge about language and the interconnection of perception and attention across various behaviors. Manschreck, Maher, & Ader (1981) call for further research in the central role of attention in motor and language dysfunction in schizophrenia.

IV. Discussion

The function of a science in its earliest stages is to define the limits and dimensions of a problem through extensive observation and exploratory research. As an area of study develops, specialization focuses on certain issues that reflect findings back to their broader context. It is hoped that these specialized areas remain true to the diversity and complexity of the original problem, modifying original insights with new, more detailed information.

In reviewing the history of language study with schizophrenic patients, it is clear that the numerous distinctions made by Kraepelin and Bleuler regarding the diversity and multidimensional nature of the various symptoms present in the schizophrenic syndrome were all but forgotten throughout most of the research. To speak of schizophrenic language production without identifying (a) the type of schizophrenia; (b) the current symptom picture when interviewed; or (c) the presence or absence of language abnormalities is to ignore much of the original observations on which the diagnostic groups were based.

Beyond this serious blind spot, the mix of clinical and experimental psychology led to many inappropriate assumptions concerning the nature of verbal behavior (see Rochester & Martin, 1979, for a history of this hybridization and its detrimental consequences for the study of schizophrenic language). In an attempt to operationalize language theories and test them in the laboratory, language was taken from its primary context of conversation and written communication and was viewed as behavior that could be simply quantified in experimental tasks designed to evoke specific types of responses. Furthermore, the study of abnormal or schizophrenic language has been hampered by our limited understanding of normal language.

A. METHODOLOGICAL PROBLEMS

In dementia praecox, where as a matter of fact countless normal associations still exist, we must expect that until we get to know the very delicate processes which are really specific to the disease the laws of the normal psyche will long continue to play their part. To the great detriment of psychopathology, where the only thing we are beginning to argue about is the ambiguity of our applied concepts, our knowledge of the normal psyche is unfortunately still on a very primitive level [Jung, 1960, p. 7].

Any model of communication must account for the social and interactive nature of language. The effects of context, interpersonal dynamics, and the subject's motivations, expectations, and apprehensions concerning the task must all be considered when examining communication patterns. Thus, the lack of naturalistic research with adequate controls has been a major difficulty in the study of schizophrenic language. Data collected in experimental situations, especially those involving the performance of a task, will vary as a function of the demand characteristics of the task and information-processing capacities utilized by the subject.

Because of the complexity of language and our limited knowledge concerning its development and maintenance, the choice of a proper control group is quite difficult. Studies have shown that such factors as age, intelligence, education, ethnic background, length of hospitalization, and medication levels can all affect a person's ability to understand and communicate. There are, no doubt, a multitude of relevant factors that should be controlled that have not yet been identified. Given our small sample sizes and the complexity of the data, any variables that can be controlled should be fully accounted for. Increased sample size from the usual 10–20 per study would also be valuable where feasible.

Several studies suggest that the nature of verbal production, especially that of schizophrenic patients, changes during the course of monologues, conversations, and interviews (Laffal, 1961; Salzinger et al., 1964). The size of the language sample must therefore be considered as an important variable in a design.

Subjects used in studies of schizophrenic language go through a variety of implicit screening criteria before they reach the point of participating in a language study. The research setting often determines such factors as level of chronicity, socioeconomic status, and educational level. Those who are actually eligible to participate are further screened for motivation, volunteerism, verbal fluency, the ability to follow directions, and so forth. Furthermore, patient groups are selected on the basis of a particular set of diagnostic criteria and the researcher's own orientation toward diagnosis. Thus, the varying selection processes of groups of subjects tend to thwart generalizability to other subclasses of schizophrenic patients, and this brings into question the adequacy and appropriateness of the applied statistical models (which often assume random selection and assignment). While at another level, cross-study comparisons are made difficult as a result of differing research settings and orientations.

Kraepelin and Bleuler, when they first attempted to categorize the disorders, were well aware of the vast number of ways in which schizophrenia could become manifest. Kraepelin described 10 categories of dementia praecox and included comments on the language and thought abnormalities for each (see Table XI).

TABLE XI
KRAEPELIN'S DIAGNOSTIC CATEGORIES OF SCHIZOPHRENIA,
WITH COMMENTS ON LANGUAGE AND THOUGHT

Dementia praecox simplex	Poverty of thought, weakness of judgment, incoherence in the train of ideas.
Silly dementia praecox, hebephrenia	The mode of speech is frequently manneristic, unctuous, didactic, sometimes noisy, or purposely obscene. The substance of conversation is often unintelligible, or there is nothing in it.
Simple depressive dementia praecox (stupor)	Train of thought changes abruptly at times and is easily diverted.
Delusional depressive dementia praecox	Confused, easily distracted perception, orientation and external perception confused.
Circular dementia praecox	Talkative, mixes up different languages, speaks nonsense, verbigerates, lets go in silly plays on words and scraps of doggeral.
Periodic dementia praecox	Marked psychic decline, weak mindedness, poverty of thought, lack of judgment.
Catatonia	Endless, repetitive verbiage.
Paranoid dementia praecox gravis	Speech incoherent and odd, driveling, verbosity, a tendency toward sounding phrases, quotations, silly plays on words, and neologisms.
Paranoid dementia praecox mitis	Odd expressions, frequently affected.
Confusional speech dementia praecox (schizophasia)	Language confusion, with thought intact.

Considering the diversity of these clinical symptoms and their varying impact on language production, it is surprising to note that, more than 50 years later, many experimental studies concerning schizophrenic language simply describe their subject population as "20 schizophrenics." It is difficult to discern why the original insights into the complexity of the disorder have continued to be glossed over, making schizophrenia appear to be a monolithic medical certainty. Research in this area needs to emphasize more stringent criteria relating to issues of diagnosis and the presence of thought disorder than have been previously applied. The process–reactive distinction that emerged during the 1960s was an important step forward in this respect. The more recent use of the SADS (Schedule of Affective Disorders and Schizophrenia) interview and the RDC (Research Diagnostic Criteria) for diagnosis have assisted in the creation of more homogeneous subject groups based on presenting symptomatology.

The renewed appreciation of the complexity of the schizophrenic syndrome has been accompanied by a renewed understanding that schizophrenia and thought disorder are not synonymous. Symptoms of thought disorder appear in over 20 different diseases, and the vast majority of schizophrenics are not exhibiting a thought disorder at any given moment. Some researchers (Manschreck et al., 1979, 1980, Manschreck, Maher, & Ader, 1981; Manschreck, Maher, Rucklos, Vereen, & Ader, 1981; Rochester & Martin, 1979) have divided their subject populations into thought-disordered and non-thought-disordered groups with positive discriminatory results. When we speak of schizophrenic language, it should be understood that we are describing a subpopulation of those individuals diagnosed as schizophrenic and that this subsample varies in the degree of overt symptomatology across individuals and over time.

Symptom changes occur as a patient goes into remission that seem to be concomitant with changes in verbal content (Reilly, Harrow, & Tucker, 1973). Some research suggests that changes in verbal production occur between the first and the second 100 words of a monologue (Salzinger et al., 1964) and between stressful versus nonstressful eliciting stimuli (Spring et al., Note 1). Thus, the stage of an individual patient in his or her symptom picture and the present level of arousal will affect data collection as will changes that occur during the data collection.

> The severity, with which the phenomenon of confusion of speech appears is subject to great fluctuation. Many patients are usually able to express themselves at first quite intelligibly, but fall into their nonsensical talk as soon as one speaks for a longer time with them or when they become excited [Kraepelin, 1919/1971, p. 180].

This is a source of variation that must be further explored and understood so as to increase the power of statistical analyses.

The clinical experience of both Kraepelin and Bleuler pointed toward the possibility of a speech pathology in schizophrenia in the absence of thought disorder as exemplified by a patient's other behaviors. This raises the interesting but as yet unexplored issue concerning the relationship between language and thought. "Schizophasia" in the absence of other overt forms of thought disorder may have a different etiology, course, and response to treatment. Kraepelin describes "confusional speech dementia":

> What distinguishes our patient here, is the sense and reasonableness in their behavior and in their actions which compels us to the assumption that there is a case not so much of severe disorder of thought but much rather of an interruption of the connections between train of thought and expression in speech [Kraepelin, 1919/1971, p. 180].

V. Overview

This chapter has traced the development of the empirical study of schizophrenic language. From the outset, the guiding principle of many of these studies has been to define and understand better those aspects of schizophrenic speech that lead to relatively reliable diagnoses of schizophrenia by both laymen and clinicians. Of course, each research paradigm combines a complex set of assumptions and methodologies, some of which can be identified through the literature, while the rest remain beyond our discernment. Because of these differences, the following summation of data across projects is done with much caution. It should be stressed that the following statements tentatively apply to a relatively small number of schizophrenic patients. While it is difficult to resist the tendency toward closure, any definitive statements at this point would be premature.

A. GRAMMATICAL COMPONENTS

In research with the type–token ratio, schizophrenic patients tend to be somewhat more repetitive in their speech than normal subjects. This suggests more theme perseveration and word repetition. The differences are small but consistent. Findings in the area of grammatical categories are inconsistent. There seems to be a slight trend toward schizophrenic patients using fewer nouns and qualifiers than do normal subjects. This may, in part, be a function of shorter clauses and fewer referent guideposts for the listener. Research into the use of personal pronouns has yet to reveal any consistent trends.

B. CONTENT

Schizophrenic patients seem to have a consistency in their verbal productions (Laffal, 1979) that covaries with changes in other symptoms as the patient goes into remission (Reilly et al., 1973). As a group, schizophrenic patients seem to have consistencies in the content areas of their speech. Generally, they seem concerned with global issues of politics, science, and religion and have many institutional concerns that are inappropriate or poorly understood. At a personal level, the language of chronic schizophrenic patients seems to exist in an intersection of interpersonal ambivalence and internal disorganization (Gottschalk & Gleser, 1979). Acutely ill patients exhibit a good deal of hostility and somatic concern as well as concern with the processes of thought and communication (Rosenberg & Tucker, 1979). Overall, their language seems to reflect an attempt at orientation in a morass of confusion, fear, and distrust. These patients seem to be attempting to defend themselves simultaneously from the chaos within and the apparent external dangers from an unusual flood of external sensation and possible threats from others. As the patient's symptoms go into remission, his or her concerns gradually shift from these issues to concerns of the future and the pragmatic interests of self and family (Reilly *et al.,* 1973).

An interesting note made by Rosenberg and Tucker (1979) is that, on the basis of "guidance" themes, as measured by their tag system of reading texts, female schizophrenics seem to behave in a semantically "masculine" manner. This is interesting in light of the feminist position that describes the negative social consequences for women who attempt to assert power and control. These results are merely suggestive and may lead to interesting psychosociological studies in the future.

C. PREDICTABILITY AND COMMUNICABILITY

The general trend is toward decreased predictability in schizophrenic speech (Rutter *et al.,* 1975; Salzinger *et al.,* 1964; Silverman, 1972, 1973). Thought-disordered schizophrenics are less predictable than are non-thought-disordered speakers (Manschreck *et al.,* 1979; Rochester & Martin, 1979), yet there may be no difference that can be discerned from their written samples (Manschreck *et al.,* 1980). At the same time, Moroz and Fosmire (1966) found no correlation between clinically rated degree of disorganization and Cloze scores, while Rutter *et al.* (1977, 1978) could not distinguish between schizophrenics and normals using the same procedure. The theory that schizophrenic speech becomes less predictable as the patient gets further away in time from the original stimulus was supported by Salzinger *et al.* (1974) but not by Rutter *et al.* (1977). A study by Spring *et al.* (Note 1) found differences in predictability between schizophrenic and normal speakers only in a neutral eliciting condition and no difference under a stress condition. This may account for some of the contradictions in previous findings.

A study of paragraph reconstruction, consisting of restringing sentences to their original order (Rutter, 1979), showed that it was more difficult to reconstruct the passages taken from schizophrenic patients than those taken from normals. (This study used the same data that failed to discriminate between these groups using the Cloze procedure.) These results suggest that the breakdown in schizophrenic communicability existed not within sentences but rather between sentences.

The cohesion and phoricity studies done by Rochester and Martin (1979) examine in detail the relationship between sentences in schizophrenic and normal speech. Using relatively young, intact thought-disordered and non-thought-disordered schizophrenics, they found that the schizophrenic subjects used shorter clauses than the normal controls and there were less cohesive ties between their sentences. Furthermore, thought-disordered speakers relied more on lexical ties (those depending on the meaning of individual words) than did the non-thought-disordered schizophrenics and normals.

Thought-disordered speakers rarely describe, but rather hint at or "point" with their words to their intended meaning. Both normal and thought-disordered speakers rely on implicit referents. However, between 33% and 50% of the implicit references used by thought-disordered speakers are obscure to the listener, whereas most from a normal speaker are readily discernable. Thought-disordered speakers appear to introduce participants inadequately into a retelling of a story and begin with general terms before describing the actual specific participant. Thought-disordered speakers also fail to discern between major and minor characters in a story retelling task.

Using a discriminative function analysis comprised of the preceding information, Rochester and Martin were able to distinguish between thought-disordered and non-thought-disordered speakers solely on the basis of language production. This suggests an empirical basis for the subjective clinical impression of "schizophrenicity" using a sophisticated linguistic model. Also, this distinction is made at a high level of language use and not at a level of severe impairment at which anyone could distinguish between thought-disordered and non-thought-disordered subjects. Thus, "stratal slips" may become a cornerstone for the diagnosis of thought-disordered speech: This model may also represent an adequate operationalization of Bleuler's descriptive theory of loose associative threads.

D. MOTOR FEATURES

From the research reviewed here, the prototypic schizophrenic patient shows signs of slow and dulled language processing. Her or his speech is generally more redundant, delivered in shorter clauses, and spoken more slowly. Rate of speech has been found to correlate with measures of affect and motor activity. High initial speech rate seems to be a good prognostic indicator (Hart & Payne, 1973). Future studies need to be done examining the relationship between medication and motor features of language production.

Besides a slower rate of speech, schizophrenics appear to pause more often than normal speakers. One study suggests that thought-disordered schizophrenics can be differentiated from non-thought-disordered schizophrenics by measuring pause length between clauses (Rochester *et al.*, 1977). These hesitations are thought to be an outward manifestation of an information-processing deficit related to distractability. Pauses within clauses are the same for normals and thought-disordered speakers but are longer for thought-disordered speakers between clauses. These possible vacuums of attention between clauses are thought to lead to the intrusion of internal and external associations that are experienced as tangential or loose to the listener. They also may explain why some schizophrenic patients seem to rely more heavily on lexical than on functional words. The fact that naming and identifying takes precedent over description of action may reflect an individual's attempt to hold onto the flow of communication in the face of a subtle breakdown in attention. Keying on individual words may, at times, represent the patient's attempt to avoid internal associations. At others, it may suggest that a distraction is diverting the patient's attention and that the ensuing repetition is a mere continuation of verbalization based more on verbal momentum than on conscious awareness and attention.

VI. Conclusion

This chapter has examined the evolution of investigations into the nature of schizophrenic language as it developed from simple counts of the parts of speech to relatively sophisticated linguistic analyses of internal referential structure. Discriminative function analyses may soon provide a multiaxial communication component to diagnosis that could foreseeably include measures of redundancy, rate of speech, hesitations, content, cohesion, and phoricity. It seems that such a model could account for original clinical insights pertaining to the complexity of loosened associative threads while at the same time offer an explanation for the often dulled and sometimes delusional content of schizophrenic language. In addition, other correlates of language production, such as motor behavior, motivation, and affect, may also come to be included not only as aids to diagnosis but also as prognostic indicators, suggestive of specific multimodal therapeutic interventions.

Reference Note

1. Spring, B. J., Briggs, D. P., Cozolino, L. J., & Manuzza, S. Predictability of schizophrenic speech: Effects of stressful and neutral eliciting conditions. Unpublished manuscript, 1982.

References

Aborn, M., Rubinstein, H, & Sterling, T. Sources of contextual constraint upon words in a sentence. *Journal of Experimental Psychology,* 1959, **57,** 171-180.

Amarel, M., & Cheek, F. Some effects of L.S.D. 25 on verbal communication. *Journal of Abnormal Psychology,* 1965, **70,** 453-456.

Amarel, M., Cheek, F. E., & Stierhem, R. J. Studies in the sources of variation in cloze scores: I. The raters. *Journal of Abnormal Psychology,* 1966, **71,** 444-448.

Astrachan, B. M., Harrow, M., Adler, P., Brauer, L., Schwartz, A., Schwartz, C., & Tucker, G. A checklist for the diagnosis of schizophrenia. *British Journal of Psychiatry,* 1972, **121,** 529-539.

Baker, S. J. A linguistic law of constancy: II. *The Journal of General Psychology,* 1951, **44,** 113-120.

Balkan, E. R., & Masserman, J. Language of fantasy. *Journal of Psychology,* 1940, **10,** 75-86.

Bleuler, E. *Dementia praecox or the group of schizophrenias.* New York: International Universities Press, 1950.

Bobon, J. Schizophrasie et schizoparaphasie. *Acta neurologica Belgica,* 1967, **67,** 924-938.

Boder, D. P. The adjective-verb quotient. *Psychological Research,* 1940, **3,** 309-333.

Cancro, R., & Sugarman, A. A. Psychological differentiation and process-reactive schizophrenia. *Journal of Abnormal Psychology,* 1969, **74,** 415-419.

Caudill, W. *Observations on the cultural context of Japanese psychiatry, in culture and mental health* (M. K. Opler, Ed.). New York: Macmillian, 1959.

Chapman, J. The early symptoms of schizophrenia. *British Journal of Psychiatry,* 1966, **112,** 225-251.

Chapman, J., & McGhie, A. A comparative study of disordered attention in schizophrenia. *Journal of Mental Science,* 1962, **108,** 487-500.

Cheek, F. E., & Amarel, M. Studies in the sources of variation in cloze scores: II. The verbal passages. *Journal of Abnormal Psychology,* 1968, **73,** 424-430.

Cooper, J., Kendall, R., Gurland, B., Sartorius, N., & Farkas, J. Cross national study of diagnosis of the mental disorders: Some results from the first comparative investigation. *American Journal of Psychiatry,* 1969, **125** (April Supp.), 21-29.

Critchley, M. The neurology of psychotic speech. *British Journal of Psychiatry,* 1964, **110,** 353-364.

Dale E., & Chall, J. S. A formula for predicting readability. *Educational Research Bulletin,* 1948, **27** (January-February), 11-20; 37-54.

Deckner, C. W., & Blanton, R. L. Effect of context and strength of association on schizophrenic verbal behavior. *Journal of Abnormal Psychology,* 1969, **74** (3), 348-351.

Dollard, J., & Mowrer, O. H. A method of measuring tension in written documents. *Journal of Abnormal and Social Psychology,* 1947, **42,** 3-32.

Ellsworth, R. The regression of schizophrenic language. *Journal of Consulting Psychology,* 1951, **15,** 387-391.

Fairbanks, H. The quantitative differentiation of samples of spoken language. *Psychological Monographs,* 1944, **56**(2), 19–38.

Feldstein, S., & Jaffe, J. Vocabulary diversity of schizophrenics and normals. *Journal of Speech and Hearing Research,* 1962, **5**, 76–78.

Fillenbaum, S., & Jones, L. V. An application of "Cloze" technique to the study of aphasic speech. *Journal of Abnormal and Social Psychology,* 1962, **65**, 183–189.

Flesch, R. *How to test readability.* New York: Harper, 1951.

Goldman-Eisler, F. *Psycholinguistics: Experiments in spontaneous speech.* New York: Academic Press, 1968.

Gottschalk, L. A. The speech patterns of schizophrenic patients: A method of assessing relative degree of personal disorganization and social alienation. *Psychiatric Research Reports,* 1958, **10**, 141–158.

Gottschalk, L. A., & Gleser, G. C. Distinguishing characteristics of the verbal communication of schizophrenic patients. In D. McRioch & E. A. Weinstein (Eds.), *Disorders of communication* (Vol. 42). Baltimore, Md.: Williams and Wilkins, 1964.

Gottschalk, L. A., & Gleser, G. C. *The content analysis of verbal behavior.* New York: Medical and Scientific Books, 1979.

Halliday, M., & Hasan, R. *Cohesion in English.* London: Longman, 1976.

Hammer, M., & Salzinger, K. Some formal characteristics of schizophrenic speech as a measure of social deviance. *Annals of the New York Academy of Sciences,* 1964, **105**, 861–889.

Hart, D. S., & Payne, R. W. Language structure and predictability in overinclusive patients. *British Journal of Psychiatry,* 1973, **123**, 643–652.

Hartman, H. *Essays on ego psychology.* New York: International Universities Press, 1964.

Honigfeld, G. The ability of schizophrenics to understand normal and pseudo-psychotic speech. *Diseases of the Nervous System,* 1963, **24**, 692–694.

Hunt, W. A., & Jones, N. F. Clinical judgment of some aspects of schizophrenic thinking. *Journal of Psychology,* 1958, **14**, 235–239.

Johnson, W. Studies in language behavior: A program of research. *Psychological Monographs,* 1944, **56**(2), 1–15.

Jung, C. G. *The psychogenesis of mental disease.* Princeton, N. J.: Princeton Univ. Press, 1960.

Kasanin, J. S. (Ed.). *Language and thought in schizophrenia.* New York: Norton, 1964.

Kelly, G. A. *A theory of personality.* New York: Norton, 1963.

Kent, G. H., & Rosanoff, A. J. A study of associations in insanity. *American Journal of Insanity,* 1910, **67** (July & October).

Kraepelin, E. *Dementia praecox and paraphrenia.* New York: Krieger Publishing Company, 1971. (Originally published, 1919.)

Laffal, J. The contextual associates of sun and God in Schreber's autobiography. *Journal of Abnormal Psychology,* 1960, **60**, 474–479.

Laffal, J. Changes in the language of a schizophrenic patient during psychotherapy. *Journal of Abnormal Psychology,* 1961, **63**, 422–427.

Laffal, J. *Pathological and normal language.* New York: Atherton Press, 1965.

Laffal, J. *A source document in schizophrenia.* Hope Valley, R.I.: Gallery, 1979.

Lorenz, M., & Cobb, S. Language patterns in psychotic and psychoneurotic subjects. *Archives of Neurology and Psychiatry,* 1954, **72**, 665–673.

MacGinitie, W. H. Contextual constraint in English prose paragraphs. *Journal of Psychology,* 1961, **51**, 121–130.

Maher, B. A. *Principles of psychopathology.* New York: McGraw-Hill, 1966.

Maher, B. A. The shattered language of schizophrenia. *Psychology Today,* November, 1968, p. 30.

Maher, B. A. The language of schizophrenia: A review and interpretation. *British Journal of Psychiatry,* 1972, **120,** 3–17.

Maher, B. A., McKean, K. O., & McLaughlin, B. Studies in psychotic language. In P. J. Stone, C. Dunphy, M. S. Smith, & D. M. Ogilvie, *The General Inquirer: A computer approach to content analysis.* Cambridge, Mass.: MIT Press, 1966.

Mann, M. B. The quantitative differentiation of samples of written language. *Psychological Monographs,* 1944, **56**(2), 41–74.

Manschreck, T. C., Maher, B. A., & Ader, D. N. Formal thought disorder, the type–token ratio, and disturbed voluntary motor movement in schizophrenia. *British Journal of Psychiatry,* 1981, **139,** 7–15.

Manschreck, T. C., Maher, B. A., & Rucklos, M. Cloze procedure and written language in schizophrenia. *Language and Speech,* 1980, **23**(4), 323–328.

Manschreck, T. C., Maher, B. A., Rucklos, M., Vereen, D. R. & Ader, D. N., Deficient motor movement in schizophrenia. *Journal of Abnormal Psychology,* 1981, **90,** 321–328.

Manschreck, T. C., Maher, B. A., Rucklos, M., & White, M. The predictability of thought disordered speech in schizophrenic patients. *British Journal of Psychiatry,* 1979, **134,** 595–601.

Martin, J. R. Learning how to tell. Unpublished doctoral dissertation, University of Essex, 1978.

Mayers, A.N., & Mayers, E. B. Grammar-rhetoric indicator. *Journal of Nervous and Mental Disease,* 1946, **104,** 604–610.

McDonald, N. Living with schizophrenia. *Canadian M.A.J.,* 1960, **82**(January 23) 218.

McGhie, A., & Chapman, J. Disorders of attention and perception in early schizophrenia. *British Journal of Medical Psychology,* 1961, **34,** 103–116.

Mittenecker, E. Eine neue quantitative Methode in der Sprachanalyse und ihre Anwendung bei Schizophrenen. *Monatsschrift fur Psychiatrie und Neurologie,* 1951, **121,** 5–31.

Moroz, M. L., & Fosmire, E. R. Application of Cloze procedure to schizophrenic language. *Diseases of the Nervous System,* 1966, **27,** 408–410.

National Institute of Mental Health. *Abnormal Involuntary Movement Scale (AIMS)* (U.S. Public Health Service Publication No. MH-9-17). Washington, D.C.: U.S. Government Printing Office, 1974.

Osgood, C. E., & Walker, E. G. Motivation and language behavior: A content analysis of suicide notes. *Journal of Abnormal and Social Psychology,* 1959, **59,** 58–67.

Pavy, D., Grinspoon, L., & Shader, R. Word frequency measures of verbal disorders in schizophrenia. *Diseases of the Nervous System,* 1969, **30,** 553–555.

Rankin, E. F. The Cloze procedure—Its validity and utility. In O. S. Causey & W. Eller (Eds.), *Starting and improving college reading programs.* Austin: Univ. of Texas Press, 1959.

Reilly, F. E., Harrow, M., & Tucker, G. J. Language and thought content in acute psychosis. *American Journal of Psychiatry,* 1973, **130**(4), 411–417.

Rochester, S. R., & Martin, J. R. *Crazy Talk.* New York: Plenum, 1979.

Rochester, S. R., Thurston, S., & Rupp, J. Hesitations as clues to failures in coherence: Studies of the thought-disordered speaker. In S. Rosenberg (Ed.), *Sentence production: A handbook of theory and practice.* Hillsdale, N.J.: Erlbaum, 1977.

Rosenberg, S. D., & Tucker, G. J. Verbal behavior and schizophrenia: The semantic dimension. *Archives of General Psychiatry,* 1979, **36,** 1331–1337.

Rutter, D. R. The reconstruction of schizophrenic speech. *British Journal of Psychiatry,* 1979, **134,** 356–359.

Rutter, D. R., Draffan, J., & Davies, J. Thought disorder and the predictability of schizophrenic speech. *British Journal of Psychiatry,* 1977, **131,** 67–68.

Rutter, D. R., Wishner, J., & Callaghan, B. A. The prediction and predictability of speech in schizophrenic patients. *British Journal of Psychiatry,* 1975, **126,** 571–576.

Rutter, D. R., Wishner, J., Kopytynska, H., & Button, M. The predictability of speech in schizophrenic patients. *British Journal of Psychiatry,* 1978, **132,** 228–232.

Salzinger, K., Portnoy, S., & Feldman, R. Verbal behavior of schizophrenic and normal subjects. *Annals of the New York Academy of Sciences,* 1964, **105,** 845–860.

Sechehaye, M. *Autobiography of a schizophrenic girl.* New York: Grune & Stratton, 1951.

Seth, G., & Beloff, H. Language impairment in a group of schizophrenics. *British Journal of Medical Psychology,* 1959, **32,** 288–293.

Silverman, G. Psycholinguistics of schizophrenic language. *Psychological Medicine,* 1972, **2,** 254–259.

Silverman, G. Redundancy, repetition and pausing in schizophrenic speech. *British Journal of Psychiatry,* 1973, **122,** 407–413.

Snyder, S. H., Banerjie, S. P., Yamamura, H. I., & Greenburg, D. Drugs, neurotransmitters, and schizophrenia. *Science,* 1974, **184,** 1243–1253.

Sommer, R., Dewar, R., & Osmond, H. Is there a schizophrenic language? *Archives of General Psychiatry,* 1960, **3,** 665–673.

Spitzer, R., & Endicott, J. *Schedule for Affective Disorders and Schizophrenia (SADS).* New York: Biometrics Research, New York State Psychiatric Institute, 1977.

Spitzer, R., Endicott, J., & Robins, E. *Research Diagnostic Criteria for a selected group of functional disorders, (RDC)* (2nd ed.). New York: Biometrics Research, New York State Psychiatric Institute, 1975.

Stone, P. J., Dunphy, C., Smith, M. S., & Ogilvie, D. M. *The General Inquirer: A computer approach to content analysis.* Cambridge, Mass.: MIT Press, 1966.

Taylor, W. L. "Cloze procedure": A new tool for measuring readability. *Journalism Quarterly,* 1953, **30,** 415–433.

Taylor, W. L. Recent developments in the use of "Cloze procedure." *Journalism Quarterly,* 1956, **33,** 42–48.

Tucker, G. J., & Rosenberg, S. D. Computer content analysis of schizophrenia: A preliminary report. *American Journal of Psychiatry,* 1975, **123,** 611–616.

Venables, P. Input dysfunction in schizophrenia. In B. A. Maher (Ed.), *Progress in Experimental Personality Research,* (Vol. 1). New York: Academic Press, 1964.

Vonnegut, M. *The Eden Express.* New York: Praeger, 1975.

Weintraub, W., & Aronson, H. The application of verbal analysis to the study of psychological defense mechanisms III: Speech patterns associated with delusional behavior. *Journal of Nervous and Mental Disease,* 1965, **141**(2), 172–179.

White, M. A. A study of schizophrenic language. *Journal of Abnormal and Social Psychology,* 1949, **44,** 61–74.

Wojcik, J. D., Gelenberg, A. J., LaBrie, R. A., & Mieske, M. Prevalence of tardive dyskinesia in an outpatient population. *Comprehensive Psychiatry,* 1980, **21,** 370–379.

THE SPECIFICITY OF THOUGHT DISORDER TO SCHIZOPHRENIA: RESEARCH METHODS IN THEIR HISTORICAL PERSPECTIVE

Philip D. Harvey and John M. Neale

DEPARTMENT OF PSYCHOLOGY
STATE UNIVERSITY OF NEW YORK AT STONY BROOK
STONY BROOK, NEW YORK

I. Introduction

Thought disorder has long been viewed as a primary feature of schizophrenia. Pioneering clinicians, such as Bleuler (1911/1950) and Kraepelin (1919, 1921), noted that schizophrenic patients had fundamental problems in both thought and expressive communication. In fact, Bleuler went so far as to say that loosened associative threads were at the root of all the other manifestations of the schizophrenic syndrome. In contrast, others, such as Schneider (1959), have focused on delusions and hallucinations as principal diagnostic features. However, none have stated that thought disorder is an unimportant variable.

Studies of thought pathology in schizophrenia have had several forms and methodologies, including clinical, natural language, and laboratory analyses. Each of these methods has its own historical niche and its own set of assumptions. Theories of the disorder have also been an important factor, influencing both the type of data collected and its interpretation. In addition, the definition of the term *thought disorder* is not well agreed upon, depending on both the research method applied and the intent of the investigation. The purpose of this chapter, therefore, is to examine each of these methods of data collection with respect to its historical perspective and current status. The primary focus will be on the information gained from each methodology regarding thought disorder in schizophrenia as a unique phenomenon, differing from the possible thought disorders of other patient groups.

II. Definition of Research Methods

Three research methods have been used in studying thought disorder. Each method yields a different data base and uses those data differently. While investigators using all three methods are usually thought to be evaluating the same phenomena, that statement may actually be more an assumption than a fact, as will be shown later.

A. CLINICAL RESEARCH

The data for clinical investigations of thought disorder are collected from either a diagnostic interview (Andreasen, 1979a), from a projective testing session (Johnston & Holzman, 1979), or from therapeutic and general interactions with patients on a hospital ward (Kraepelin, 1919). The roles of the participants are clearly delineated, with the schizophrenic in a patient role. The speech is analyzed in terms of clinical criteria for deviance, much the same as other symptoms are evaluated to see if they meet diagnostic criteria. The amount of interpretation of the speech deviance may differ, from considering it as limited to speech and overt communication (e.g., Andreasen, 1979a, 1979b) to viewing disordered speech as an indicator of underlying disordered thought (e.g., Johnston & Holzman, 1979).

B. NATURAL LANGUAGE RESEARCH

Natural language studies differ only slightly in data collection procedures from clinical studies. The speech need not be collected from a diagnostic interview, but speech from such an interview could be analyzed. The interviewer is not required to be a clinician or professional, but can be. The natural language method simply requires a sample of speech, gained by any means. Some investigators have used samples of writing (Maher, McKean, & McLaughlin, 1966), others have recorded speech generated in the presence of a nonreactive observer (Gottschalk & Gleser, 1964), while still others have used as data subjects' verbatim repetition of a story read to them (Rochester & Martin, 1979). The crucial difference between natural language and clinical methods is in the categories used to analyze the speech. Generally, psycholinguistic categories and the frequency of common speech elements or parts of speech are examined in the natural language studies. The level of interpretation of the speech data can vary, from examination of the speech at face value to inferences about thought processes. In addition, in some studies in which easily countable and definable units are examined, a computer can be utilized to rate the speech. One advantage of the natural language method is that normals can be compared directly to psychotics. In a clinical study this comparison is usually not meaningful, because deviant units are very rare in normals' speech.

C. LABORATORY RESEARCH

Laboratory studies of thought disorder come the closest to assessing thought processes. Laboratory tasks are used to assess cognitive processes or usage of small units (words, sentences) of speech. Typically the performance of schizophrenics is compared to that of some contrast group, usually normals but sometimes patients in other diagnostic categories. Such content areas as attention (Neale & Cromwell, 1970), conceptual performance (Goldstein, 1959), word association (Kent & Rosanoff, 1910), and many others have been examined. Discourse is rarely studied, because of the obvious difficulties in manipulating large amounts of speech in cognitive tasks. However, if subjects are not evaluated on their speech as well as their laboratory task performance, then the processes measured in laboratory studies may not be related to subjects' speech production.

Determining where the research methods diverge and their remaining common ground will make examination of the concept of thought disorder easier. Therefore, a historical review of the research on thought disorder, covering examplars of all three methodologies, will be provided. At the conclusion of that review, we will be in a better position to examine the specificity of thought disorder to schizophrenia.

III. Clinical Studies of Thought Disorder

A. KRAEPELIN

The first major studies of thought disorder in schizophrenia were the extensive clinical reports of Kraepelin (1919, 1921). His orientation was largely descriptive and offered very little in the way of explanatory and unifying principles. Kraepelin described the symptoms and course of the disorder he called dementia praecox, proposing that it consisted of progressive mental and social deterioration beginning in the early years of life. One of the features of this deterioration was that speech became unintelligible and, therefore, thought was inferred to be disordered.

Two important observations of Kraepelin were that speech is often disordered in manic psychosis as well as schizophrenia and that there is an important distinction between the *content* and the *form* of disordered speech. Speech content is defined as the topics discussed by the patient and his or her beliefs. These topics and beliefs are often very deviant, especially in delusional patients. The form of speech has typically been defined as its rules of organization (e.g., syntax). Most studies of speech disorder in schizophrenia have focused on "formal thought disorder" and that concentration will be continued in this chapter.

Although subsequent researchers often used the accurate and complete descriptions of thought disorder provided by Kraepelin, for most of this century his work had only moderate impact, especially in America. One reason for this lack of impact may be that Kraepelin was atheoretical, going no further than describing the symptomatology and course of the disorder. While some of the earliest laboratory research into schizophrenic thought disorder was completed in Kraepelin's laboratory, his influence on laboratory research was not nearly as great as that of some later scientists.

B. BLEULER

The next major figure on the scene was Eugen Bleuler, who, in fact, invented the term *schizophrenia*. Bleuler also was a clinically oriented scientist but differed from Kraepelin in offering a theoretical explanation for the disorder, contained in the term *schizophrenia* itself. Although recognizing the symptomatic heterogeneity of schizophrenia, he thought that there was a common feature, an associative disturbance, in all patients, leading speech to be unintelligible.

In order to understand Bleuler's (1911/1950) view of speech deviance, it is first important to appreciate his view of normal speech. He was a verbal associationist, believing that elements of speech are generated because of their associative relationship to previous elements. A disruption in the ability to produce associations would lead speech to drift, with new ideas being only tangentially related to previous ones. Schizophrenic speech, with its most salient phenomena being its apparently purposeless drift from topic to topic, seems to be accurately described by this early conceptualization.

This specification of an essential feature in schizophrenia served the purpose of providing testable predictions about the disorder. But the key issue of the specificity of thought disorder to schizophrenia was not well addressed. Although Bleuler discussed other patient groups, his treatment of them was affected by his theoretical belief that the similar speech disorders of other patient groups, such as manics, were caused by different factors.

Much of the early work by both Kraepelin and Bleuler, although differing in certain respects, had the common purpose of describing observed phenomena in patients' speech. Categories of deviant speech were observed and given conceptual labels. Many of the early names for aspects of formal thought disorder were created by Kraepelin himself (1919) and have remained to this day—*poverty of thought* (lowered frequency of spontaneous speech), *neologisms* (individually created words with a special meaning), and many others. A list of many of the currently used terms for various aspects of formal thought disorder, adapted from Andreasen (1979a), is presented in Table I.

C. More Recent Investigations

More recent investigations have studied thought disorder in schizophrenia with generally the same procedures and goals as the early clinical studies, modifying some of the early descriptive terms (e.g., Wing, Birley, Cooper, Graham, & Isaacs, 1967; World Health Organization, 1973) and adding new ones. However, until recently the prevalence rates of thought disorder in schizophrenics as a whole and of each of these descriptive categories were not well established. Most investigators tended to go along with the Bleulerian hypothesis that all schizophrenics were thought disordered and simply assumed that deviant speech was present in the majority of patients.

A major investigation, the International Pilot Study of Schizophrenia (IPSS) (World Health Organization, 1973), included assessment of thought disorder. The subcategories of thought disorder were taken from the Present State Exam (Wing *et al.,* 1967) and consisted of several Kraepelinian categories (e.g., incoherence, circumstantiality, poverty of speech). Prevalence of thought disorder ranged from a low of 4% (Moscow) to a high of 12% (Prague), much lower than Bleulerian theory would predict. However, subjects in the IPSS were on medication. At the time of Bleuler's

TABLE I

DEFINITIONS OF CLINICAL THOUGHT DISORDER CATEGORIES[a]

Poverty of speech	Restriction in the amount of spontaneous speech
Poverty of content of speech	Speech adequate in amount but low in information
Pressure of speech	Increase in the amount of spontaneous speech
Distractible speech	Interruption of a train of discourse, with focus shifted to an external object
Tangentiality	Replying to a question in a manner not related to the question
Derailment	Ideas expressed in spontaneous speech are obliquely related or are unrelated to previous speech
Incoherence	Speech that makes no sense, ignoring grammatical and syntax rules
Illogicality	Overtly expressed reasoning that breaks logical rules
Clanging	Speech that creates links on the basis of phonological rather than semantic rules
Neologisms	Uniquely created words with a special meaning
Word approximations	Use of old words in a new and unconventional way
Circumstantiality	Indirect and lengthy speech gets to a goal slowly, if at all
Loss of goal	Speech that never reaches logical end points
Perseveration	Repetition of words, ideas, or concepts to an extreme degree
Echolalia	Patient repeats whole words or phrases of the examiner
Blocking	Interruption of a train of speech, with patient comment that thought is blocked
Stilted speech	Excessively pompous or formal speech
Self-reference	Repeated references to self

[a] Adapted from Andreasen (1979a).

theorizing, medication was not used, making it impossible to judge whether Bleuler was accurately reporting a more prevalent rate of thought disorder or whether his theoretical position led him to make highly inferential judgments.

In the IPSS, diagnostic subcategory of schizophrenia was highly related to presence or absence of speech disorder. Hebephrenics were much more likely than catatonics or paranoids to have thought disorder. Although this finding makes logical sense, as unintelligible speech was one of the diagnostic criteria for the hebephrenic subtype, it is of interest that the prevalence of the hebephrenic subtype of schizophrenia varied cross-nationally, ranging from a high of 35% (Taipei) to a low of 0% (Moscow and Washington). This cross-national variation was moderately related to overall prevalence of thought disorder. Therefore, not only were all schizophrenics not thought disordered, but country of investigation was also related to the prevalence of thought disorder.

D. SPECIFICITY OF THOUGHT DISORDER IN CLINICAL STUDIES

While Bleuler stated that other patients suffered from speech disorders, he believed that their problems were not caused by associative disturbance. Consequently, Bleuler's followers compared schizophrenics and normals, as the disordered speech of other psychiatric patients was seen as a confound to studying associative deficits in a pure form. The experimental, clinical, and natural language research that followed from Bleuler's theorizing presumed that speech disorder, caused by an underlying associative deficit, was unique to schizophrenia. Inclusion of other patients as contrast subjects was, until the late 1970s, extremely rare.

Andreasen (1979a, 1979b) has shattered a few of the myths about the prevalence of thought disorder in general and the frequency with which the various descriptive categories of disordered speech occur. Using an extremely liberal cutoff for a global rating of thought disorder (a rating of 1 [mild] or more on a 5-point scale), she found that a large proportion of schizophrenics were thought disordered. She also showed that subcategories of thought disorder based on the Bleulerian conception of associative loosening were not useful for discriminating depressives and manics from schizophrenics. When Andreasen grouped together the conceptual categories of tangentiality (vague and drifting answers to questions), derailment (rapid changes in topic during speech), incoherence, and clanging—the conceptual categories of psychotic speech more often described as being related to loose associations—there was virtually no difference between manics and schizophrenics.[1]

In addition, Andreasen found that in psychotic affective disorder, primarily mania, some of the classical clinical categories were as prevalent or even more prevalent than in schizophrenia itself. These categories included distractible speech (abrupt changes in topic elicited by an irrelevant environmental stimulus), pressure of speech (excessive amount of rapid speech), and perseveration (repeating the same word, phrase, or topic over and over). However, another method of dividing the subcategories of thought disorder, into positive versus negative signs, was successful in discriminating schizophrenics and manics. Positive signs of thought disorder are florid psychotic speech elements, such as the ones just described. Negative signs include poverty in the amount of speech and poverty of content of speech (speech adequate in amount but containing very little information). The F

---

[1]The last point, failure to differentiate schizophrenics from manics on the primary features of thought disorder as defined by Bleuler's theory, casts serious doubt upon that theory and other work based solely upon it. However, as the majority of the subjects in Andreasen's study were medicated, the findings are not a clear refutation of Bleuler's theory.

for the MANOVA on negative signs was highly significant, indicating that the schizophrenics had more negative signs than the manics. Depressives also tended to have more negative signs of thought disorder (poverty of speech and poverty of content of speech) than manics. Manic patients could be discriminated from both depressives and schizophrenics by higher ratings on derailment, tangentiality, and pressure of speech.

Data from the IPSS were similar to Andreasen's findings. A discriminant function analysis revealed that manics and schizoaffectives could be discriminated from schizophrenics by the exclusive presence in schizophrenics of poverty of content of speech and neologisms. However, both the IPSS and Andreasen found that neologisms were a rare (about 5%) phenomena in schizophrenics, indicating that presence of neologisms is not a generally useful discriminating factor. Both Andreasen and the IPSS concluded that an overall rating of thought disorder, weighting all signs equally, would be useless for a differential diagnosis among psychoses.

Thus, it appears that the simple designation of a patient as thought disordered or not on the basis of a clinical evaluation of speech is not a useful diagnostic sign. The clinical method does, however, allow for the subtyping of patients on the basis of their most common pattern of speech disturbance. Andreasen, for example, found that thought disorder was relevant to diagnosis, but only when speech disorder was divided into positive and negative signs. Further investigators could profit from these findings when trying to make specific statements about schizophrenic thought disorder. Evaluating speech of schizophrenics is necessarily limited by this type of analysis, however, as it appears that the major sign of communication problems in schizophrenia is an absence of speech. One direction to follow would be to try to find the basis for this lack of speech. Does lack of speech mean lack of thought? Or are schizophrenics more afraid than other psychotic patients of talking to an interviewer? While Andreasen's results indicate that thought disorder in a global sense is not a uniquely schizophrenic phenomenon, her data can certainly serve to inspire more productive research in the future by delineating specific areas that need to be examined.

IV. Natural Language Studies

A. Content Analysis

Natural language studies of speech have evaluated either the form or the content of psychotic speech. Many of the earliest studies of the form of speech used human raters to count words and the frequency with which various parts of speech were used. For example, Fairbanks (1944) found that schizophrenics used fewer nouns, conjunctions, prepositions, and adjectives than a college student contrast group.

Studies of speech content tried to isolate themes present in the speech of schizophrenic patients. Gottschalk and Gleser (1964), for example, developed coding categories after examining the speech of schizophrenic and normal subjects. Schizophrenics, compared to several contrast groups, including other psychiatric patients, general medical patients, and normals, produced more speech units interpreted as indicating concerns with others avoiding them, self avoiding others, physical and psychological malfunctioning, unsureness of performance, denial of affect, need for control, and disorientation. Also analyzed were such categories as sentences where the main theme was other people avoiding the subject and incomplete, blocked, or bizarre sentences. Therefore, the rating categories did not always separate the form and the content of the disordered utterance. Furthermore, criteria for rating a phenomena as present were not clearly defined, severity ratings had reference points that were not clearly specified, and reliability was not adequately reported. Even more importantly, the ratings were based on raters' inferences about speech content (e.g., underlying meaning and motives), rather than on the observable speech itself.

B. THE GENERAL INQUIRER

The first totally objective method of studying the form and content of schizophrenic speech was presented in the General Inquirer studies. Maher *et al.* (1966) were seeking a way of classifying subjects as thought disordered that tapped the decision processes used by clinical judges. They used a computer system to analyze the formal and thematic patterns in passages written by schizophrenics. Their procedure involved a computerized sorting procedure on 50-word samples and then a replication on 100-word samples. They found that psychiatric patients, both schizophrenics and others, rated as thought disordered (TD) by lay judges were likely to have a higher ratio of objects to subjects in their writing than non-thought-disordered (NTD) psychiatric patients. Nine other formal categories, however, did not discriminate among the groups. In the 100-word sample replication, the object–subject ratio statistic was used to try to discriminate TD patients from NTD patients. Unfortunately, the measure failed to discriminate, casting doubt on object–subject ratios as a reliable indicator of thought disorder.

The results for the thematic categories indicated that the TD group made fewer references to personal experiences and themselves in general than did the NTD group; on the replication with the 100-word samples, level of self-reference continued to discriminate among the groups. In addition, TD patients made more references to general themes, such as politics, religion, law, and war. These references were often presented in complex and abstract ways, indicating little personal involvement on the part of the speaker. However, the other 16 thematic categories did not discriminate among the groups.

The results of the preceding lines of research make an interesting methodological point. In the Gottschalk and Gleser studies, using human coders and a loosely specified rating scheme with unassessed reliability, the speech of normals and schizophrenics was easily discriminated. In contrast, the General Inquirer studies used a highly systematic and reliable rating system and found much smaller differences between schizophrenics and normal speakers. It is impossible to determine from these studies if a highly systematic rating scheme or nonhuman raters account for the differences in the discriminating power of the measures used in the studies. This confound is not, however, unresolvable, as the study described next demonstrates.

C. Cohesion and Reference

Perhaps the most interesting of the naturalistic studies are those of Rochester (Rochester & Martin, 1979; Rochester, Martin, & Thurston, 1977). In these studies, Rochester and her co-workers closely analyzed the speech of 20 TD schizophrenics (defined by a priori clinical ratings), 20 NTD schizophrenics, and an equal number of normals. A rating system derived from Halliday and Hasan (1976) was used to examine the cohesiveness and patterns of reference of speech. Cohesion is the process whereby persons link together the main ideas in their speech (e.g., linking sentences together), and reference is the process of referring to information that the listener shares with the speaker.

Their data provide intriguing insights into the differences in the speech of normals, NTD schizophrenics, and TD schizophrenics. They found that TD schizophrenics could be discriminated from both NTD schizophrenics and normals on several variables. The TD schizophrenics did not present a pattern of discourse that was easy for a listener to follow. They provided fewer cohesive ties than did NTD schizophrenics and normals, and their cohesion was of a less useful type. Clauses were linked by repeating main elements verbatim or by using synonyms or general words, rather than pronouns, to substitute for initially presented items in order to skillfully weave a connected stream of discourse. TD schizophrenics occasionally attempted to relate segments of speech on the basis of similar sounding words in the to-be-linked segments. For example, words taken from the same root tended to be used as links (e.g., *I know some people who have a house near the sand dunes. The beach there is quite sandy*). In contrast, normals tended to use more conjunctions, connections that express a logical relationship between clauses.

The patterns of reference, defined as the ability to tie several sentences together under a main idea by referring the listener back to the initial theme, were poor in TD patients. They tended to use more references that were unclear, frequently using pronouns with no clear referent (e.g., talking about "him" or "her" without mentioning a male or female previously: *The boy was walking down the street. Then she turned around and left*). Another common error of TD schizophrenics was making ambiguous references (e.g., *The two girls were walking down the street. Then she turned around and left*). TD schizophrenics' reference failures often misled listeners, who appeared to be forced into the position of having to guess who or what was the object of the reference. In the terminology of Rochester and Martin, a listener is instructed to "retrieve" unavailable information. This failure, combined with a less frequent correct use of complicated reference patterns, provides the general picture of the linguistic deviance as described by Rochester and Martin.

Perhaps the most important finding of these studies was the unexpected competence of NTD schizophrenics. They spoke less than normals and TD schizophrenics, but their speech was nevertheless competent. Their patterns of reference and cohesion were similar to those of the normals, although somewhat impoverished. They did not tend to mislead listeners in the same way as did the TD patients. When student raters read all of the transcripts with the task of identifying deviant segments, NTD patients had only about 5% deviant clauses; normals were deviant in about .5% of their speech units. TD patients were also more competent than most investigators would assert, with only about 10% of their speech units being deviant. If Rochester and Martin had failed to subdivide their patient groups, they would have found that schizophrenics were more deviant than normals. But the large performance difference between the TD and NTD schizophrenics would have been impossible to detect.

The advantage of the Rochester *et al.* studies was that a specifically outlined, reliable, and discriminating set of coding procedures was used. Previous studies had either depended on intuition for the rating of the speech deviations (e.g., Gottschalk & Gleser, 1964), with high levels of discrimination between groups, or had used an inflexible, computer-based system, with a loss of much discriminating power (e.g., General Inquirer). While the Rochester *et al.* procedures are presently not convertible to a computerized system, they are an improvement in the objectivity of naturalistic observations.

D. SPECIFICITY OF THOUGHT DISORDER IN NATURAL LANGUAGE STUDIES

A frequent problem with natural language studies of thought disorder is that they, like some early clinical studies, failed to compare schizophrenics with other relevant patient groups. The Gottschalk and Gleser (1964) studies, however, used brain-damaged patients, nonschizophrenic psychiatric patients, and general medical patients, in addition to normals. Schizophrenic patients, although not subdivided into TD and NTD categories a priori, could be discriminated from all patients other than the brain-damaged ones.

In another study reported in the previously cited Maher *et al.* (1966) paper, process and reactive schizophrenics were compared to nonschizophrenic psychiatric patients on several speech measures. Reactive schizophrenics produced more nouns and a lower ratio of objects to verbs than did process schizophrenics. Nonschizophrenics could be discriminated from the combined schizophrenic group by their greater use of ambivalent terms (*but, however, if, probably*) and a lower ratio of nouns and verbs to adjectives and adverbs. These results were interpreted as indicating that schizophrenics produced speech that was less elaborated than that of nonschizophrenics. Again, however, the issue of specificity was not well addressed by the use of a heterogeneous nonschizophrenic contrast group.

Rochester and Martin (1979), although stating that disordered speech is not specific to schizophrenia, did not examine the disordered speech of other patients. One study that examined the speech of manics (Durbin & Marshall, 1977), found that manics also made the same type of errors as Rochester and Martin's TD schizophrenics. The manics made errors in *semantic anaphora* (failing to provide adequate links between sentences), leaving listeners with a feeling that they needed more information in order to understand exactly what was being said. However, there are problems in making comparisons between groups using observations collected with slightly different coding systems and diagnostic criteria. Thus far, there have not been any studies that have simultaneously compared the cohesion and reference patterns of schizophrenics and other psychiatric patients.

V. Laboratory Studies of Thought Disorder

The most prevalent type of investigation of thought disorder in schizophrenia has been laboratory research on cognitive processes. The key assumption in this research is that cognitive processes found to be deviant in schizophrenics are directly related, possibly in a causal fashion, to the production of disordered speech. Most of the early research was inspired by the theorizing of Bleuler and investigated his theoretical construct of associative loosening. It will be shown, however, that the majority of these researchers overlooked Bleuler's own point: that thought and language are not one and the same. Later on, research expanded into many areas of cognitive functioning. We will explore three major areas of interest: associations, attention and memory, and conceptual ability.

A. Associations

Many of the early studies of thought disorder concentrated on associative difficulties. Kent and Rosanoff's classic (1910) study on word associations demonstrated that schizophrenics were quite likely to produce individual associations (i.e., associations that were not produced by any of 1000 normals) when presented with a single stimulus word.

Many other studies have examined schizophrenics' tendency to produce indiosyncratic associates. These findings have been criticized, however, on several conceptual (O'Brian & Weingartner, 1970) and methodological (Moon, Mefferd, Wieland, Pokorny, & Falconer, 1968) grounds. For example, does a deviant response to a stimulus necessarily indicate a permanent associative deficit? O'Brian and Weingartner showed that normal subjects do not always give high-frequency associates and that these responses are a function of several external conditions required by the task. Poor receptive ability, leading to mishearing the stimulus, could also lead to idiosyncratic or even bizarre responses. In fact, schizophrenics are worse than normals at simply repeating the stimulus word back to an examiner (Moon *et al.,* 1968). Maher (1972) reviewed many association studies that used auditory presentation of stimuli and found that none had controlled for schizophrenic problems in attention to auditory stimuli. He concluded that the results from these studies were difficult to interpret because of this methodological problem.

More sophisticated studies of associative difficulties in schizophrenia have demonstrated that schizophrenics differ from normals in their use of associates and word meanings in a laboratory context. Chapman, Chapman, and Miller (1964) have shown that schizophrenics have problems in identifying a correct lower frequency word meaning of a target word when an incorrect, as defined by task demands, high-frequency word meaning is present. The study involved presenting subjects with a sentence with a word underlined. The subjects then had to choose the correct definition of the underlined word from one of three alternatives. The target words used as referents had both highly frequent (high meaning) and less frequent (low meaning) usages, and the present meanings were defined solely by the sentence context. Schizophrenic patients performed more poorly than normals only when a less frequently occurring use of the word (e.g., *pen,* a fenced enclosure) was presented in the sentences. When this happened, schizophrenics tended to choose the most frequently encountered meaning (e.g., *pen,* a writing implement) as the definition.

It seems, therefore, that schizophrenics ineffectively screen presented word stimuli for their semantic context, choosing instead to utilize frequency characteristics in generating a response to a task demand. Chapman *et al.* interpreted their findings as meaning that schizophrenics were yielding to the normal bias of responding to a word in terms of its most frequent usage. They later developed a theory of disordered thought in schizophrenia on the basis of this and other findings.

B. INFORMATION PROCESSING

Other researchers followed a different course in investigating disordered thought and pursued attentional deficits as possible causes. Chapman and McGhie (1962) reported the results of several experimental tasks that attempted to show that deficits in selective attention were present in schizophrenia. Their battery of tasks included a visual Stroop task, auditory and visual distraction tasks, and others. Schizophrenics performed more poorly than normals in the presence of distraction, but not in neutral conditions. However, errors in their data reporting (e.g., combinations of means and standard deviations that were mathematically impossible) were noted by Chapman and Chapman (1973), and their neutral and distraction tasks were not matched for ability to discriminate between groups. This discriminating power problem is common in many studies (Chapman & Chapman, 1973) and makes interpretation of measured differences between groups impossible.

Another series of studies on perceptual distractibility was performed by Oltmanns, Ohayon, and Neale (1978). These investigators studied the effects of diagnostic criteria and antipsychotic medication on distractibility. Chronic schizophrenics, both on and off antipsychotic medication, were tested on a digit span distraction task, with neutral and distraction conditions matched for discriminating power. The task was an auditory presentation of a digit series, which subjects were instructed to recall immediately. The distraction condition contained opposite-sexed voices interspersed between target digit presentations. Antipsychotic medication was observed to decrease distractibility in chronic patients, and schizophrenics identified by Research Diagnostic Criteria (RDC) (Spitzer, Endicott, & Robins, 1978) were more distractible than DSM-II schizophrenics. Therefore, with the discriminating power problem controlled, some schizophrenics are indeed especially distractible. Furthermore, diagnostic criteria are an important variable to be considered in evaluation of studies on distractibility. Finally, antipsychotic medication does not spuriously produce differences between normals and schizophrenics on this type of distractibility measure, as the differences between the groups were suppressed by these drugs.

Another view of schizophrenic distractibility, the ability to attend to internally generated information, was investigated in a series of studies by Cohen and his associates (Cohen & Cahmi, 1967; Cohen, Nachmani, & Rosenberg, 1973; Rosenberg & Cohen, 1964) that examined the ability of schizophrenic subjects to consider a listener's needs while communicating. Their first task was a password-type situation, where a subject was presented with two words, with one identified as the referent. The subject's task was to provide a clue that would allow a listener to discriminate the referent from the nonreferent word. Schizophrenics performed both as speakers (providing clues) and as listeners (choosing the referent on the basis of the speaker's clues). Schizophrenics performed equivalently to normals in the listener role, but performed significantly more poorly in the speaker role.

Subsequently, Cohen et al. (1973) replicated and extended this finding by having subjects try to provide clues that would allow a listener to differentiate among similarly colored disks. Normals and hospitalized schizophrenics were told to use free speech to provide information that would allow a listener to discriminate the referent disk. As the closeness in hue of the disks increased, so did the likelihood that schizophrenics would start to emit associates of the common color of the disks. Rather than describing the color differences, they emitted chains of high associates to the disks' common features. Cohen proposed that this associative chaining meant that the attentional dysfunction of schizophrenics consisted of a tendency to perseverate on similarities combined with an inability to break out of that pattern.

Another commonly investigated attentional deficit in schizophrenia is ability to shadow material dichotically. Payne, Hochberg, and Hawks (1970) found that schizophrenics performed significantly more poorly than normals in the presence of distraction, while not differing from them in the absence of distraction. Another finding in the area (Schneider, 1976) adds a qualification. Schneider found that schizophrenics' dichotic-shadowing performance was only inhibited by distraction if the distracting information was of a personal nature (e.g., material from an active delusional system). A more recent study (Pogue-Geile & Oltmanns, 1980) found that schizophrenics tended to make many more errors in dichotic shadowing than normals and that their errors were likely to be semantically irrelevant (i.e., not based on reasonable projections of the train of thought of the presented message). An example of a semantically irrelevant error is that of a patient who shadows the message *Let's go boating tomorrow. I'll meet you at the dock.* with *Lets go boating. I'll meet you at the museum.* A semantically relevant error would be: *Lets go boating. I'll meet you at the shore.* The semantically irrelevant errors may indicate that schizophrenics are not using knowledge of semantic relations to help them out when they are overloaded during processing. Normals are better able to predict what might be presented, and their errors are words that fit into the context of the presented utterance.

Maher, Manschreck, and Rucklos (1980) reached a similar conclusion from data they collected on the Miller and Selfridge (1950) contextual constraint task. They found that TD patients benefited significantly less from contextual constraint than did NTD schizophrenics and normals. The TD schizophrenics differed more and more from NTD patients and normals as the level of constraint increased. Their interpretation of these findings is that schizophrenics, particularly those with thought disorder, are less able to utilize knowledge of semantic rules to their benefit.

Further studies of schizophrenic attentional dysfunction include those involving size constancy (Weckowicz & Blewett, 1959), size estimation (Silverman & Gaarder, 1967), incidental learning (Venables, 1963), reaction time (Shakow, 1962), and many other areas. However, a review by Neale and Cromwell (1970) effectively demonstrated that the majority of these studies were flawed by methodological problems. Some of the major problems in the attentional research that were pointed out by Neale and Cromwell were failure to subdivide schizophrenic subjects on relevant dimensions (acute–chronic, paranoid–nonparanoid, etc.), failure to integrate research findings and clinical phenomena, and the use of simple-minded, single, dependent variables. At that time no studies met their criteria for being relevant to the understanding of thought disorder. Furthermore, much of the data from the various studies were contradictory. A clear picture of the actual attentional deficits present in schizophrenics was not available, to say nothing of the relationship of these deficits to clinical phenomena, such as disordered speech.

In addition to the methodological problems present in the studies, many of the areas of attentional research were poorly interrelated. The construct of attentional deficit was quite broadly defined with various tasks all thought to measure attention. Yet, none of the studies had combined measures of multiple deficits and examined their coexistence within patients. Later, Kopfstein and Neale (1972) found that these measures of attentional deficit shared little variance. Few changes have occurred in the years since 1972. Researchers still continue to examine single measures of attention, failing to include multiple dependent measures that could be related to each other.

C. CONCEPTUAL ABILITY

Many researchers do not believe that information-processing deficits are the principal causes of disordered speech. Another major area of laboratory study in schizophrenic thought disorder is conceptual ability. K. Goldstein (1939, 1944/1964, 1959) proposed that the key aspect of thought disorder lies in schizophrenic patients' loss of ability to think abstractly. This thinking problem, called concrete thought, was initially measured with an object-sorting test, developed by Goldstein and Scheerer (1941). The patient is asked to sort a set of objects into a variety of groupings, involving both subject-generated groups and alternatives suggested by the examiner. Sortings are scored as either adequate or concrete on the basis of predetermined criteria. Schizophrenics were less able than normals to sort objects on the basis of abstract groupings, behaving instead as if an object had only one meaning and one characteristic. In addition, the schizophrenics were less able than normals to separate their own experiences from the characteristics of the objects, often mentioning personal experiences in their descriptions of the task objects and using their own unique experiences as a basis for grouping the objects together. In many cases the subjects also tended to include fewer objects per group than did the normals.

Other investigators did not agree with the loss of abstraction explanation for the poor performance of schizophrenics on the object-sorting test. Cameron (1939), for example, stated that patients often responded to extremely broad and non-test-specific aspects of the situations, and subsequently a whole body of research on the "overinclusiveness" of conceptual performance of schizophrenics emerged. Payne, Matussek, and George (1959), using a somewhat different object-sorting task, found that schizophrenics were likely to hand over more objects in a predefined conceptual category than were neurotic controls. Their interpretation of the results was that schizophrenics were reacting to irrelevant stimuli and were therefore overincluding items because of an inability to select out items that did not reasonably belong together.

The proverb interpretation task was also used to investigate schizophrenics' conceptual problems. The task was initially designed by Benjamin (1944), and performance on it has been used as a measure of schizophrenic concreteness (e.g., R. Goldstein & Salzman, 1967). An example of the proverb interpretation research is a study by Gorham (1956), who used a multiple-choice format and found that schizophrenics chose significantly fewer abstract interpretations of common proverbs and significantly more concrete interpretations than did normals.

The controversy about whether schizophrenics were showing inability to reason abstractly because of underinclusiveness or overinclusiveness extended to the proverb interpretation task as well. Payne *et al.* (1959) interpreted the fact that schizophrenic patients used more words than did normals in specifying the meaning of the proverbs as indicating that proverbs meant more to them. Therefore, they concluded that schizophrenics were overinclusive in their thought.

There have been problems with the Payne reinterpretation of the proverbs task and with replication of his object-sorting results. First, using more words in a description does not necessarily imply that the proverb has more meaning to the person. Deficits in knowledge of the words required to describe a complicated concept and simple verboseness could both lead a patient to produce many words. The issue of replication of the Payne *et al.* (1959) study was addressed by Payne himself (Hawks & Payne, 1971). His three tests of overinclusion (proverb word count, number of objects sorted, unusual sorting) correlated so poorly and were so variable from study to study that they could not reasonably measure the concept of overinclusion. In addition, a measure of simple talkativeness correlated well with all three measures, higher in fact than the measures intercorrelated with themselves. A reasonable alternative is that schizophrenics were simply more talkative than the contrast groups in Payne's studies.

The conflict between over- and underinclusiveness of schizophrenic conceptual abilities is hard to resolve for one important reason: The concepts are so loosely defined that vastly different dependent measures can be used to index them. Goldstein and his co-workers evaluated object groupings for their concreteness or adequacy. On the other hand, Payne and his co-workers counted the number of objects handed over by a subject in response to a request from the experimenter. The proverb task has the same problems. Payne and associates counted the number of words used to interpret the proverb, whereas Benjamin had a multiple-choice format in his task, with responses compared to predetermined norms to evaluate acceptability. These differences make the data collected by the two different orientations incompatible. In addition, other issues are raised by Andreasen, as the next section will demonstrate.

D. SPECIFICITY OF THOUGHT DISORDER
IN LABORATORY STUDIES

One of the early studies of deviant associations indicated that manics and schizophrenics performed equivalently. Aschaffenburg (cited in Maher & Maher, 1979) found that in a continuous association task manics gave as many deviant associations to a target stimulus as did schizophrenics. However, he, like Bleuler, postulated that schizophrenics and manics had differing underlying reasons for their similar performance, with manics having a motor problem and schizophrenics an attentional problem. He did not, however, offer any evidence to support this view, other than that manics' overall problems seemed due to motor overactivity.

In a much later study, Harrow and Quinlan (1977) compared schizophrenics and other psychiatric patients (depressives, latent schizophrenics, personality disorders) on object sorting, proverb interpretation, and Rorschach tests. They reported that more severe levels of thought pathology were more often present in the schizophrenic group. However, severe thought pathology was not present in every schizophrenic, weakening its usefulness as a discriminator. Moderate levels of thought pathology were not good discriminators of the groups at all. The phase of the illness contributed strongly to the differences between the groups, with such differences being largest at the acute phase.

The object-sorting task used by Harrow and Quinlan and many others has a poor history of being able to discriminate schizophrenics and other psychiatric groups. Goldstein (1939) first reported on the similarities between schizophrenics and organics and built his theory of schizophrenic thought on those similarities. Later, however, the similarities were no longer mentioned, and the schizophrenics tended to be discussed as if they alone manifested pathology on that task. Many subsequent studies failed to include an organic contrast group or glossed over the similarities between the groups. For example, Tutko and Spence (1962) presented a scoring scheme that "differentiated" schizophrenics and brain-damaged subjects. However, they were only marginally able to discriminate the two groups ($p < .10$).

Research on overinclusivity, a psychological deficit also measured by object-sorting tasks and supposedly linked to schizophrenic thought disorder, also has failed to reveal unique schizophrenic deficits. Andreasen and Powers (1974) found that manics were more overinclusive than schizophrenics in that they produced more words to interpret proverbs and sorted many more objects than did the schizophrenics in each category. Andreasen and Powers pointed out that their inability to replicate Payne's findings was likely due to the types of contrast groups used and diagnostic criteria. Payne used depressives as a contrast group; they probably tend to be even more motorically and cognitively retarded than schizophrenics. Also, Payne's clinical descriptions of his acute schizophrenics sound as if they were instead manic or schizoaffective because of their talkativeness and hyperactivity.

Depressives were used as a contrast group by Hemsley (1976), who compared them to schizophrenics on several tasks. He could discriminate depressives and schizophrenics on Bannister's Grid Test of Thought Disorder, a choice reaction-time task, the digit symbol subtask of the WAIS, associative intrusions in the Chapman (1958) task, and Payne's object-sorting task (overinclusion). Schizophrenics made more associative errors than the depressives on the Chapman task, made more overinclusive responses on the object-sorting task, and received lower scores on the digit symbol subtask.

The fact that schizophrenics could be discriminated from the depressive group might initially be seen as evidence that these tasks were measuring specific deficits. But the issue of specificity can only be properly addressed if all groups who might perform similarly are assessed. Manic patients have been shown to have communication problems similar to those of schizophrenics. Therefore, Hemsley's results do not conclusively show that any of these deficits are unique to schizophrenia.

Another finding casts doubt on another view of schizophrenic thought disorder. Naficy and Willerman (1980) used the Chapman, Chapman, and Miller (1964) task to compare the performance of manics, schizophrenics, and normals. They found that manics yielded to normal biases, as operationalized by responding to words in terms of their most frequent meaning, to the same extent as schizophrenics. Therefore, it cannot be concluded that excessive yielding to normal biases is a purely schizophrenic phenomenon.

Another area of schizophrenic cognitive deficit that may be shared by other groups is information processing. Oltmanns (1978) found that manics were as distractible as schizophrenics on a general measure of distraction—the digit span distraction task of Oltmanns and Neale (1975). A much more specific examination of the performance of the groups (serial position analysis of a word span task) did, however, provide a discrimination; schizophrenics showed a greater recall deficit on the primary portion of items presented during distraction than did the manics. Russell and Beekhuis (1976) found that depressives performed as poorly as schizophrenics on a memory task. A similar result was obtained by Sternberg and Jarvik (1976). Filtering ability was examined by Hemsley and Zawada (1976), who found that unipolar depressives performed as poorly as schizophrenics. Korboot and Yates (1973) also found that the visual search (visual attention) performance of depressives was not discriminable from that of schizophrenics. Therefore, many investigators evaluating different areas of information processing have reported few significant differences between schizophrenics and other psychotic patients.

Maher et al. (1980) were able to discriminate TD schizophrenics from NTD schizophrenics and other psychiatric patients. They found that a mixed group of unipolars and bipolars benefited from contextual constraint significantly more than did TD schizophrenics, while not differing from NTD schizophrenics and normals. These findings once again point out the need to subdivide schizophrenic patients on the basis of speech disorder. If the schizophrenic group had not been divided, no significant differences may have been present at all. This subdivision issue is also relevant to the contrast groups used in these studies. Many investigations have used a mixed affective control group composed of unipolar and bipolar patients, with resulting problems in making statements about specificity of deficits found. If manic and unipolar patients were subdivided, differences between them could also be meaningfully examined.

Finally, patients may not be the only groups who differ from normals on experimental tasks that try to identify "schizophrenic" deficits. Many other groups, some fully normal and none suffering from anything resembling clinical thought disorder, also show deficits on tasks purporting to find unique schizophrenic deficits. Harvey, Weintraub, and Neale (Note 1), for example, found that learning-disabled children were more overinclusive than normals of the same age as measured by an object-sorting task. They were also deficient in the ability to produce adequate clues in the Cohen and Cahmi (1967) word communication task. The magnitude of the differences found between the groups on both of these measures was quite large, similar to the ones typically observed between schizophrenics and normals on these tasks. Overinclusiveness may also be present in nonpatients, as demonstrated by Andreasen and Powers' (1975) finding that highly creative writers were quite overinclusive on an object-sorting task. In fact, these writers were much more overinclusive than schizophrenics and performed similarly to manic patients. In a similar vein, Rierdan (1980) found that the continuous word associations of socially isolated, not otherwise disturbed, adolescents were more idiosyncratic than those of nonisolates.

Therefore, the tasks that claim to be testing psychological deficits related to thought disorder in schizophrenics are assessing processes that may not even be correlated with psychosis. While there is an occasional study that reports a unique schizophrenic deficit (e.g., Pogue-Geile & Oltmanns, 1980), most laboratory studies fare poorly when other psychotics are compared to the schizophrenic group.

E. GENERAL PROBLEMS
WITH THE LABORATORY METHOD

Many of the methodological problems in psychological deficit research have been fully discussed elsewhere. Here we want to describe a major conceptual problem: the lack of concern with relating deficits on cognitive tasks to speech deviance. On the basis of the speech dysfunction of schizophrenics, many investigators claim that schizophrenics necessarily have *thought* disorder. Rochester and Martin (1979) note that investigators who make this claim are making a double inference: The listener is confused, hence it is assumed that the speaker is also confused, and the talk is strange, so therefore the thought is as well. Thus, an investigator who measures a cognitive deficit is making a triple inference and an additional assumption. The assumption is that the measurement device is measuring cognitive deviance accurately, and the extra inference is that the deviant cognitive process is correlated with disordered speech. Chapman and Chapman (1973) have shown that nearly every investigator has been wrong in assuming accurate measurement, and it seems likely that this third level of inference is out of line as well. There is very little evidence to date that suggests that speech and cognitive disorders are related.

Treating task-measured cognitive performance deficits as one and the same as disordered speech (and disordered thought) has led to a whole tradition of defining patients as thought disordered on the basis of laboratory task performance, independent of actual speech production. Even worse, in terms of generality of results, is the common practice of not categorizing patients on the basis of speech disorder before laboratory testing and yet attempting to make general statements about thought disorder.

This problem of relating speech disorder and laboratory task performance is an important one for examining the specificity of thought disorder to schizophrenia. If schizophrenics and some other group perform equivalently on laboratory tasks, yet do not have the same communication problems, what is to be concluded? This problem cannot even be addressed if thought disorder is defined in terms of laboratory task performance. Many researchers have lost track of the fact that thought disorder was originally defined in terms of *speech* that was very difficult to understand and often nonsensical.

VI. Future Directions and Suggestions for Improvements

The problem of defining thought disorder in terms of laboratory task performance is a good example of the current problems in thought-disorder research. There has been very little effort expended in linking the various methods of research. Because various methodologies are associated with different topics of investigation, investigators are therefore in a position to make different statements about factors that may either cause or coincide with disordered speech. Ideally, researchers using the laboratory method should examine variables that might underlie deviant speech (i.e., deficits that cause deviant speech phenomena), while researchers using the natural language method should try to describe aspects of speech that make it appear deviant and hard to understand for a listener. These methodologies should form a hierarchy, with the most molar phenomena described by clinical studies. The most molecular data are collected in laboratory studies, with the goal of discovering causes of speech deviance. However, no investigator to date has utilized all three perspectives on disordered speech simultaneously. All the thousands of studies in the area of disordered thought in schizophrenia are mere bits and pieces of several different puzzles, impossible to put together.

In general, an emphatic "no" can be answered to the question "Is thought disorder specific to schizophrenia?" The harder question to answer, in terms of feasibility and significance, is whether different aspects of thought disorder are more characteristic of one diagnostic group than another. As of now, the only solid evidence comes from clinical studies. Andreasen (1979b), it will be recalled, found that schizophrenics display negative subtypes of thought disorder at a much higher rate than manics do.

We have several recommendations for the improvement of research attempting to differentiate the thought disorders of various patient groups. First, the term *thought disorder* in its present use is misleading and should be split into two categories. The first should be discourse failure, as described by Rochester and Martin (1979). The second should be thought disorder, which could be defined as the deviant cognitive processes that relate to discourse failure.

Second, a closer relationship between studies of discourse failure and thought disorder are required. While clinical investigators are the only ones with any consistent success in differentiating subtypes of deviant communication, laboratory studies in which investigators subdivide schizophrenics on the basis of speech disorder (e.g., Maher *et al.*, 1980) show promise of being able to do so. Investigators in the laboratory modality should attend to the differences found in the clinical or natural language studies and should concentrate on identifying the specific cognitive processes that are at the root of the differences. Researchers conducting natural language studies should expand their patient samples to include multiple patient groups and variables other than cohesion and reference. This expansion would enable them to be on the same footing as clinical investigators in identifying variables that discriminate among diagnostic groups. Their studies would then be able to provide the basis for laboratory studies of the kind described here (i.e., closely linked to observed speech). As the most pressing problem in laboratory studies has been one of content validity (e.g., assessing a different phenomenon than one is trying to explain), close relationships with actual speech phenomena would be a great improvement. Previous problems in psychological deficit research, such as trying to define a central deficit, trying to have one type of cognitive dysfunction explain the whole variety of disordered utterances, or measuring deficits unrelated to speech, would then be avoided.

An example of this proposed linking process can be seen in Rochester and Martin's (1979) attempt to relate stratal slips to Oltmanns's (1978) findings. Speech strata are levels of speech competence and include the ability to link sounds into words, words into sentences, and sentences together to put across a main idea. Stratal slips are defined as a loss of ability to use one level of speech competence. Oltmanns found that schizophrenics are unable to use certain levels of information processing. Rochester and Martin proposed that loss of a level of speech competence is analogous to loss of a level of information-processing ability. Therefore, Rochester and Martin are hypothesizing a relationship between speech phenomena and a cognitive deficit. However, because they did not identify the specific information-processing deficits that could lead to stratal slips, the actual relationship between Oltmanns's results and their findings remains to be tested. This kind of empirical linkage between experimental findings and natural language speech phenomena is necessary for any progress in research on thought disorder and discourse failure to take place.

A study that meets our proposed criteria for being an acceptable study in linking research in thought disorder and discourse failure is that by Manschreck, Maher, and Rucklos (1981). They used a patient sample that included schizophrenics and other psychotics and subdivided the schizophrenic patients on the basis of clinically rated speech disorder. Utilizing both natural language and clinical evaluations of thought disorder, they related various indices of thought disorder to each other, as well as correlated speech and motoric disorders. They found that lower type–token ratios, which are generally interpreted as indicating that speech is low in information, were related to presence of clinically rated poverty of content in thought-disordered schizophrenics. They also assessed voluntary motor behavior (e.g., clapping hands, shaking head) for clumsiness, stereotypy, and motor blocking, and found that thought-disordered schizophrenics were most disturbed. In addition, speech disorder correlated significantly with motoric difficulties. This study demonstrates that appropriate methodological refinements help to generate studies that advance our knowledge of language and communication disorders in psychosis. This study also links other psychotic phenomena, such as motor difficulties, with disordered speech. As schizophrenia is not a disorder of communication alone, research that investigates several aspects of schizophrenia at once is even more valuable.

The most likely reason that psychological deficits of schizophrenics are nonspecific and not clearly linked to speech is that long ago the link between actual speech and psychological deficits was blurred. At the time of the blurring, too little was known about normal information processing and cognition for subtle differentiation in an experiment. Therefore, more molar deficits were studied, deficits that would be present in any group suffering from cognitive problems. Because of the guiding assumption that only schizophrenics would show thought disorder, the correlation, if any, between psychological deficits and disordered speech was not even assessed. Now, however, the study of cognition is more advanced, and there is promise that more discriminating studies can be conducted. We may at last be able to conduct laboratory studies of the processes related to the differences between patient groups demonstrated by clinical studies, in order to answer the questions "Which parts of thought disorder are specific to schizophrenia?" and "Which dysfunctional thought processes are related to discourse failure?"

Reference Note

1. Harvey, P. D., Weintraub, S., & Neale, J. M. Specificity of cognitive deficits to schizophrenia: The need for multiple control groups. Paper presented at the annual meeting of the Eastern Psychological Association, Hartford, 1980.

References

Andreasen, N. C. Thought language and communication disorders: I. Clinical assessment, definition of terms, and evaluation of their reliability. *Archives of General Psychiatry,* 1979, **36,** 1315–1321. (a)

Andreasen, N. C. Thought, language, and communication disorders: II. Diagnostic significance. *Archives of General Psychiatry,* 1979, **36,** 1325–1330. (b)

Andreasen, N. C., & Powers, P. Overinclusive thinking in mania and schizophrenia. *British Journal of Psychiatry,* 1974, **125,** 452–456.

Andreasen, N. C., & Powers, P. S. Creativity and psychosis: An examination of conceptual style. *Archives of General Psychiatry,* 1975, **32,** 70–73.

Benjamin, J. D. A method for distinguishing and evaluating formal thinking disorders in schizophrenia. In J. S. Kasanin (Ed.), *Language and thought in schizophrenia.* New York: Norton, 1944.

Bleuler, E. *Dementia praecox: or the group of schizophrenias.* New York: International Universities Press, 1950. (Originally published, 1911.)

Cameron, N. Reasoning, regression, and communication in schizophrenics. *Psychological Monographs,* 1939, **50** (Whole No. 1).

Chapman, L. J. Intrusion of associative responses into schizophrenic conceptual performance. *Journal of Abnormal and Social Psychology,* 1958, **56,** 374–379.

Chapman, L. J., & Chapman, J. P. *Disordered thought in schizophrenia.* New York: Appleton, 1973.

Chapman, L. J., Chapman, J. P., & Miller, G. A. A theory of verbal behavior in schizophrenia. In B. A. Maher (Ed.), *Progress in experimental personality research* (Vol. 1). New York: Academic Press, 1964.

Chapman, J., & McGhie, A. A. A comparative study of disordered attention in schizophrenia. *Journal of Mental Science,* 1962, **108,** 487-500.

Cohen, B. D., & Cahmi, J. Schizophrenic performance on a word communication task. *Journal of Abnormal Psychology,* 1967, **72,** 240-246.

Cohen, B. D., Nachmani, G., & Rosenberg, S. Referent communication disturbances in schizophrenia. *Journal of Abnormal Psychology,* 1973, **72,** 1-13.

Durbin, M., & Marshall, R. L. Speech in mania: Syntactic aspects. *Brain and Language,* 1977, **4,** 208-218.

Fairbanks, A. The quantitative differentiation of samples of spoken language. *Psychological Monographs,* 1944, **56,** 19-28.

Goldstein, K. The significance of special mental tests for the diagnosis and prognosis of schizophrenia. *American Journal of Psychiatry,* 1939, **96,** 575-587.

Goldstein, K. Concerning the concreteness in schizophrenia. *Journal of Abnormal and Social Psychology,* 1959, **59,** 146-148.

Goldstein, K. Methodological approach to the study of schizophrenic thought disorders. In J. S. Kasanin (Ed.), *Language and thought in schizophrenia.* New York: Norton, 1964. (Originally published, 1944.)

Goldstein, K., & Scheerer, M. Abstract and concrete behavior: An experimental study with special tests. *Psychological Monographs,* 1941, **53** (Whole No. 239).

Goldstein, R. H., & Salzman, L. F. Cognitive functioning in acute and remitted psychiatric patients. *Psychological Reports,* 1967, **21,** 24-26.

Gorham, D. R. Use of the proverbs test for discriminating schizophrenics and normals. *Journal of Consulting Psychology,* 1956, **20,** 435-444.

Gottschalk, L. A., & Gleser, G. C. Distinguishing characteristics of the verbal communications of schizophrenic patients. In D. McRioch & E. A. Weinstein (Eds.), *Disorders of communication.* Baltimore: Williams & Wilkins, 1964.

Halliday, M. A. K., & Hasan, R. *Cohesion in English.* London: Longman, 1976.

Harrow, M., & Quinlan, D. Is disordered thinking unique to schizophrenia? *Archives of General Psychiatry,* 1977, **34,** 15-21.

Hawks, D. V., & Payne, R. W. Overinclusive thought disorder and symptomatology. *British Journal of Psychiatry,* 1971, **118,** 663-670.

Hemsley, D. R. Problems in the interpretation of cognitive abnormalities in schizophrenia. *British Journal of Psychiatry,* 1976, **129,** 32-35.

Hemsley, D. R., & Zawada, S. L. "Filtering" and the cognitive deficit in schizophrenia. *British Journal of Psychiatry,* 1976, **128,** 456-461.

Johnston, M. H., & Holzman, P. S. *Assessing schizophrenic thinking: A clinical research instrument for measuring thought disorder.* San Fransisco:Jossey-Bass, 1979.

Kent, H., & Rosanoff, A. J. A study of association in insanity. *Journal of Insanity,* 1910, **67,** 326-390.

Kopfstein, J. H., & Neale, J. M. A multivariate study of attention dysfunction in schizophrenia. *Journal of Abnormal Psychology,* 1972, **36,** 294-298.

Korboot, P. J., & Yates, A. J. Speed of perceptual functioning in chronic nonparanoid schizophrenics: Partial replication and extension. *Journal of Abnormal Psychology,* 1973, **81,** 296-298.

Kraepelin, E. *Dementia praecox and paraphrenia.* Edinburgh: Livingstone, 1919.

Kraepelin, E. *Manic-depressive insanity and paranoia.* Edinburgh: Livingstone, 1921.

Maher, B. A. The language of schizophrenia: A review and reinterpretation. *British Journal of Psychiatry,* 1972, **120,** 3-17.

Maher, B. A., & Maher, W. B. Psychopathology. In E. Hearst (Ed.), *The first century of experimental psychology*. Hillsdale, N.J.: Erlbaum, 1979.

Maher, B. A., Manschreck, T. C., & Rucklos, M. E. Contextual constraint and the recall of verbal material in schizophrenia: The effect of thought disorder. *British Journal of Psychiatry*, 1980, **137**, 69–73.

Maher, B. A., McKean, K. O., & McLaughlin, B. Studies in psychotic language. In P. J. Stone, R. F. Bales, Z. Namenworth, & D. M. Ogilve (Eds.), *The General Inquirer: A computer approach to content analysis*. Cambridge, Mass.: MIT Press, 1966.

Manschreck, T. C., Maher, B. A., & Rucklos, M. E. Formal thought disorder, the type-token ratio, and voluntary motor movement in schizophrenia. *British Journal of Psychiatry*, 1981, **139**, 7–15.

Miller, G. A., & Selfridge, J. Verbal context and the recall of meaningful material. *American Journal of Psychology*, 1950, **63**, 176–185.

Moon, A. F., Mefferd, R. B., Wieland, B. A., Pokorny, A. D., & Falconer, G. A. Perceptual dysfunction as a determinant of schizophrenic word associations. *Journal of Nervous and Mental Disease*, 1968, **146**, 80–84.

Naficy, A., & Willerman, L. Excessive yielding to normal biases is not a distinctive sign of schizophrenia. *Journal of Abnormal Psychology*, 1980, **89**, 697–703.

Neale, J. M., & Cromwell, R. L. Attention and schizophrenia. In B. A. Maher (Ed.), *Progress in experimental personality research* (Vol. 5). New York: Academic Press, 1970.

O'Brian, J. P., & Weingartner, H. Associative structure in chronic schizophrenia. *Archives of General Psychiatry*, 1970, **22**, 136–142.

Oltmanns, T. F. Selective attention in schizophrenic and manic psychoses: The effect of distraction on information processing. *Journal of Abnormal Psychology*, 1978, **87**, 212–225.

Oltmanns, T. F., & Neale, J. M. Schizophrenic performance when distractors are present: Attentional deficit or differential task difficulty. *Journal of Abnormal Psychology*, 1975, **84**, 205–209.

Oltmanns, T. F., Ohayon, J., & Neale, J. M. The effect of diagnostic criteria and antipsychotic medication on distractibility in schizophrenia. *Journal of Psychiatric Research*, 1978, **14**, 81–91.

Payne, R. W., Hochberg, A. C., & Hawks, D. V. Dichotic stimulation as a method of assessing disorder of attention in overinclusive schizophrenic patients. *Journal of Abnormal Psychology*, 1970, **76**, 185–193.

Payne, R. W., Matussek, P., & George, E. I. An experimental study of schizophrenic thought disorder. *Journal of Mental Science*, 1959, **105**, 627–652.

Pogue-Geile, M. F., & Oltmanns, T. F. Sentence perception and distractibility in schizophrenic, manic, and depressed patients. *Journal of Abnormal Psychology*, 1980, **89**, 115–124.

Rierdan, J. Word associations of socially isolated adolescents. *Journal of Abnormal Psychology*, 1980, **89**, 98–100.

Rochester, S. R., & Martin, J. R. *Crazy talk: A study of the discourse of schizophrenic speakers*. New York: Plenum, 1979.

Rochester, S. R., Martin, J. R., & Thurston, S. Thought process disorder in schizophrenia: The listener's task. *Brain and Language*, 1977, **4**, 95–114.

Rosenberg, S. D., & Cohen, B. D. Speakers' and listeners' processes in a word-communication task. *Science*, 1964, **145**, 1201–1203.

Russell, P. N., & Beekhuis, M. E. Organization in memory: A comparison of psychotics and normals. *Journal of Abnormal Psychology*, 1976, **85**, 527–534.

Schneider, K. *Clinical psychopathology*. New York: Grune & Stratton, 1959.

Schneider, S. J. Selective attention in schizophrenia. *Journal of Abnormal Psychology*, 1976, **85**, 527–534.

Shakow, D. Segmental set. *Archives of General Psychiatry,* 1962, **6,** 1-17.

Silverman, J., & Gaarder, K. Rates of saccadic eye movements in and size judgements of normals and schizophrenics. *Perception and Motor Skills,* 1967, **25,** 661-667.

Spitzer, R. L., Endicott, J., & Robins, E. *Research diagnostic criteria (RDC) for a selected group of functional disorders.* New York: Biometrics Research, 1978.

Sternberg, D. E., & Jarvik, M. E. Memory functions in depression. *Archives of General Psychiatry,* 1976, **33,** 219-224.

Tutko, T. A., & Spence, J. T. The performance of process and reactive schizophrenics and brain injured subjects on a conceptual task. *Journal of Abnormal and Social Psychology,* 1962, **65,** 387-394.

Venables, P. H. Selectivity of attention, withdrawal, and cortical activation. *Archives of General Psychiatry,* 1963, **9,** 74-78.

Weckowicz, T. E., & Blewett, D. B. Size constancy and abstract thinking in schizophrenics. *Journal of Mental Science,* 1959, **105,** 909-934.

Wing, J. K., Birley, J. L. T., Cooper, J. C., Graham, P., & Isaacs, A. D. Reliability of a procedure for measuring and classifying "present psychiatric state". *British Journal of Psychiatry,* 1967, **113,** 499-515.

World Health Organization. *The International Pilot Study of Schizophrenia.* Geneva: WHO, 1973.

PSYCHOPHYSIOLOGICAL PROCESSES IN DELINQUENCY-PRONE YOUNG ADULTS[1]

*William M. Waid**

INSTITUTE OF PENNSYLVANIA HOSPITAL AND UNIVERSITY OF PENNSYLVANIA
PHILADELPHIA, PENNSYLVANIA

I. Introduction

Antisocial behavior is a form of social pathology that ranges from mildly troublesome "victimless" trangressions, such as cheating on tests, repeated motor vehicle violations, and recreational illicit drug use, to flagrant violations of social codes, such as robbery, embezzlement, assault and battery, and even homicide. Such behavior encompasses white collar as well as organized and street crime. While some serious forms of antisocial behavior,

*Present address: New Jersey Psychological Institute, 93 West Main Street, Freehold, New Jersey 07728.

[1]The research reported here was supported in part by the Institute for Experimental Psychiatry.

such as homicide, may often reflect relatively specific behavioral disorders or isolated outbursts (e.g., White, McAdoo, & Megargee, 1973), there is nonetheless considerable consensus that much antisocial behavior forms a pattern in which an individual repetitively transgresses social rules and laws (e.g., Wolfgang, Figlio, & Sellin, 1972).

Although social conditions have long been held to be at the root of antisocial behavior, and undoubtedly account for much of it, the last two decades have seen a reemergence of interest in biological determinants. This interest has been heightened by sociological findings indicating that about 50% of the crime in a given locale is accounted for by a very small percentage of repetitively antisocial individuals (e.g., West & Farrington, 1973; Wolfgang, Figlio, & Sellin, 1972) and by a growing body of research consistently finding that identical twins are likelier both to have criminal records than are fraternal twins (e.g., Mednick & Christiansen, 1977).

Constitutional explanations of crime and delinquency that emerged early in psychology's history were based on such global biological concepts as body build and skull shape and fell into disrepute (e.g., Nassi & Abramowitz, 1976). Modern biomedical technology, however, has made possible the investigation of more fundamental biological processes and has permitted studying their relationship to theoretically relevant processes of learning and perception as these processes ensue. Macroneurophysiological (i.e., psychophysiological) processes, such as the galvanic skin reflex or electrodermal response (EDR), the electroencephalogram (EEG), and several cardiovascular processes (e.g., heart rate and peripheral constriction and dilation of blood vessels), can be recorded continuously and noninvasively from human subjects during learning or perceptual tasks or even during social interaction. Such measures do not permit the exquisitely fine-grained analyses of the biological substrates of behavior that are permitted in animal preparations, but they permit a much more fine-grained analysis of the possible role of biological, particularly neurophysiological, processes in behavior, including antisocial behavior, than was possible when constitutional theories were first proposed. Findings using psychophysiological variables may ultimately be integrated with even more fine-grained analyses at the microneurophysiological, biochemical, and neuroanatomic levels of analysis that can typically be carried out only with infrahuman beings.

It should be noted that the psychophysiological approach, although biological, is neutral with regard to any hereditary contribution to antisocial behavior. Psychophysiological differences, such as those described in the following discussion, might well mediate hereditary contributions, as has been suggested by Mednick and Volavka (1980), but this is an empirical question. The psychophysiological differences between antisocial and other individuals might also result from early experience (Thompson & Grusec,

1973) or from learning processes such as habituation (Kimmel, 1973). Regardless of how these differences emerge, they may play a role in antisocial behavior.

Most of the psychophysiological research on this problem over the past two decades has focused on the sociopathic personality (e.g., Hare, 1978). This work has typically compared prisoners diagnosed as sociopathic with prisoners diagnosed as nonsociopathic (e.g., less recidivist) and/or nonprisoner controls. This chapter reviews a conceptually related program of research on the psychophysiological correlates of antisocial or delinquency-prone personality in the normal, noninstitutionalized population. The results of this research provide a link between the research on incarcerated clinical sociopaths and that in the related areas of delinquency per se (e.g., Mednick & Volavka, 1980) and hyperactivity (e.g., Satterfield & Dawson, 1971). This chapter does not attempt a complete review of the psychophysiological studies of psychopathy, delinquency, or hyperactivity, but the studies cited are the most representative. Reviews have been presented on the psychophysiology of psychopathy (Hare, 1978), delinquency (Mednick & Volavka, 1980), and hyperactivity (Hastings & Barkley, 1978), and Cantwell (1978) has reviewed studies indicating the apparent strong overlap of these dimensions.

Psychophysiological research on antisocial personality has been based on the theory that sociopathic behavior may develop partly as a result of a deficiency in fear conditionability that renders an individual relatively impervious to punishment (e.g., Lykken, 1957). Mowrer's (1947) two-stage theory of avoidance learning provided a framework for this research. According to Mowrer's (1947) theory, cues associated with punishment acquire, in the first stage, the capacity to elicit classically conditioned fear responses. In the second stage, responses that are instrumental in removing the organism from the fear-producing cues are reinforced by fear reduction. The relevance of a theory of avoidance learning to sociopathic behavior is that failure to learn to inhibit behavior in response to aversive contingencies and weak emotional reactivity have been standard criteria for the diagnosis "sociopathic personality disturbance" (American Psychiatric Association, 1952; Cleckley, 1964).

Two stable findings about sociopathic individuals are consistent with this theory of the development of sociopathic behavior: First, they show significantly smaller anticipatory or conditioned electrodermal responses (EDRs) than do nonsociopaths (e.g., Hare, 1965a, 1965b; Hare & Quinn, 1971; Lippert & Senter, 1966; Lykken, 1957), and second, they do not perform well in tasks that can be assumed to be mediated by fear or anxiety (Lykken, 1957; Rosen & Schalling, 1971; Schachter & Latane, 1964; Schmauk, 1970; Schoenherr, 1964). In aversive situations, anticipatory electrodermal activity (EDA) is assumed to reflect fear aroused by a stimulus that consistently precedes an aversive stimulus and, theoretically, represents the first stage of avoidance learning. Grings and Lockhart (1966) and Waid (1976a) have both presented evidence that the EDR is indeed correlated with avoidance learning.

Virtually all of this research has been carried out at the extremely antisocial end of the socialization continuum, usually with institutionalized subjects and virtually always with subjects who are explicitly labeled as criminal or delinquent. Thus, the physiological characteristics of antisocial individuals may be sequelae rather than antecedents of the behavior pattern. Only a finding by Mednick and Hutchings (1977) that poor electrodermal conditioning around age 10–12 was predictive of registered delinquency about 10 years later provides evidence that the physiological characteristics are antecedents of the behavior patterns rather than sequelae. Although this prospective study is an important one, it unfortunately obtained a very small sample of delinquents. Only 7 subjects had registered delinquency at 10-year follow-up, compared to 98 with no delinquency. Furthermore, any sample relying on registered delinquency as a criterion confounds antisocial behavior with the vagaries of the law enforcement and judicial processes. Subjects with registered delinquency are those who are apprehended and adjudicated. Otherwise similar "delinquents" may avoid apprehension (Nye, 1958). Thus, the study is sufficiently limited in scope to make supporting studies highly desirable.

The series of studies reported here support the physiological mediation hypothesis but use a different strategy: If the physiological characteristics are antecedent to rather than sequelae of delinquency, then even in a normal, noninstitutionalized, nonlabeled population of young adults, individuals who are electrodermally hyporesponsive in anticipation of noxious stimulation should be less well socialized and have greater, though as yet perhaps unregistered, delinquent tendencies than their more responsive counterparts. One purpose of the series of studies reported here was to test this hypothesis.

The chronically reduced EDR associated with antisocial personality has been attributed to several factors. One view has been that it reflects depressed functioning of the physiological arousal substrates of fear and anxiety. Mawson and Mawson (1977) have proposed that the differences are, in contrast, due to innate differences in neurotransmitter functioning. These are not mutually exclusive propositions, of course, but rather theories addressing different levels of analysis, one psychological and the other biochemical. Another psychological view has been that the differences may be due to acquired cognitive or attitudinal mechanisms.

Lykken, Hare, and Schalling, for example, have each proposed that sociopaths may have greater tolerance for noxious stimulation resulting from what might be called a "repressive" coping style. The main evidence for such a model has been the observation that sociopaths show heart rate increases in anticipation of noxious stimuli that are as large or larger than those of control subjects. Since such heart rate increases reported elsewhere have been interpreted as indicating a reject, as opposed to an intake, mode of processing stimuli (Lacey, 1967), these data have been interpreted as evidence that sociopaths use signals of impending noxious stimuli to reduce the impact of the subsequent noxious stimuli. Although these data are interesting, the chain of inferences seems rather long. The studies I will describe have, in part, attempted to evaluate similar hypotheses by setting up conditions that should either enhance or depress the hypothesized ability of antisocial personalities to reduce the impact of noxious stimuli.

Notably lacking in the literature on psychophysiological correlates of antisocial behavior is evidence that the apparently reduced EDR of sociopathic and delinquency-prone individuals actually plays a role in their behavior problems. Few if any studies have examined both physiological responses and relevant behavior in the same sample. A third purpose of this research, addressed in the final studies, is to examine both physiological response and relevant behavior in the same sample of delinquency-prone and control subjects to determine whether the apparently reduced EDR of sociopathic and delinquency-prone individuals actually correlates with the kinds of antisocial behaviors they presumably engage in.

II. Assessing Delinquency Proneness in Noninstitutionalized Samples

The concept of antisocial personality may have different definitions depending upon an investigator's orientation regarding the relationship of personality to behavior and the nature of abnormal behavior. The research reported here is guided by an orientation consistent with Berlyne's (1968) definition of personality theory as "the theory of individual differences." The implication of this definition is that a concept such as sociopathy, for example, will be considered a dimension or an attribute of behavior on which individuals may vary, rather than either a personality type necessarily entailing a coherent pattern of individuality (Berlyne, 1968) or a disease entity (cf. Ullman & Krasner, 1969). From this point of view, a person categorized as sociopathic, for example, according to a questionnaire score (e.g., the Minnesota Multiphasic Personality Inventory [MMPI] Psychopathic deviate [Pd] scale) or life history data and clinical impression (e.g., Cleckley, 1964) is viewed as being at one extreme of the dimension of antisocial behavior, and the term *sociopathic* is regarded as a summary label applied to observed behavior (Mischel, 1973). This point of view is implicit in some previous research on sociopathy (Hare, 1965c; Hetherington & Klinger, 1964; Schachter & Latane, 1964) in which the subjects were college students and has been made explicit by Wiggins (1968), who observed that "psychopathy . . . *or at its positive pole,* 'socialization,' [is] among the most prominent of trait dimensions currently under active investigation [p. 317]." The Pd scale of the MMPI and the Socialization (So) scale of the California Psychological Inventory (CPI) are the most prominent questionnaire measures of the dimension (Wiggins, 1968), and the terms *psychopathic, sociopathic,* and *undersocialized* are treated as virtually synonymous.

Hogan's (1973) definition of the socialization dimension is consistent with the clinical concept of the sociopathic end of the dimension and with the definition of the dimension scaled by the CPI scale:

> A person may be considered socialized to the degree that he regards the rules, values, and prohibitions of his society as personally mandatory. Conversely, to the extent that one feels estranged from the rules and norms of his social group, he tends to be unsocialized [p. 221].

Consistent with this, the So scale of the CPI is described (Gough, 1964) as indexing the degree to which a person has internalized the rules, values, and conventions of his or her society.

The So scale (Gough, 1964) was used to assess delinquency-proneness in the present research because of the sizable literature supporting its validity. In addition to reliably discriminating between delinquents and nondelinquents (Gough, 1965) in a wide variety of nations and cultures (Gough, 1965), this scale has been found to work well at various levels of socialization (Hogan, 1973). At the upper level, Holland (1959) found that scores significantly predicted academic achievement among National Merit Scholars, and Hetherington and Feldman (1964) found that college students who cheated, both in the classroom and in a disguised, contrived situation, scored significantly lower on the scale than did students who did not cheat. Holland's evidence is consistent with that of Kipnis (1971). At the lower end, Vincent (1961) found that the scale differentiated between female welfare recipients with one illegimate child and those with two or more. The importance of these findings for the present discussion is that they indicate that the So scale is capable of measuring significant differences in socialization at several levels of the dimension.

Studies by Widom (1976) and others have found a reasonably good overlap of the clinical ratings of sociopathy and So scale scores even within the somewhat restricted range of a prison sample, and, regardless of this relationship to clinical ratings, many studies document that the scale correlates highly with delinquent behavior. A particularly illustrative finding is that of Kendall, Deardorf, and Finch (1977), who found that, among juveniles, first offenders score significantly lower on the So scale than nonoffender controls and that repeat offenders scored significantly lower than first offenders. Kipnis (1971) reported extensive research on this dimension within the normal population, linking underachievement in intellectually competent individuals to impulsiveness, which is in turn associated with several sociobehavioral manifestations of undersocialization. Impulsiveness is assessed by means of the Impulsiveness Index (Kipnis, 1971), which incorporates the Impulsiveness scale (Kipnis, 1971) and the So scale. Finally, Schalling, Lidberg, Levander, and Dahlin (1973) found that prison inmates scoring low on the scale gave smaller EDRs than those scoring high, a finding analogous to the comparisons of EDRs of psychopathic and nonpsychopathic prisoners (Hare, 1978).

III. General Method

Although different stimulus materials and procedures were used from study to study, depending upon its purpose, all shared a common basic methodology. The subjects in each study were young adults ranging from 18 to 28 years of age, recruited for participation by advertisements on the campuses of Rutgers University and the University of Pennsylvania. Scores on the So scale were obtained for each subject, as were electrodermal recordings. The EDR or skin conductance response was recorded using a constant .75-V source (Beckman Skin Conductance Coupler) applied to a pair of .64 cm^2 Beckman biopotential electrodes attached to the palmar surfaces of the first phalanx of the third and fourth fingers of the left hand. Johnson & Johnson K-Y Jelly was used as the electrode medium (Edelberg, 1967). The skin was cleaned with acetone prior to electrode placement, and adhesive rings were used to maintain a uniform area of contact with the skin. When subjects completed the So scale, it was identified to them only as the California Psychological Inventory: Scale VII. Most studies of the psychophysiological correlates of antisocial personality have examined only male subjects, as was the case in some of the studies presented here. In the two studies in the present series that included male and female subjects, statistical analyses indicated that sex did not account for any of the effects of interest. The electrodermal–socialization relationship was the same for females as for males.

IV. Origins of the Physiological Correlates of Antisocial Personality

A. CONDITIONAL VERSUS UNCONDITIONAL STIMULI

Figure 1 illustrates some findings from the first sample (Waid, 1976b), in which subjects had been exposed to a series of pairings of a visual stimulus with a 93-dB noise burst. The low-socialization (LS) subjects tended to give significantly smaller EDRs both to the warning stimulus and to the noise bursts than did high-socialization (HS) subjects. These results confirmed a negative relationship between electrodermal responsivity and delinquent tendencies in a normal, noninstitutionalized population, a finding analogous to comparisons of prison sociopaths with nonprison control subjects or nonsociopathic inmates and to the prospective study of Loeb and Mednick (1977).

The other feature of Figure 1 that requires comment is that the most stable and profound differences between groups are in the unconditional EDR. These are present at early trials, whereas the differences between groups on the conditional EDRs emerge across time. Although further work certainly needs to be done on the temporal emergence of the differences between groups, these data do suggest that HS and LS subjects differ in a fundamental way in their response to noxious stimuli and that the reduced

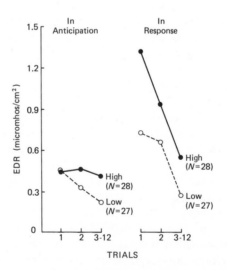

FIG. 1. Amplitude of the EDR of high- and low-socialization subjects in anticipation of and in response to noise burst as a function of trials.

conditional EDR typically shown by such subjects may result from the fact that the unconditional stimulus ultimately has less impact on them.

B. Warning Utilization

Before coming to the conclusion that the unconditional EDR is the locus of the differences between HS and LS subjects, there is another aspect of the conditional–unconditional response relationship that must be considered. Badia and Defran (1970), Lykken (1962), and others have shown that the occurrence of a conditional stimulus or warning signal results in a reduction in the amplitude of the unconditional response. Lykken and others have interpreted this phenomenon in terms of coping processes; that is, the signal permits the person to partially negate or ignore the unconditional stimulus, reducing its impact. Without going into the details of the controversy over how this occurs (e.g., Badia & Defran, 1970; Furedy & Klajner, 1974; Lykken, 1962; Waid, 1979), we should just note that most of the studies discussed so far used a conditioning paradigm, so that the noxious stimulus was always preceded by some sort of conditional or warning stimulus.

Thus, it might be that the reduced EDR of LS subjects might be due to a differential effect of the conditional stimulus rather than to differences in the reaction to the unconditional stimulus per se. For example, LS subjects might be more vigilant than HS subjects, such that they would make better use of the warning information inherent in a conditional stimulus to reduce the impact of the unconditional stimulus. As the saying goes, "Forewarned is forearmed," with the hypothesis being that LS subjects might be more able to make use of subtle forewarnings than their more socialized counterparts.

To test this hypothesis, subjects (Waid, 1976b) were exposed to 30 pairings of a 93-dB 5-sec noise burst with a visual stimulus, a slight change in the illumination of the room. The light change randomly occurred either 11, 3, 1, .5, or 0 sec before the noise burst and terminated simultaneously with it. If LS subjects typically show reduced EDRs to unconditional stimuli because they are better able to use signals of its advent in order to cope with the unconditional stimulus, then these usual differences between groups should be observed at long warning intervals, such as 11 or 3 sec, but not at the 0-sec warning interval.

Figure 2 depicts the results (Waid, 1976b). In both groups a warning of 1 sec or longer significantly reduces the EDR in comparison with the 0-sec or no warning condition. The LS subjects give smaller EDRs to the noise burst than do the HS subjects regardless of warning interval. Since the differences between groups are equally large with a 0-sec warning as with a 3-

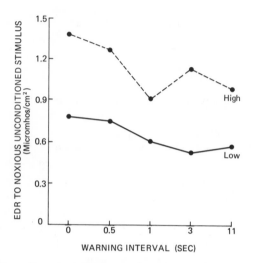

FIG. 2. Electrodermal response of high- and low-socialization subjects in response to noise bursts as a function of warning interval.

or 11-sec warning, the differences cannot be attributed to a differential effect of the warning stimulus.

C. ORIENTING RESPONSE

It might be hypothesized that LS subjects would be less responsive than HS subjects to any stimulus that would cause them to orient, so a similar condition to that described in Section II, B was run (Waid, 1976b) with an innocuous 65-dB tone as the unconditional stimulus. There was no difference between groups in the EDR to these tones, suggesting that the differences between groups do not reside in mechanisms relating to the orienting response, but rather in differences between groups in the processing of noxious stimulation.

D. SENSORY PROCESSES

Another explanation of the differences in EDR to noxious stimuli might be that LS subjects do not perceive the stimuli to be as intense as do HS subjects; that is, they might have an attenuation of the perceptual processing of intense stimuli. To examine this possibility, the subjects (Waid, 1976b) were instructed to make magnitude estimations of the loudness of the noise bursts and the tones. As can be seen in Table I, there were no significant differences between HS and LS subjects in their magnitude estimations.

TABLE I
MEAN MAGNITUDE ESTIMATIONS OF NOISE
BURSTS AND TONES MADE BY TWO
SOCIALIZATION GROUPS

Level of socialization	Type of stimulus	
	Noise	Tone
High	114.8	98.4
Low	112.0	102.6

These results are conceptually consistent with those of Hare and Thorvaldson (1970) using electric shock.

To summarize, LS subjects give smaller EDRs to noxious noise bursts than do HS subjects despite roughly equal perceptions of the intensity of the stimuli and regardless of the presence or absence of a warning. These findings are inconsistent with the hypothesis that the reduced EDR of individuals with antisocial tendencies results from enhanced coping mechanisms.

E. SOCIOEMOTIONAL STIMULI

These results are consistent with predictions based upon the theory that poorly socialized behavior develops at least in part as the result of insufficient physiological arousal in response to, as well as in anticipation of, stress, particularly punishment. If such a theory is valid, however, the reduced EDR shown by LS subjects should be also observed in response to social stimuli or behavior that might be conceptualized as noxious or disturbing.

In a study done in collaboration with Martin Orne and Stuart Wilson (Waid, Orne, & Wilson, 1979a), deception was chosen as the social behavior to examine. The EDR of HS and LS subjects was recorded in the context of a laboratory lie detector test administered by a professional polygraph examiner. Among subjects who were attempting deception, the correlation between socialization and the mean EDR accompanying deception was $r(13) = .45$, $p < .05$. LS subjects also showed a significantly smaller EDR to an unexpected, loud stimulus, an approximately 90-dB hand clap administered at the end of the final series of questions. This result replicates earlier findings (Hare, 1978; Waid, 1976a). The relatively reduced EDR to deception given by LS subjects resulted in their being less likely to be detected as deceptive than their HS counterparts. The fact that LS subjects show reduced EDRs in response to a relevant social behavior such as deception further supports the view that poorly socialized behavior develops at least in part as the result of insufficient physiological arousal in response to such stressful events. The detection of deception paradigm, however, did not permit addressing the question of likelihood of deception as a function of level of socialization. Sections IV, B and C address this question using other relevant social behaviors.

F. AWARENESS

In every study in this area known to the writer, subjects as a matter of course have been aware that their physiological responses are under scrutiny. Further, the ability of people to modulate their EDR to stimuli has been demonstrated by a number of investigators, though there are, of course, great individual differences in such abilities (Stern & Kaplan, 1967). Thus, it might be hypothesized that, when poorly socialized individuals are aware that their physiological responses are being scrutinized, they might successfully exert more control over their responsivity. In an unaware condition, they might be just as responsive as more highly socialized people.

In contrast, it might be that HS individuals may be inordinately aroused by the awareness that their responses are being scrutinized. Alternatively, awareness of recording may have no such differential effects. We (Waid, Orne, & Wilson, 1979b) used a situation developed by Thackray and Orne (1968), who found that deception could be detected even when subjects were apparently unaware that their physiological responses were being monitored, though detection was somewhat attenuated compared with an aware condition.

A polygraph examiner administered a lie detector test using a Stoelting field polygraph situated next to the subject. Recordings of electrodermal activity were made simultaneously and unobtrusively on a Beckman Type R Dynograph in another room. The lie detector test per se was the "aware" condition, while a preceding period during which the examiner reviewed the questions with the subject, with the Stoelting turned off, was the "unaware" condition.

Although in any laboratory study suspicion might exist that monitoring was taking place, the present procedures, in which a recording apparatus next to the subject was used at certain times, appeared successful in making the actual recordings (which were made even when this apparatus was not operating) quite unobtrusive. Detailed postexperimental interviews revealed no indication that subjects were aware that any recording took place at times when the Stoelting polygraph was not operating.

The results are illustrated in Figure 3. LS subjects gave significantly

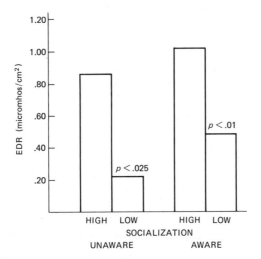

Fɪɢ. 3. Electrodermal response to deception given by high- and low-socialization subjects under unaware and aware conditions.

smaller EDRs than HS subjects when attempting deception during the polygraph test. They also gave significantly smaller responses than the HS subjects during the question review period, during which time they were apparently unaware that their physiological responses were being recorded.

Replication of the reduced EDR to social stress among LS subjects under unaware conditions strengthens the view that such reduced arousal plays an important role in their social conduct. Awareness of physiological monitoring apparently does not explain the finding that HS subjects are markedly aroused and LS subjects little aroused by stress.

G. ROUTINE SOCIAL STIMULI

Another set of data from this study (Waid *et al.,* 1979b) is relevant. Before the lie detector test, the examiner conducted a 10–15-min biographical interview, also under unaware conditions. Figure 4 summarizes a basic finding from the interview. LS subjects gave significantly smaller EDRs than did HS subjects to questions asking about any history of illegal conduct. In contrast, there were no significant differences between groups in EDR to routine information questions. These findings with social stimuli are analogous to those of the earlier study with physical stimuli in which HS and LS subjects differ on responses to noxious stimuli but not on responses to innocuous tones eliciting orienting responses.

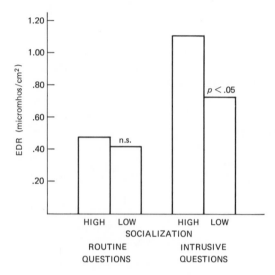

FIG. 4. Electrodermal response given by high- and low-socialization subjects to routine and to intrusive questions during an interview.

H. SLEEP VERSUS WAKING STATES

The weight of the evidence mustered so far argues against the hypothesis that the physiological differences between antisocial and other individuals may be due to cognitive-perceptual or coping processes, rather than to basic differences in visceral centers regulating the reaction to noxious conditions. Nonetheless, for heuristic purposes it was hypothesized that a cognitive mechanism of an entirely different order than had been previously considered—the waking state itself—might mediate the electrodermal differences. If the differences in EDR to stress between HS and LS subjects originate in aspects of the central nervous system (CNS) involved with waking functioning (e.g., certain cortically mediated processes), then the positive relationship between level of socialization and EDR to noxious stimuli should be observed in the waking state but not during sleep. If, in contrast, the differences in physiological response originate in visceral regulatory components of the CNS that are normally always functioning (e.g., such subcortical areas as the limbic system that regulate visceral processes), then changing from waking brain activity to sleeping brain activity should have little or no effect on the EDR differences. That is, LS subjects should continue to give smaller EDRs than HS subjects to noxious stimuli administered during sleep. This hypothesis was tested in a study by Waid and Dinges (Note 1).

After adaptation to the laboratory on a first visit and a nap in bed on a second visit, subjects returned for a third day, on which they napped in a cushioned recliner–chair. Recordings performed during this nap constitute the present data. Subjects were not told how long they would be permitted to nap. The nap period was 60 min and was terminated by a 93-dB bell. Subjects then performed a number of cognitive tasks. About 15 min after the end-of-nap bell, a second identical bell was presented. Palmar EDR and four channels of EEG were recorded throughout the nap. EEG electrode placement, recording parameters, and sleep–wakefulness stage scoring were accomplished using standardized criteria (Rechtschaffen & Kales, 1968). For the present analyses, subjects were classified as either asleep (i.e., in Stage 1, 2, 3, or 4 sleep) or awake at the time of the 93-dB awakening bell.

Twenty-three subjects were already awake before the first bell occurred. Preliminary analyses contrasting the 23 awake subjects and the 44 asleep subjects indicated that time since awakening and total sleep time affected the relationship between socialization and the EDR. Since our original hypotheses were concerned with waking versus sleep state, subgroups of HS and LS subjects were selected who were asleep at the first bell and who were matched on the parameters of total sleep time and time since awakening at the second bell. These 7 LS (score ≤ 31) and 14 HS (score ≥ 40) subjects comprise the data of this report.

The results of this analysis are presented in Table II. The table presents the amplitude of the EDR to the first and second bells in the LS and HS groups. For these subjects, the first bell occurred while subjects were asleep, while the second occurred about 15 min after awakening.

At the second bell, 15–20 min after the nap, while in the waking state, LS had significantly lower EDR amplitude than HS subjects, as expected from previous research. At the bell ending the nap, however, LS subjects averaged larger EDRs than HS subjects, though these mean amplitude dif-

TABLE II

MEAN EDR (KILOHMS) OF LOW- AND HIGH-SOCIALIZATION SUBJECTS
MATCHED FOR TOTAL SLEEP TIME, STAGE AT NAP END,
AND TIME SINCE AWAKENING

| | Socialization | | | |
| | Low ($N = 7$) | High ($N = 14$) | | |
Stimulus			t	p
93-dB bell				
Ending nap period	274.7	200.9	1.29	n.s.
15–20 min post nap	44.7	78.1	1.87	< .05

ferences were nonsignificant. Both groups had a significant decrease in mean EDR amplitude from the first bell (asleep) to the second bell (awake), but these decreases were much greater for the LS subjects. Although the present study did not permit counterbalancing the sleep and waking state presentations of the bell, habituation is unlikely to account for the present pattern of results. Previous studies have shown LS subjects to give smaller EDRs to the first of a series of noxious stimuli as well as to single presentation of such a stimulus. In the present study, the two presentations were separated by about 15 min of performance on several cognitive tasks. The groups did not differ in tonic electrodermal levels at either bell.

Some aspects of having slept disrupted the typically observed positive correlation between socialization and EDR to a noxious stimulus. When LS and HS subjects were matched on nap sleep characteristics, LS subjects were less responsive electrodermally than HS subjects when a loud bell was presented during the waking state, consistent with previous research, but they were just as responsive as HS subjects when it was presented during the sleep state. It is important to note that this disruption of the typical relationship was accompanied by greater EDR amplitudes among both HS and LS subjects, rather than by reduced amplitudes, in comparison with the waking state.

It would appear that some process active only during wakefulness is the basis for attenuated electrodermal reactivity in LS individuals. It is possible that the attenuated electrodermal responsivity results from some cortically mediated cognitive process that is active only during wakefulness. In light of the marked lack of effect of other cognitive-perceptual processes, such as vigilance, sensory sensitivity, and habituation, however, this seems unlikely. Whether this disruption results instead from some cortically mediated modulation in waking arousal levels or from other underlying physiological processes, independent of cognitive function, remains to be determined.

I. REDUCED EDR TO CONFLICT

The evidence reviewed so far can be summarized as indicating that HS and LS subjects do not differ in the EDR to innocuous orienting stimuli such as mild tones or routine personal information questions, that HS subjects come to respond more than LS subjects to such stimuli when they are paired with noxious stimuli, and that HS subjects generally respond more than LS subjects to noxious stimuli. The differences in the EDR to noxious stimuli do not appear to be accounted for by differences between groups in judgments of the intensity of stimuli, vigilance to warning cues, habituation across blocks of trials, or greater control of responsivity when aware that their responses are being recorded. These findings seem consistent with a model that holds that LS subjects have a defect in the motivational and/ or affective processes underlying noxious stimulation, resulting in a reduced EDR to noxious stimuli and stimuli associated with them, at least in the waking state.

Recent theoretical formulations, however, have focused on the EDR as reflecting the operation of a behavioral inhibition system (Fowles, 1980) and have attributed the development of antisocial behavior patterns to a reduction in the strength of this system with a consequent disinhibitory psychopathology (Fowles, 1980; Gorenstein & Newman, 1980). Most of the physiological findings with regard to antisocial personality have involved physically noxious stimuli, however, and while these results may well be interpreted in terms of disinhibitory processes as well as in terms of reduced aversive processes, it is not possible to distinguish between the two interpretations.

Suggestive evidence is provided by findings that undersocialized subjects are less detectible, using the EDR, in the physiological detection of deception (Giesen & Rollison, 1980; Ingersoll, 1977; Waid, Orne, & Wilson, 1979a). For example, Waid, Orne, and Wilson (1979a) found that subjects who tended to give larger EDRs when attempting deception than when answering control questions had higher Socialization scale scores than did subjects who did not respond differentially. Although this differential EDR to questions involving deception, in comparison with control questions, was attributed to the presumed aversiveness of deception, it might be more accurately attributed to *response conflict* (Davis, 1961) and the inhibitory processes it evokes. Aside from any aversiveness attached to deception, presumably through conditioning (Davis, 1961), deception involves inhibiting one response, the truthful one, and substituting another. Laboratory tasks involving analogous response conflicts (i.e., the inhibition of a dominant behavioral response and the substitution of another) in the absence of aversive stimuli have been found to induce considerable physiological response (Elliott, Bankart, & Light, 1970; Frankenhaeuser, Mellin, Rissler, Bjorkvall, & Patkar, 1968). The present study examines the EDR of HS and LS subjects under nonaversive conditions requiring inhibitory control. If the disinhibitory model is a useful one, then LS subjects should respond electrodermally to response conflict in the absence of aversive stimuli less frequently than do HS subjects, analogously to their less frequent differential EDR to deception. Positive findings would suggest the inadequacy of conceptualizing the reduced EDR of undersocialized subjects solely in terms of reduced aversive processes and would support the utility of a model based on the concepts of response conflict and reduced inhibition of dominant behaviors.

A task based on the Stroop color–word interference task was designed in such a way as to permit auditory presentation of stimuli and the measurement of EDRs on each trial (Waid & Orne, in press). The task was not designed to be stressful, but rather to accustom the subject to making a certain kind of response, the "dominant" response, and then to require him or her to inhibit that response and make another.

Windes (1968) found that interference effects similar to the Stroop color–word effect could be obtained with numerical stimuli. Such stimuli were adapted to auditory presentation. The task consisted of the numbers 1–25 presented serially, through earphones, with the numbers 6, 9, 11, 15, 20, and 24 presented out of order. The subject was instructed:

> I will read a list of numbers to you, one number every 10–15 seconds. You are to count the numbers aloud. When you hear the first number you would say "one," when you hear the second one say "two," and so forth regardless of what number I read to you. If you respond incorrectly that will count as an error. We will record your verbal reaction time to each number you hear, so respond as quickly as possible after I've read each number. If you respond before I've finished reading the number that will count as an error also. Respond as quickly as possible, without making any errors. I'll start reading the numbers in 10–15 seconds.

The subject then heard the numbers 1–25, with six of the numbers being presented out of order (e.g., 9 occurring where 6 should be). Thus, on the majority of trials, including the first five, the subject repeated, as quickly as possible, precisely the number he or she heard, whereas on six trials the subject was required to inhibit such a response and supply a different number. The latter trials will be referred to as the response conflict trials.

Electrodermal activity was monitored throughout, and the experimenter recorded the subject's verbal response to each item. Approximately an hour after the task, a third experimenter had the subject complete the Socialization scale and a questionnaire that asked the subject to recall the numbers that had been presented out of order. The exposure–recall interval was 1 hr. The memory measure was taken to assess whether any effects observed might be due to differential attention to or processing of the task stimuli. Studies of the role of physiological arousal in human attention and memory (e.g., Corteen, 1969; Waid, Orne, Cook, & Orne, 1978; Waid, Orne, & Orne, 1981) suggest that response conflict events that evoke large EDRs might be recalled better than those that evoke smaller EDRs. If LS subjects are less aroused electrodermally by response conflict, it might be due to reduced attention, rather than to reduced inhibitory control.

A summary score analogous to the frequency of detection of deception measure that has been found to discriminate between HS and LS subjects was derived for the EDR to response conflict. Each EDR to a response conflict trial was compared to the EDR on the immediately preceding and following trials. The frequency (0–6) with which the EDR to response conflict was greater than the EDR to both of the adjacent control trials was the score. The number of items recalled could range from 0 to 6.

The task was pretested using 12 pilot subjects. It was counterbalanced with a presentation of the same stimuli with instructions to "just listen." The pretesting indicated that a substantial EDR was evoked by the out-of-order items and that the differentially large EDR to these numbers could be attributed to the response conflict rather than to dishabituating characteristics of the stimuli. The mean number of differentially large EDRs in the count reaction-time condition ($M = 3.92$, $SD = 1.24$) was significantly larger than that in the "just listen" condition ($M = 1.08$, $SD = 1.24$, $t(11) = 4.44$, $p < .001$). Three of the 12 pilot subjects made at least one error on a response conflict trial.

Ninety male college students then completed the task as described here. Analysis of variance indicated that level of socialization (high, medium, or low) had a significant positive relationship with the number of EDRs to response conflict ($F(2,87) = 3.94$, $p < .05$).

To simplify examining the relationships of interest, extreme groups of HS (≥ 43, $N = 17$) and LS (≤ 31, $N = 10$) subjects were compared. These results are presented in Table III. LS subjects gave a differentially large EDR to response conflict less frequently than did HS subjects. The two groups did not differ significantly in the number of response conflict stimuli recalled. Consistent with previous studies (e.g., Waid *et al.,* 1981), items

TABLE III
EDR and Memory Measures as a Function of Level of Socialization

	Level of socialization			
Measure	High ($N = 17$)	Low ($N = 10$)	t	p^a
EDR				
Mean	4.53	3.60	2.06	< .025
SD	1.23	1.07		
Number recalled				
Mean	2.71	3.00	0.55	n.s.
SD	1.72	1.05		

[a] One-tailed test.

recalled were associated with larger EDRs than were items not recalled, and LS subjects showed a different pattern of results related to the EDR as a function of recall of the response conflict stimuli. For each subject, the mean EDR to response conflict stimuli that were recalled was expressed as a percentage of the mean EDR to such stimuli that were not recalled. HS subjects had a significantly larger EDR to recalled as compared to not-recalled stimuli ($M = 199\%$) than did LS subjects ($M = 149\%$, $t = 1.89$, $p < .05$).

A between-subjects analysis also suggested a dissociation between the EDR and recall among LS subjects. Table IV presents the number of EDRs to response conflict as a function of high- and low-socialization crossed with high (four or more items) and low recall (three or fewer items recalled). HS subjects tended to have more EDRs to response conflict if they recalled many such events than if they recalled few, as expected from previous research (e.g., Waid *et al.*, 1978). Among LS subjects, however, recall was unrelated to the EDR, and the differences between HS and LS subjects are more pronounced when subjects with poor recall are not included.

In sum, LS subjects tended to give differentially large EDRs to response conflict less frequently than did HS subjects. This result suggests the inadequacy of conceptualizing the reduced EDR of undersocialized subjects solely in terms of reduced aversive processes. Other studies (Hare, 1978; Waid, 1976b) indicate that these differences are not due to differences in orienting or attentional processes.

Subsequent recall of the response conflict stimuli was approximately equal

TABLE IV

NUMBER OF DIFFERENTIALLY LARGE
EDRs TO RESPONSE CONFLICT
AS A FUNCTION OF SOCIALIZATION
AND LATER RECALL

	Later recall	
Socialization	High	Low
High		
Mean	4.88	4.22
SD	1.13	1.30
Low		
Mean	3.25	3.83
SD	0.96	1.17
t	2.61	0.60
p	< .025	n.s.

in HS and LS subjects, indicating that the increased errors and reduced EDRs among LS subjects were not due to inattention, at least as indexed by subsequent memory. The LS subjects, however, showed a dissociation between the EDR and memory. Among HS subjects, those who later recalled many items had given more EDRs to response conflict than those who recalled few, as expected from previous research (e.g., Waid *et al.*, 1978). This was not the case among LS subjects. Moreover, within subjects, the EDR–memory relationship was significantly stronger among HS than among LS subjects.

The dissociation between memory and the EDR in LS subjects is analogous to the dissociation between EDR conditioning and acquisition of awareness of stimulus contingencies among clinical sociopaths reported by Ziskind, Syndulko, and Maltzman (1978). Following aversive EDR conditioning, they assessed subjects' learning of stimulus contingencies and, analogously to the present memory results, found no difference between sociopaths and nonsociopaths in their awareness of stimulus contingencies. Conditioning was demonstrated only among nonsociopaths who showed awareness, however. Nonsociopaths showed a dissociation between EDR conditioning and cognitive learning: Even sociopaths who verbalized awareness did not show conditioning of the EDR.

These findings of dissociation are consistent with the view that cognitive learning, even of aversive conditioning stimulus contingencies or memory for noxious events or for response conflicts, is unimpaired in antisocial personalities, whereas the learning of associated behavioral (i.e., inhibition) or emotional (e.g., EDR) responses is impaired. It may be that several discrete psychological or physiological mechanisms will ultimately be shown to account for the differences in EDR between highly and poorly socialized individuals revealed under distinct conditions, such as noxious stimulation, the detection of deception, or the present response conflict task. In lieu of such evidence, however, it is parsimonious to account for the differences observed under different conditions in terms of a single process. In light of the results of this study, such a process would seem to involve something other than the capacity to respond to noxious stimulation. It would be difficult for the latter model to account for the differences between HS and LS subjects on the present response conflict task since the stimuli were not regarded as noxious in any way. A deficit in the processes underlying response inhibition might, on the other hand, mediate the reduced EDR to both physically and socially noxious stimuli since such stimuli may well evoke conflicting response tendencies in the subject. The results of this study are consistent with such a model, one that has been proposed independently by several investigators (Fowles, 1980; Gorenstein & Newman, 1980).

V. Delinquency Proneness, Physiological Response, and Disinhibited and Asocial Behavior

A. REDUCED EDR TO CONFLICT AND FAILURE TO INHIBIT DOMINANT BEHAVIORS

Regardless of whether the electrodermal differences between highly and poorly socialized individuals originate in aversive or in inhibitory processes, these differences have been viewed as playing a role in asocial behavior (e.g., Mednick & Volavka, 1980). Although several studies are consistent with a physiological mediation model, few studies have adequately tested this role by examining both physiological responses and relevant behavior concurrently in the same sample. The best established finding is that undersocialized subjects are poorer at passive avoidance learning than are their more socialized counterparts (Chesno & Killman, 1975; Lykken, 1957; Schachter & Latane, 1964; Schmauck, 1970) and that poor avoidance learning is associated with reduced electrodermal activity during task performance (Schmauk, 1970; Waid, 1976a).

Consistent with the hypothesis that the reduced EDR is associated more directly with reduced inhibitory control than with reduced aversive processes, we hypothesized (Waid & Orne, in press) that undersocialized subjects would show poorer performance on tasks involving inhibition of dominant responses even in the absence of aversive stimuli. Positive findings would further support the utility of a response conflict or disinhibitory pathology model of the processes underlying antisocial personality. Poor inhibitory control (i.e., impulsiveness) has been proposed by other investigators as a model of processes underlying antisocial behaviors (Kipnis, 1971). Restraining aggressive impulses, for example, may be conceptualized as involving the inhibition of aggressive responses and the substition of others. Apart from any aggressive or other antisocial drives that might be dominant in an individual, reduced ability to inhibit dominant response tendencies and to substitute others could lead to considerable antisocial behavior. Individuals who are little aroused physiologically by response conflict, as undersocialized subjects are hypothesized to be, might have more difficulty inhibiting the dominant impulse. The response conflict task used in Waid and Orne (in press), modeled on the Stroop color–word interference task, provided a relevant context for such a test.

Few subjects made errors on the task. Nonetheless, using the dichotomy of errors versus no errors as the independent variable, the 10 subjects who made one or more errors had significantly lower socialization and EDR scores than those who made no errors ($M = 32.4$ and $M = 38.1$, $t = 3.64$, $p < .0005$, respectively, and $M = 3.0$ and $M = 4.1$, $t = 2.26$, $p < .01$, respectively). The subjects who made errors did not differ from the no-error subjects on number of items recalled. Analogous results were obtained when subjects were split on socialization. The 10 subjects with the lowest socialization scores had significantly more errors ($M = 1.1$, $SD = 1.9$) than did the 17 with the highest scores ($M = 0$, $SD = 0$, $t = 1.77$, $p < .05$).

The physiological processes underlying the EDR have been proposed as playing a mediating role in the development of socialized behavior (Mednick & Volavka, 1980). While some suggestive evidence has been reported (Loeb & Mednick, 1977; Lykken, 1957; Schmauk, 1970), this study attempted to present more explicit evidence by concurrently examining electrodermal activity and a theoretically relevant behavior—inhibition of dominant responses in a conflict or interference situation. If the reduced EDR plays a role in the development of antisocial behavior, and does so through its deleterious effects on the inhibition of impulses, then more errors on a response conflict task, as well as reduced EDRs, would be expected among LS subjects. The results substantially confirmed such a view.

In summary, poorly socialized subjects gave differentially large EDRs to response conflict less frequently than their more highly socialized counterparts. They were also more likely to make errors on the task by failing to inhibit a dominant response. These results are consistent with a model that holds that poorly socialized behavior develops in part as a result of reduced physiological reactions that make it more difficult to inhibit dominant responses in conflict situations.

B. PUNCTUALITY: TIMELY ANTICIPATION OF FUTURE EVENTS

Although both avoidance learning and interference task performance correlates of socialization and the EDR are consistent with the physiological mediation model, evidence that the physiological component mediates more ecologically representative types of antisocial behavior that typify the construct is still lacking. Suggestive evidence comes from the finding by Mednick and Hutchings (1977) that poor electrodermal conditioning around age 10–12 was predictive of registered delinquency about 10 years later and from the finding by Waid, Orne, and Wilson (1979a, 1979b) that LS subjects were less responsive electrodermally when engaging in a relevant social behavior—deception. However, studies that have directly observed such behavior—for example, cheating (Hetherington & Feldman, 1964) or aggression (Wilkins, Sharff, & Schlottman, 1974) in delinquency-prone and control subjects—have not obtained physiological data. The present study (Waid, Orne, & Orne, Note 2) reports personality, physiological, and behavioral observations on the same sample.

Punctuality of fulfilling social commitments was chosen as the behavior of interest. Punctuality data are typically highly variable because of the effects of extraneous factors (e.g., one receives an important telephone call just when due to leave for the appointment). However, they have the virtue of transcending the laboratory context, with its attendant problems of external validity, since the planning and behavior required to arrive punctually occur considerably prior to arrival for the appointment itself.

Individuals who are insensitive to other people, as are the delinquency prone, should be more likely to arrive late, causing inconvenience to another person. Several studies have found that delinquents have a shorter future time perspective than do nondelinquents (cf. Barabasz, 1968–1969; Barndt & Johnson, 1955; Black & Gregson, 1973; Brock & Del Guidice, 1963; Matulef, 1967; Stein, Sarbin, & Kulik, 1968). Such findings have been interpreted (Cottle & Klineberg, 1974) as consistent with the weak anticipation of future events reflected in the diminished acquisition of conditioned EDRs in the delinquency prone. Since reduced EDR to conflict is hypothesized to underlie reduced social responsiveness, we also hypothesized the electrodermally hyporesponsive subjects would tend to arrive late regardless of socialization score.

Each subject's appointment time and exact arrival time were unobtrusively recorded. The appointment time minus the arrival time provided a punctuality score. Each subject was exposed to the mild response conflict task (see Section IV, I) while palmar electrodermal activity was recorded, and completed questionnaires, including the Socialization scale. The frequency with which a subject gave a larger EDR to response conflict than to control items provided a measure (0–6) of EDR to conflict.

LS subjects had significantly lower EDR scores than did HS subjects ($p < .025$). They also tended to arrive significantly later than HS subjects ($p < .05$). To examine the role of the EDR measure in these relationships, subjects were also split on this measure for purposes of analysis. Subjects who responded strongly in the EDR to response conflict (score = 6) had both higher socialization scores ($p < .025$) and earlier arrival times ($p < .025$) than subjects who responded weakly in the EDR to response conflict (score ≤ 2). Although there was some overlap in the subjects selected by splitting on socialization or splitting on the EDR, the overlap did not approach significance.

Thus, socialization was significantly predictive of both the EDR and punctuality, and the EDR was predictive, at least partially independently, of both socialization and punctuality. The apparent overlap of the dimensions of delinquency proneness and hyperactivity was alluded to in Section I, as were the similar electrodermal findings contrasting delinquents and hyperactives with control subjects. The present Socialization scale–punctuality data permit a compelling juxtaposition with a 10-year follow-up study on hyperactive children. Weiss, Hechtman, and Perlman (1978) found that at 10–13-year follow-up, subjects who had been diagnosed as hyperactive around 6–7 years of age scored significantly lower on the CPI Socialization scale and were rated by their teachers (last year of high school) as significantly less punctual in school activities than carefully matched control subjects. Several studies have found hyperactive children to be less responsive electrodermally than control children (e.g., Satterfield & Dawson, 1971). Taken together, these studies strongly suggest that the electrodermal differences are precursors rather than sequelae of delinquency and antisocial behavior.

Future research using path analytic techniques will explore causal models of the interrelations of the socialization, electrodermal, and punctuality data of the present study. The most compelling model, based on such previous findings as those of Loeb and Mednick (1977), is that individuals fail to become adequately socialized, and thus they frequently fail to conform to social expectations and rules partly because of reduced physiological arousal, as indexed by the EDR, to conditions involving conflict.

C. POLYDRUG USE

A final study provides further evidence that relevant nonlaboratory behaviors may be mediated by reduced underlying physiological responsivity indexed by the EDR.

Although an essentially victimless form of delinquency, the illegal use of marijuana, amphetamines, and other psychoactive drugs has evoked considerable public concern. Recent events have heightened concern over the extent of psychoactive drug use on the job, particularly where errors can be fatal. Although many factors may contribute to the decision to experiment with psychoactive substances, personality factors related to the willingness to violate societal rules may be an important one. Consistent with such a view, Hogan, Mankin, Conway, and Fox (1970) found that, among college students, frequent marijuana use was significantly negatively correlated with Socialization scale score. The present study (Waid, Dinges, Wilson, & Orne, Note 3) sought to replicate this finding and in addition examine the interrelations of socialization and illicit drug use with electrodermal activity.

Study 1: On separate days, each of 23 subjects (*a*) were exposed to a 93-dB bell while the EDR was recorded (the bell followed a 15-min period devoted to performance on a number of cognitive tasks reported elsewhere); (*b*) completed the Socialization scale (Gough, 1964); and (*c*) completed an extensive inventory of sleep-related behavior, including questions concerning the frequency of use of marijuana, LSD, and other illicit drugs. The polydrug use scores computed for each subject could range from 0 to 10. *Study 2:* On Day 1 each of 90 subjects (*a*) were exposed to the interference task described in Section IV, I, while the EDR was recorded and (*b*) completed the Socialization scale. On Day 2 subjects were given an interview that included questions about marijuana use. Subjects' answers were scored on a scale from 0 (has not used marijuana) to 6 (marijuana smoked more than once a week). The mean Socialization scale score of 38 in both studies was comparable to norms for a college sample. Since the Socialization scale, as well as the EDR, was predicted to relate to polydrug use, it is important to note that the scale does not contain illegal drug use items, though it has two questions about excessive alcohol use. Rather, the scale focuses on poor interpersonal relations, social insensitivity, sensation seeking, disturbed family and school life, lack of anxiety, and socially disinhibited behavior.

The results of the two samples are presented in Table V. In both studies socialization was positively correlated with the electrodermal measure and with drug use, replicating previous work. In addition, the electrodermal measure was significantly correlated with drug use in the expected direction. Although the partial correlations were not significant in the small first sample, in Study 2 the electrodermal measure was significantly correlated with socialization, with drug use held constant and with drug use with socialization held constant. The multiple correlation of drug use with both socialization and the electrodermal measure was .43 ($p < .025$) in Study 1 and .35 ($p < .005$) in Study 2. Although there was some overlap in the subjects selected by splitting on socialization or splitting on the EDR, the overlap was not significant.

TABLE V

INTERCORRELATIONS OF ILLEGAL DRUG USE, SOCIALIZATION, AND ELECTRODERMAL MEASURES IN TWO STUDIES

	Study 1 (N = 23)		Study 2 (N = 88)	
	Electro-dermal	Drug use	Electro-dermal	Drug use
Socialization	.48*	−.41*	.39**	−.30*
Electrodermal	—	−.32	—	−.29*
Drug Use		—		—

*p < .025
*p < .005
**p < .0001

Thus, the EDR was predictive of both polydrug use and socialization, and socialization was, at least partially independently, significantly predictive of both the EDR and polydrug use. The most compelling causal model of the interrelations of these variables, based on such previous findings as those of Mednick and Volavka (1980), is that individuals fail to become adequately socialized and thus frequently fail to conform to social regulations partly because of reduced physiological processes indexed by the EDR. Future work utilizing path analytic techniques will seek to document this causal model.

VI. Conclusions

The Socialization scale of the California Psychological Inventory has been used to study the electrodermal characteristics of delinquency-prone subjects from a noninstitutionalized, nonlabeled population. Differences in the EDR, particularly to noxious stimuli, have been reliably observed between subjects scoring high and low on the scale. These findings appear to be analogous to findings comparing HS with LS prison inmates or sociopathic with nonsociopathic inmates. The observation of these analogous differences in noninstitutionalized, nonlabeled subjects strengthens the view that the physiological characteristics are antecedents rather than sequelae of antisocial dispositions. In addition, several processes have been empirically discounted as possible mediators of the differences between highs and lows on the EDR to noxious stimuli. These include the utilization of warning cues, orienting or attention, sensory differences, and differential effects of awareness of being monitored. One process, however, the waking state itself, was found to be critical to the reduced EDR of LS subjects. When administered during daytime sleep, confirmed by EEG criteria, a loud bell evoked similar EDRs in LS and HS subjects. The similarity was not due to lack of response in the sleep condition, since these EDRs were larger than when the same stimulus was evoked during the waking state, particularly among LS subjects.

Evidence has also been offered to the effect that a deficit in processes underlying response conflict, rather than a deficit in the capacity to respond to noxious stimuli, should be conceptualized as being the most parsimonious explanation for the observed differences in EDR. It may be that several discrete psychological or physiological mechanisms may ultimately be shown to account for the differences in EDR between HS and LS subjects shown under such distinct conditions as noxious stimulation and the present response conflict task. In lieu of such evidence, however, it seems more parsimonious to account for the differences observed under different conditions in terms of a single process. In light of these results, this process would seem to involve something other than the capacity to respond to noxious stimulation. It would be difficult for the latter model to account for the differences between HS and LS subjects on the present response conflict task since the stimuli were not regarded as noxious in any way. A deficit in the processes underlying response conflict might, on the other hand, be at the root of the reduced response to both physically and socially noxious stimuli since such stimuli may well evoke conflicting response tendencies in the subject.

Finally, evidence was presented consistent with the view that the electrodermal characteristics of LS subjects do indeed play a role in their problem behavior as implied by several theorists (e.g., Mednick & Volavka, 1980). Both the Socialization scale and electrodermal activity were found to be predictive of relevant behaviors—response inhibition, punctuality, and polydrug use. These findings are, of course, subject to the limitations of correlational data. Nonetheless, these findings contribute to a growing body of literature that is highly consistent with the physiological mediation hypothesis. Loeb and Mednick's predictive study has already been described. Stimulant medication, such as amphetamine, produces at least temporary improvement in such behavior as self-control among both hyperactives (Barkley, 1977) and delinquents (Eisenberg, Lachman, Molling, Lockner, Mizelle, & Conners, 1963; Maletzky, 1974). Such medication has been found elsewhere (Lader, 1969) to augment the EDR to noxious stimuli. These pharmacological findings are consistent with the view that physiological processes that underlie electrodermal activity and that can be manipulated by amphetamine and other stimulants indeed play a role in delinquency-prone behavior.

Acknowledgments

I thank David F. Dinges, Emily Carota Orne, Martin T. Orne, and Stuart K. Wilson, who collaborated in many of the studies, for their helpful comments during the preparation of this chapter.

Reference Notes

1. Waid, W. M., & Dinges, D. F. Level of socialization and electrodermal response in sleep and wake states. Paper presented at the 52nd Annual Meeting of the Eastern Psychological Association, New York, April 1981.
2. Waid, W. M., Orne, E. C., & Orne, M. T. Reduced electrodermal response, failure to

fulfill social commitments punctually, and delinquency-proneness. Paper presented at the 15th Annual Meeting of the Society for Psychophysiological Research, Washington, D. C., October 1981.
3. Waid, W. M., Dinges, D. F., Wilson, S. K., & Orne, M. T. Electrodermal activity as predictor of polydrug use and level of socialization. Paper presented at the meeting of the Eastern Psychological Association, Baltimore, April 1982.

References

American Psychiatric Association. *Diagnostic and statistical manual: Mental disorders.* Washington: American Psychiatric Association, 1952.

Badia, P., & Defran, R. H. Orienting responses and GSR conditioning: A dilemma. *Psychological Review,* 1970, **77,** 171–180.

Barabasz, A. F. Time constriction in delinquent and non-delinquent girls. *Adolescence,* 1968–1969, **3,** 435–440.

Barkley, R. A. A review of stimulant drug research with hyperactive children. *Journal of Child Psychology and Psychiatry,* 1977, **18,** 137–165.

Barndt, R. J., & Johnson, D. M. Time orientation in delinquents. *Journal of Abnormal and Social Psychology,* 1955, **55,** 343–345.

Berlyne, D. E. Behavior theory as personality theory. In E. F. Borgatta & W. W. Lambert (Eds.), *Handbook of personality theory and research.* Chicago: Rand McNally, 1968.

Black, W. A., & Gregson, R. A. Time perspective, purpose in life, extraversion and neuroticism in New Zealand prisoners. *British Journal of Social and Clinical Psychology,* 1973, **12,** 50–60.

Brock, T. C., & Del Guidice, C. Stealing and temporal orientation. *Journal of Abnormal and Social Psychology,* 1963, **66,** 91–94.

Cantwell, D. P. Hyperactivity and antisocial behavior. *Journal of the American Academy of Child Psychiatry,* 1978, **17,** 252–262.

Chesno, F., & Kilman, P. Effects of stimulation intensity on sociopathic avoidance learning. *Journal of Abnormal Psychology,* 1975, **84,** 144–150.

Cleckley, H. *The mask of sanity* (4th ed.). St. Louis, Mo.: Mosley, 1964.

Corteen, R. S. Skin conductance changes and word recall. *British Journal of Psychology,* 1969, **60,** 81–84.

Cottle, T. J., & Klineberg, S. L. *The present of things future: Explorations of time in human experience.* New York: Free Press, 1974.

Davis, R. C. Physiological responses as a means of evaluating information. In A. D. Biderman & H. Zimmer (Eds.), *The manipulation of human behavior.* New York: Wiley, 1961.

Dinges, D. F., Orne, E. C., Evans, F. J., & Orne, M. T. Performance after naps in sleep-conducive and alerting environments. In L. C. Johnson, D. I. Tepas, W. P. Colquhoun, & M. J. Colligan (Eds.), *The 24-hour workday: A symposium on variations in work-sleep schedules.* Washington, D. C.: National Institute for Occupational Safety and Health, 1981.

Edelberg, R. Electrical properties of the skin. In C. C. Brown (Ed.), *Methods in psychophysiology.* Baltimore: Williams & Wilkins, 1967.

Eisenberg, L., Lachman, R., Molling, P., Lockner, A., Mizille, J., & Conners, C. A psychopharmacologic experiment in a training school for delinquent boys. *American Journal of Orthopsychiatry,* 1963, **33,** 431–447.

Elliott, R., Bankart, B., & Light, T. Differences in the motivational significance of heart rate and palmar conductance: Two tests of a hypothesis. *Journal of Personality and Social Psychology,* 1970, **14**, 166–172.

Fowles, D. C. The three arousal model: Implications of Gray's two-factor learning theory for heart rate, electrodermal activity, and psychopathy. *Psychophysiology,* 1980, **17**, 87–104.

Frankenhaeuser, N., Mellin, I., Rissler, A., Bjorkvall, C., & Patkar, P. Catecholamine excretion as related to cognitive and emotional reaction patterns. *Psychosomatic Medicine,* 1968, **30**, 109–120.

Furedy, J. J., & Klajner, F. On evaluating autonomic and verbal indices of negative preception. *Psychophysiology,* 1974, **11**, 121–124.

Giesen, M., & Rollison, M. A. Guilty knowledge versus innocent associations: Effects of trait anxiety and stimulus context on skin conductance. *Journal of Research in Personality,* 1980, **14**, 1–11.

Gorenstein, E. E., & Newman, J. P. Disinhibitory psychopathology: A new perspective and a model for research. *Psychological Review,* 1980, **87**, 301–315.

Gough, H. G. *Manual for the California Psychological Inventory.* Palo Alto, Calif.: Consulting Psychologists Press, 1964.

Gough, H. G. Conceptual analysis of psychological test scores and other diagnostic variables. *Journal of Abnormal Psychology,* 1965, **70**, 294–302.

Grings, W. W., & Lockhart, R. A. Galvanic skin response during avoidance learning. *Psychophysiology,* 1966, **3**, 29–34.

Hare, R. D. Temporal gradient of fear arousal in psychopaths. *Journal of Abnormal Psychology,* 1965, **70**, 442–445. (a)

Hare, R. D. Acquisition and generalization of a conditioned fear response in psychopathic and nonpsychopathic criminals. *Journal of Psychology,* 1965, **59**, 367–370. (b)

Hare, R. D. Psychopathy and choice of immediate versus delayed punishment. *Journal of Abnormal Psychology,* 1965, **16**, 499–502. (c)

Hare, R. D. Electrodermal and cardiovascular correlates of psychopathy. In R. D. Hare & D. Schalling (Eds.), *Psychopathic behavior: Approaches to research.* London: Wiley, 1978.

Hare, R. D., & Quinn, M. J. Psychopathy and autonomic conditioning. *Journal of Abnormal Psychology,* 1971, **77**, 223–235.

Hare, R. D., & Thorvaldson, S. A. Psychopathy and response to electrical stimulation. *Journal of Abnormal Psychology,* 1970, **76**, 370–374.

Hastings, J. E., & Barkley, R. A. A review of psychophysiological research with hyperkinetic children. *Journal of Abnormal Child Psychology,* 1978, **6**, 413–447.

Hetherington, E. M., & Feldman, S. E. College cheating as a function of subject and situational variables. *Journal of Educational Psychology,* 1964, **55**, 212–218.

Hetherington, E. M., & Klinger, E. Psychopathy and punishment. *Journal of Abnormal and Social Psychology,* 1964, **69**, 113–115.

Hogan, R. Moral conduct and moral character: A psychological perspective. *Psychological Bulletin,* 1973, **79**, 217–232.

Hogan, R., Mankin, D., Conway, J., & Fox, S. Personality correlates of undergraduate marijuana use. *Journal of Consulting and Clinical Psychology,* 1970, **35**, 58–61.

Holland, J. L. The prediction of college grades from the California Psychological Inventory and the Scholastic Aptitude Test. *Journal of Educational Psychology,* 1959, **50**, 135–142.

Ingersoll, B. D. Detection of deception in primary psychopaths. Unpublished doctoral dissertation, Pennsylvania State University, 1977.

Kendall, P. C., Deardorf, P. A., & Finch, A. J. Empathy and socialization in first and repeat juvenile offenders and normals. *Journal of Abnormal Child Psychology,* 1977, **5**, 93–97.

Kimmel, H. D. Habituation, habituability, and conditioning. In H. V. S. Peeke & M. J. Herz (Eds.), *Behavioral studies* (Vol. 1). New York: Academic Press, 1973.

Kipnis, D. *Character structure and impulsiveness.* New York: Academic Press, 1971.

Lacey, J. I. Somatic response patterning and stress: Some revisions of activation theory. In M. H. Appley & R. Trumbell (Eds.), *Psychological stress: Issues in research.* New York: Appleton, 1967.

Lader, M. Comparison of amphetamine sulphate and caffeine citrate in man. *Psychopharmacologia,* 1969, **14,** 83–94.

Lippert, W. W., & Senter, R. J. Electrodermal responses in the sociopath. *Psychonomic Science,* 1966, **4,** 25–26.

Loeb, J., & Mednick, S. A. A prospective study of predictors of criminality: 3. Electrodermal response patterns. In S. A. Mednick & K. O. Christiansen (Eds.), *Biosocial bases of criminal behavior.* New York: Gardner Press, 1977.

Lykken, D. T. A study of anxiety in the sociopathic personality. *Journal of Abnormal and Social Psychology,* 1957, **55,** 6–10.

Lykken, D. T. Preception in the rat: Autonomic response to shock as a function of length of warning interval. *Science,* 1962, **137,** 665–666.

Maletzky, B. M. d-amphetamine and delinquency. *Diseases of the Nervous System,* 1974, **35,** 543–547.

Matulef, N. J. Future time perspective and personality characteristics of male adolescents, delinquents and non-delinquents. *Dissertation Abstracts International,* 1967, **28,** 1204–1205.

Mawson, A. R., & Mawson, C. D. Psychopathy and arousal: A new interpretation of the psychophysiological literature. *Biological Psychiatry,* 1977, **12,** 49–74.

Mednick, S. A., & Christiansen, K. O. (Eds.). *Biosocial bases of criminal behavior.* New York: Gardner Press, 1977.

Mednick, S. A., & Hutchings, B. Some considerations in the interpretation of the Danish adoption studies. In S. A. Mednick & K. O. Christiansen (Eds.), *Biosocial bases of criminal behavior.* New York: Gardner Press, 1977.

Mednick, S. A., & Volavka, J. Biology and crime. In N. Morris & M. Tonry (Eds.), *Crime and justice: An annual review of research.* Chicago: Univ. of Chicago Press, 1980.

Mischel, W. Toward a cognitive social learning reconceptualization of personality. *Psychological Review,* 1973, **80,** 252–283.

Mowrer, O. H. On the dual nature of learning—a reinterpretation of "conditioning" and "problem solving." *Harvard Educational Review,* 1947, **17,** 102–148.

Nassi, A. J., & Abramowitz, S. I. From phrenology to psychosurgery and back again: Biological studies of criminality. *American Journal of Orthopsychiatry,* 1976, **46,** 591–607.

Nye, F. I. *Family relationships and delinquent behavior.* New York: Wiley, 1958.

Rechtschaffen, A., & Kales, A. (Eds.), *A manual of standardized terminology, techniques, and scoring system for sleep stages of human subjects.* Washington, D. C.: Public Health Service, U. S. Government Printing Office, 1968.

Rosen, A., & Schalling, D. Probability learning in psychopathic and nonpsychopathic criminals. *Journal of Experimental Research in Personality,* 1971, **5,** 191–198.

Satterfield, J. H., & Dawson, M. E. Electrodermal correlates of hyperactivity in children. *Psychophysiology,* 1971, **8,** 191–197.

Schachter, S., & Latane, B. Crime, cognition, and the autonomic nervous system. In D. Levine (Ed.), *Nebraska Symposium on Motivation.* Lincoln: Univ. of Nebraska Press, 1964.

Schalling, D., Lidberg, L., Levander, S. E., & Dahlin, Y. Spontaneous autonomic activity as related to psychopathy. *Biological Psychology,* 1973, **1,** 83–97.

Schmauk, F. J. Punishment, arousal and avoidance learning in sociopaths. *Journal of Abnormal Psychology,* 1970, **76,** 325–335.

Schoenherr, J. C. Avoidance of noxious stimulation in psychopathic personality (Doctoral dissertation, University of California, Los Angeles, 1964). Dissertation, 1964, Vol. 25, 2055 (University Microfilms No. 64-8334).

Stein, K. B., Sarbin, T. R., & Kulik, J. A. Future time perspective: Its relation to socialization process and the delinquent role. *Journal of Consulting and Clinical Psychology,* 1968, **32,** 257-264.

Stern, R. M., & Kaplan, B. E. Galvanic skin response: Voluntary control and externalization. *Journal of Psychosomatic Research,* 1967, **10,** 349-353.

Thackray, R., & Orne, M. T. Effects of the type of stimulus employed and the level of subject awareness on the detection of deception. *Journal of Applied Psychology,* 1968, **52,** 234-239.

Thompson, W. R., & Grusec, J. Studies of early experience. In P. H. Munsen (Ed.), *Carmichael's manual of child psychology.* New York: Wiley, 1970.

Ullmann, L. P., & Krasner, L. *A psychological approach to abnormal behavior.* Englewood Cliffs, N. J.: Prentice-Hall, 1969.

Vincent, C. *Unmarried mothers.* New York: Free Press, 1961.

Waid, W. M. Skin conductance response to punishment as a predictor and correlate of learning to avoid two classes of punishment. *Journal of Abnormal Psychology,* 1976, **85,** 498-504. (a)

Waid, W. M. Skin conductance response to both signaled and unsignaled noxious stimulation predicts level of socialization. *Journal of Personality and Social Psychology,* 1976, **34,** 923-929. (b)

Waid, W. M. Perceptual preparedness in man: Brief forewarning reduces electrodermal and psychophysical response to noxious stimulation. *Psychophysiology,* 1979, **16,** 214-221.

Waid, W. M., & Orne, M. T. Reduced electrodermal response to conflict, failure to inhibit dominant behaviors, and delinquency-proneness. *Journal of Personality & Social Psychology,* 1982, **43,** 769-774.

Waid, W. M., Orne, E. C., Cook, M. R., & Orne, M. T. Effects of attention, as indexed by subsequent memory, on electrodermal detection of information. *Journal of Applied Psychology,* 1978, **63,** 723-733.

Waid, W. M., Orne, E. C., & Orne, M. T. Selective memory for social information, alertness, and physiological arousal in the detection of deception. *Journal of Applied Psychology,* 1981, **66,** 224-232.

Waid, W. M., Orne, M. T., & Wilson, S. K. Effects of level of socialization on electrodermal detection of deception. *Psychophysiology,* 1979, **16,** 15-22. (a)

Waid, W. M., Orne, M. T., & Wilson, S. K. Socialization, awareness, and the electrodermal response to deception and self-disclosure. *Journal of Abnormal Psychology,* 1979, **88,** 663-666. (b)

Weiss, G., Hechtman, L., & Perlman, T. Hyperactives as young adults: School, employer, and self-rating scales obtained during ten-year follow-up evaluation. *American Journal of Orthopsychiatry,* 1978, **48,** 438-445.

West, D. J., & Farrington, D. P. *Who becomes delinquent?* London: Heinemann, 1973.

White, W. C., McAdoo, W. G., & Megargee, E. I. Personality factors associated with over- and under-controlled offenders. *Journal of Personality Assessment,* 1973, **37,** 473-478.

Widom, C. S. Interpersonal and personal construct systems in psychopaths. *Journal of Consulting and Clinical Psychology,* 1976, **44,** 614-623.

Wiggins, J. S. Personality structure. *Annual Review of Psychology,* 1968, **19,** 293-350.

Wilkins, J. L., Scharff, W. H., & Schlottman, R. S. Personality type, reports of violence, and aggressive behavior. *Journal of Personality and Social Psychology,* 1974, **30,** 243-248.

Windes, J. D. Reaction time for numerical coding and naming of numerals. *Journal of Experimental Psychology,* 1968, **78**, 318–322.

Wolfgang, M. E., Figlio, R. M., & Sellin, T. *Delinquency in a birth cohort.* Chicago: Univ. of Chicago Press, 1972.

Ziskind, E., Syndulko, K., & Maltzman, I. Aversive conditioning in the sociopath. *Pavlovian Journal of Biological Science,* 1978, **13**, 199–205.

INDEX